American film and politics
from Reagan to Bush Jr

edited by

Philip John Davies and Paul Wells

D0060761

Manchester University Press
Manchester and New York

distributed exclusively in the USA by Palgrave

Copyright © Manchester University Press 2002

While copyright in the volume as a whole is vested in Manchester
University Press, copyright in individual chapters belongs to their
respective authors, and no chapter may be reproduced wholly or in part
without the express permission in writing of both author and publisher.

Published by Manchester University Press
Oxford Road, Manchester M13 9NR, UK
and Room 400, 175 Fifth Avenue, New York, NY 10010, USA
www.manchesteruniversitypress.co.uk

Distributed exclusively in the USA by
Palgrave, 175 Fifth Avenue, New York,
NY 10010, USA

Distributed exclusively in Canada by
UBC Press, University of British Columbia, 2029 West Mall,
Vancouver, BC, Canada V6T 1Z2

British Library Cataloguing-in-Publication Data
A catalogue record for this book is available from the British Library

Library of Congress Cataloging-in-Publication Data applied for

ISBN   0 7190 5864 3   *hardback*
        0 7190 5865 1   *paperback*

First published 2002

10 09 08 07 06 05 04 03 02   10 9 8 7 6 5 4 3 2 1

Typeset by Illuminati, Grosmont
Printed in Great Britain
by Bell & Bain Limited, Glasgow

Contents

Contributors

Albert Auster is Associate Professor in the Department of Communications and Media Studies at Fordham University, New York. His publications include co-authorship with Leonard Quart of *American Film and Society Since 1945.*

Philip John Davies AcSS is Director of the Eccles Centre for American Studies at the British Library, and Professor of American Studies at De Montfort University. He is Chair of the British Association for American Studies. He was co-editor of *Cinema, Politics and Society in America*, and his recent publications include *US Elections Today*, co-authorship of *The History Atlas of North America*, and co-editing of *Political Parties and the Collapse of the Old Orders.*

Mary Ellison, Reader in American Studies at the University of Keele, teaches on the representation of African Americans and American Indians in film, and is the author of several books and articles on African American music and film. Her publications include *Extensions of the Blues*, and *Lyrical Protest.*

Phil Melling is the author of *Vietnam in American Literature, Fundamentalism in America*, and *American Literary Documents of the 1920s*. He is also a playwright and biographer and the author of *Man of Amman*, an oral history of Welsh sport.

Brian Neve is author of *Film and Politics in America: A Social Tradition*, co-editor of *Cinema, Politics and Society in America*, and has written many articles and chapters on politics and film He is an Associate Editor of *Cineaste.*

Leonard Quart, Professor of Cinema Studies at the College of Staten Island and at the CUNY Graduate Center, has been Associate Editor, Editor, and Contributing Editor of *Cineaste* since 1978. His publications include co-authorship with Albert Auster of *How the War Remembered: Hollywood and Vietnam*, and *American Film and Society Since 1945*.

Carol R. Smith lectures in American Studies and English and is Director of the Cultural Studies Research Centre at King Alfred's College, Winchester. She researches into the debates surrounding American identity and contemporary culture and has recently published work on Saul Bellow, *Dumbo*, sitcoms and family values, and is co-author of *Gender, Ethnicity and Sexuality in Contemporary American Film*.

Paul Watson is Senior Lecturer in Media Studies at the University of Teesside, with special interests in Animation, New Digital Interfaces in Film, and Theoretical Determinacy in Film Studies. He is co-author (with Paul Wells) of *The Animation Handbook* (forthcoming).

Paul Wells is Professor of Media and Cultural Studies and Head of the Media Portfolio at the University of Teesside. He is the author of *Understanding Animation, Animation and America, Animation: Genre and Authorship*, and curator of *Animation at the Ark* at the Children's Cultural Centre in Dublin.

Ralph Willett recently retired from a career of teaching American Studies at the University of Hull. He now lives in the south-west of England, where he chairs Yeovil Cinematheque and pursues research interests in crime fiction and fine art. His numerous popular culture publications include *The Naked City: Urban Crime Fiction in the USA*.

Acknowledgements

The editors would especially like to thank the contributors and Matthew Frost at Manchester University Press for their patience and support in what has been a protracted and complex project, sometimes beset by unforeseen difficulties.

The editors would also like to acknowledge the support of their colleagues at De Montfort University and the University of Teesside.

This book is dedicated with affection to our children, Andrew, Carolyn, Freddie and Lola.

Part 1

'Life is not like a
box of chocolates'

Introduction

Philip John Davies and Paul Wells

If the end of a century duly prompts *fin-de-siècle* anxiety, and signals all manner of doom and despondency, what, then, of the dawning of a new millennium? As we enter the brave new world of the twenty-first century, analysis of what we are, what we have become, where we are going to, and why it matters, proliferates. Are we 'dumbing down' or 'growing up'? Are we merely part of a postmodern mediated age which refuses any notion of consensual reality? What, given this scale of relativity and ambiguity, is the status of 'Politics' big 'P' – governmental, strategic, democratic – and 'politics' small 'P' – personal, localised, unstable? These questions beg many further questions, and belie easy answers, but as the United States enters its post-Clinton (and Lewinsky) era, it remains a useful exercise to take stock of 'politics', ideologically determined and otherwise, as it has underpinned Hollywood movies of the contemporary era.

As ever, and ironically, even more than politicians themselves, in the mass mediated era, it is the implied ideological agenda of cinema which still offers significant clues to the popular understanding of sociocultural identity and political existence. The deep theme of much American cinema is still the simultaneous longing to acknowledge the profound effects of late industrial capitalism and technological innovation, yet also a nostalgic desire to look back upon our past in the spirit of loss for supposedly better times. It was always thus. While sustaining a model of progress, the United States has always been anxious about the values and achievements it may have left behind. American cinema provides a specific locus by which this seemingly contradictory yearning is played out artistically and commercially. Hollywood – the spectacular epitome of a globally expansive entertainment industry, and the defining example of a cinematic apparatus embracing institutional, economic and techno-logical flux – speaks to the world; aesthetically constructing, uncon-sciously reflecting, sometimes accidentally determining sociocultural experience.

The defining issue in film production over the last twenty years, the broad terrain of the discussions in this book, has been the return to what might be understood as 'corporate movie-making' – films produced less in accordance with the authorial distinctiveness of the independent film-makers of the 1960s and 1970s, and more in accord-ance with predetermined market research; formulaic stories; high spectacle; limited narrative and thematic complexity; and pat, often naive resolutions. First among equals here, particularly during the 1980s, are the films produced by Don Simpson and Jerry Bruckheimer – the unremittingly vacuous *An Officer and a Gentlemen* (Taylor Hackford, 1982), *Flashdance* (Adrian Lyne, 1983), *Top Gun* (Tony Scott, 1986), *Days of Thunder* (Tony Scott, 1990) – yet all these films are extremely well executed, and were commercially successful. Argu-ably, such films are 'mere products': the visual equivalent of a Burger and Fries; extremely popular but 'artless' on the terms and condi-tions laid down by the masters – Wyler, Huston, Zinnemann and Stevens; the auteurs – Welles, Ford, Hawks, and Hitchcock; the 'movie-brats' – Spielberg, Scorsese, Lucas, and De Palma; or the 'iconoclasts' – Altman, Kubrick and Friedkin. This, of course, is a dangerous and ill-informed generalisation. 'Event' or 'High Concept' movies, which have accompanied the rise of the multiplex cinemas and the rejuvenation of the cinema audience, are merely of a different order.

While those movies may have satisfied the popcorn-munching, post-teen, sub-adolescent sensation-seekers of the 1980s, there were always those by the more authorially distinctive Jim Jarmusch, John Sayles, David Lynch, and Joel and Ethan Coen for other more demanding, niche audiences. Interestingly, though, whether 'High Concept' or 'My Concept', what characterises many of these films and film-makers is an apoliticised or taken-for-granted political stance that either implicitly endorses the Reagan years, or ignores them altogether. Spike Lee and Oliver Stone are, with some caveats, honourable exceptions here. Susan Mackey-Kallis has suggested of Stone that '[I]n order to create a political perspective, [his] films create arguments out of images and icons out of individuals', emphasising a rhetorical rather than an aesthetic agenda.[1] In this model, social redeemers, embodying a leftist stance, fail in the light of the oppressive conservatism and hypocrisy of middle American power-broking. Stone's technique – emphatic, overdetermined, archetypical – sustains the 'entertainment' factor alongside the often simplistically polemical and, in doing so, maintains the box-office returns that continue to legitimise his practice. Without commercial success, Stone's 'radicalism' could not be endorsed, but it should be noted that Stone may be perceived as radical only in the light of the ideology-free, liberally centrist or politically naive tendencies in mainstream Hollywood cinema. More prominent in 1980s cinema are the laughable ideological currencies of *Top Gun*, for example, which reinforces Cold War antagonisms and, congruent with 'the need for speed', hastens past the obvious global political and military meltdown that would actually have been occasioned if the events of the movie had really taken place. Unsurprisingly, it is not the politics we remember, however, but little Tom Cruise giving taller people 'high fives'; winning the girl; and enjoying a sky-riding 'shoot 'em up' with an unseen enemy, who is self-evidently disadvantaged by not having Tom's charisma or teeth.

Making claims about the ways in which American cinema has served historical accuracy, political agendas and dominant social tendencies is perhaps anathema to the very premiss of cinema as a populist, storytelling entertainment medium, but this is to neglect the potentially powerful effects of film as a medium. A whole canon of work has addressed this complex medium, discerning 'messages' and 'meanings'. The difficulty remains that it can never be certain if these messages and meanings are authorially intended, commercially created, academically invented or genuinely embraced by real people in actual audiences. No analysis is devoid of informed speculation, and in a period within Film Studies which is fast rejecting coherent ideological readings in favour of a more open approach to the possible ways in which films might be experienced and acted upon by the audiences who watch them, it is right to be cautious about critical positions and outcomes. The fact remains, though, that the politics of the most powerful nation in the world cannot be divorced from the most far-reaching entertainment medium in the world.

Powers, Rothman and Rothman argue that the determination and evaluation of social and political themes in American film are too often compromised by the jargonistic and subjective vagaries of film theories rooted in aesthetic or narrow ideological frames, unsupported by substantive empirical evidence.[2] While this is probably true, it does much to discredit the significance of reading specific American movies as *emblematic* examples of sociocultural knowledge and political ideas. Work which delineates the impact and effect of Hollywood's creative elites within their institutional structure, *and* the actual representational presence of key social paradigms within a range of texts, is especially welcome, but it should not discredit the project of this volume, in which more subtle textual readings are directly related to models which problematically entwine populist narratives with political/politicised issues. Work by Martin Barker, though not explicitly developing the '(P)olitical' as a category of interpretation, nevertheless offers an approach in which the 'processes, patterns and principles of the film' itself offer clues to the ways in which film narrative plays out the social principles of the 'real world' in relation to the generic agendas of the film and, in so doing, 'opens a door to further exploration of the relations between rules operative in the *film* and the external referents of those rules in the social world'.[3]

This is an especially useful point of focus when we seek to evaluate the kind of movie-making which has followed on from the 1980s bravura movies. Hollywood cinema in the 1990s has arguably developed and enhanced its modes of spectacle since the 1980s, fully embracing the benefits of digital post-production technologies, and the extraordinary impact of computer-generated imagery. James Cameron, Paul Verhoeven, Joel Schumacher and Roland Emmerich have emerged as auteurs in the CGI era, enhancing the scale of their dramatic conflict with previously unimaginable vistas. Arguably, each is more concerned with the instigation of sensation in audiences – the 'wow' factor – than with the overt delineation of a political stance or an ideological exploration. Their preoccupation with the medium does not preclude them, however, from creating the kind of filmic infrastructure which, Barker suggests, is the determinant of a relationship between generic expectation and the known variables of the politically determined world. Roland Emmerich's *Independence Day* (Roland Emmerich, 1996), for example, is a *tour de force* of 'having your cake and eating it too' in using state-of-the-art digital cinema to depict the destruction of politically meaningful sites in the United States, most notably the White House, only to resurrect the populist meanings enshrined in those sites in the gung-ho durability of the American military and the community rearguard action against the alien 'other'. This is generically predictable science-fiction cinema as much as it is a set of narrative conditions whereby the 'what if' of invasion is played out against the human actions that will oppose it. This is not so far from Capra at his populist best in *It's A Wonderful Life* (Frank Capra, 1946) – still a touchstone in American cinema for the recovery of a view of the value of 'right-acting' individuals in a world that seems inevitably corrupt, dissolute, and increasingly threatened from within and without.

Crucially, this kind of cinema, addressed comprehensively in the series of essays in this volume, is most notable for its acts of political 'smuggling', often playing out tensions between a discredited model of a liberal-democratic and consensual 'centre', and the dynamics of alternative and contradictory positions both at the heart and at the margins of American life. In this sense, American cinema remains remarkably resilient in still offering audiences stories in which the personal can be political, and where the 'Political' can still be subject to creative interrogation and critique. The space between the specificity of 'cinema' and the tenets of the music video, or advertising films, or television programmes has been much reduced. The models of 'synergy' between film texts and their cross-media spin-offs in advertising, promotion and publicity have impacted upon the particularity of 'cinema', rendering it merely as a part of an image culture, rooted in marketing principles. This does not necessarily undermine the idea of film as art, nor film as ideology, but it changes the way in which audiences may understand the relationship between cinema and politics.

In order to illustrate this, one might usefully choose two directors – Michael Bay and David Fincher – who have risen to prominence in recent years, but who – being versed in the particular hybridity of aesthetics that has evolved out of the Simpson/Bruckheimer years, the proliferation of the music video, and the third generation of 'movie bratism' – have a signature style that is no longer rooted in challenging classical narrative cinema, or its 'invisible' ideologies, but in the rhetorical and highly stylised presentation of the immediacy of moral or ethical dilemmas as the substantive consequence of the *lack* of political effect. The implicit idea both in the making of films, and in their ultimate completion as a historically determined, socially influenced, cultural artefact is that style has triumphed over substance because there has been little that is politically substantive – which is not in itself a vindication of style and 'spin'. In other words, there has been a convergence of the presentation of 'real-world' politics and the execution of contemporary cinema as an exercise in image-making and the 'styling' of mythic principles.

Michael Bay, director of Simpson and Bruckheimer's *Bad Boys* (1995), *The Rock* (1996), *Armageddon* (1998) and *Pearl Harbor* (2001), honed his skills on Meatloaf and Tina Turner videos, before making advertisements for Coca-Cola and Nike campaigns. The slickness and efficiency of Bay's action sequences, and his ability to recall and facilitate archetypes of American heroism – most notably in the figures of Ben Affleck and Bruce Willis in *Armageddon*, as the United States once again bails out the rest of the world – has given Bay a currency as a 'Stars and Stripes' director, properly reflecting the prominence and interventionary nature of the United States on the world stage in the post-Cold War era. Interestingly, as an aside here, it is worth noting that notoriously right-wing screenwriter and director John Milius, a stalwart from the first generation of 'movie brats' who include Spielberg and Scorsese, once observed: 'When the United States is politically weak or vulnerable, it needs its muscular movie heroes, Conan, Rocky, Rambo, to suggest that we have things worth fighting for, worth preserving, even if those things are not easy to talk about, or describe anymore. They just *are*.'[4] In a certain way, Bay's films follow this dictum. They are self-righteous endorsements of both the American movie-making tradition *and* the flag-waving agendas naturalised within them; their actual social referents seem increasingly different. *Pearl Harbor* – given the largest ever budget in advance by a major studio, the Walt Disney Motion Pictures Group, and produced by Jerry Bruckheimer – echoes *From Here to Eternity, 30 Seconds Over Tokyo* and *Tora! Tora! Tora!* Although it is self-evidently in the mould of a Simpson/Bruckheimer movie of the 1980s, it encompasses other trends, most notably the stress on dialogue re-emphasised by the success of Quentin Tarantino, and the aesthetic self-consciousness in action sequences played out by John Woo.[5] *Pearl Harbor* refuses to let the politics of the bombing of Pearl Harbor on 7 December 1941 affect the clarity of the spectacle, or the inevitable endorsement of 'big government' as the instigator of big decisions and big guns. The 'political' impact echoes that of *Saving Private Ryan* (Steven Spielberg, 1998), which essentially works as another opportunity to embrace a story which signals that the contemporary era should be proud and grateful for the preservation of the principle of democracy in itself, rather than evaluate or criticise its systematic abuse in the postwar era.

It is in this that David Fincher, also of the music video generation, differs. His stylistic bravura is very much directed at the mythic 'underbelly' of American culture. Fincher's take on democracy is one that foregrounds its dystopic tendencies. *Alien³* (1992), *Se7en* (1995), *The Game* (1997) and *Fight Club* (1998) all demonstrate aspects of a seemingly irredeemable social malaise. *Se7en* plays out theological tropes as metaphors for not merely spiritual collapse but the irrecoverable demise of the late capitalist urban infrastructure. 'Politics' has singularly failed in this context, and no amount of macho bravura is going to revive a corporate culture which is destroyed by its own excessive and brutalist consumption – a theme developed in a similarly bleak, morally ambivalent critique of masculinity in crisis, *Fight Club*. Fincher's stylisation, unlike that of the Simpson/Bruckheimer school, insists upon its generic credentials recalling social referents and, in doing so, posits a way in which even the 'blockbuster' movie may be the textual embodiment of a contemporary political terrain. The two models epitomised by Bay and Fincher provide apt parentheses for the range of positions in between, explored in this book.

Powers, Rothman and Rothman's sociological approach suggests that 'movie content reflects more sophisticated and cynical views than people in the audience would independently hold',[6] partially confirming Michael Medved's anxiety about a radical (and destructive) misrepresentation of American culture in movies, far removed from the conservative ethos of the audience.[7] This, like any other generalisation, is contentious. Hollywood movies have always embodied a tension between art and commerce, which at one level necessitates a commitment to aesthetic quality at the level of execution, even if there is often less aspiration to exploit and advance the distinctiveness of film form for the purpose of a level of expression which embraces depth and potential longevity. Sometimes telling a story is enough. Ephemeral, superficial, yet engaging, a movie in itself may demand no more than to be enjoyed for what it is. Again – reinforcing Barker's position – it is likely to signify its own intentions and relationships beyond that, and seek out debate rather than decision.

Arguably, then, far from being a mere repository of conservative values – clearly the most readily perceived function of American film

– Hollywood cinema may be viewed as the embodiment of the shifting agendas in the postwar period. In the last twenty years, Hollywood cinema has become a site in which the film text has increasingly called attention to itself and its own terms and conditions. It is the ways in which those terms and conditions may be interpreted which afford the critic the points of access to the *socially signifying referents* which have questioned and challenged American political life. In many senses, this has amounted to an address of relationship between the traditionally sanctioned institutions of the military and the church, and the changing paradigms of gender, race and morality. By looking properly at the socially signifying referents as they may be configured from the generically determined constructions of contemporary film, it is possible to address the extent to which a film is 'protopolitical' or significantly politicised. The niche films produced by Miramax, or the work of young aesthetes and polemicists in the 1990s like Todd Solondz, Neil La Bute, Paul Thomas Anderson, Harmony Korine, Guy Maddin and Kimberley Pierce, for example, may be viewed as 'protopolitical' because they foreground a social critique which implies political ineptitude or decay; while movies like *Bulworth* (1998), *Wag the Dog* (1997) and *Primary Colors* (1998) self-evidently suggest that they are both 'Political' and politicised in directly addressing the American political system.

This collection of essays seeks to address the space between the protopolitical and the self-consciously issue-led fictions, taking up post-1980 cinema as the embodiment of destabilised political flux, uncertain in its address and nostalgic in its desire for archetypical simplicities and lifestyles which may be reconciled in their purpose and achievement. Politics in the 1990s are abstracted to accommodate this urgent need for redemption, and American cinema – often banal in its spectacle, but potent in its projection of socially oriented wishes and desires – provides the key context in which the postmodern concept of 'an end to history' is reconciled. Looking back in order to look forward characterises policy and pictures in the United States, and it is this concept – the past as the redeemer of the future, and the mythic method by which America finds its identity – that resides at the heart of this set of detailed studies.

It is perhaps apt to conclude this introductory piece by making some comment about the seminal film of the mid-1990s, *Forrest Gump* (Robert Zemeckis, 1995). The central cloying metaphor of Robert Zemeckis' phenomenally (and inexplicably) successful film,

'Life is like a box of chocolates: you never know what you're going to get', offers a springboard from which to view the range of critical commentaries in this volume. Both at the box office and at the Academy, *Forrest Gump*'s simple, seemingly visionary statement became extraordinarily persuasive. For those of us who feel that in any one box of chocolates you know exactly what you are going to get and eat them in accordance with preference and need, and that the only certainty is that the orange creams will be left until last, *Gump*'s metaphor comes unstuck. Zemeckis' knowing treatment of the *Gump* narrative, however, and the deliberate 'dumbing down' of the received effect of American cultural history played out through Forrest (Tom Hanks), has more in common with the more pragmatic consumption of the box of chocolates than we might initially think. American film has long preferred a simplistic mode to send direct, reassuring messages about American society and the legacy of its political impact. *Gump* speaks to a tradition in American film which pays lip service to the socially framing figures and structural mechanisms of government in the United States, only to rely ultimately on the impact of accessible ideologically charged images and actions as the most *actually* affecting method of endorsing 'the American way'. In truth, movies like *Gump* become a robust reiteration of attractive myths which still desire 'an American dream' to survive in the face of social and cultural destabilisation, and ironically, while they might inspire other movies like *Independence Day* in the emphatic reiteration of the same point, they also encourage the complacency of the *Dumb and Dumber* (1994)-style movie, epitomised by the Farrelly Brothers. While it is possible to derive subversive and transgressive satisfactions from such comedies, it may be equally true that this kind of work reiterates a view of the United States in which it remains content to sit smugly within the confines of its own ideologically secure but politically abject regimes, uncomfortable with any genuinely progressive repertoires of social development.

It is the intention of the essays that follow to explore these issues, looking at the political context in which movies have been made; the ways movies address overtly 'political' themes (though this term in itself has taken on significant cultural breadth); the modes in which American political figures and frameworks have been represented, perhaps repositioned, inevitably redefined; and finally, how such seemingly 'serious' ideas and issues have found a populist base. The 'unpredictability' of opening a box of American 'chocolates' will be

resolved in a series of essays which will unpack the very pre-
dictabilities of American film yet, at the same time, reveal that
Hollywood films are not necessarily the conservative texts received
wisdom might have us believe. Contradiction is often at the centre of
both destabilised cultures and those which exhibit liberal pluralist
agendas; it is this contradiction which has characterised American
film in the last twenty years, and is an underpinning theme in the
explorations presented here.

American cinema, political criticism and pragmatism: a therapeutic reading of *Fight Club* and *Magnolia*

Paul Watson

> If the American Left is to revitalize itself, it will have to relearn plain English, return to the actual and resistant world and it will never do that with its present encumbrance of theory.
>
> Robert Hughes, *Culture of Complaint*

'*You wanna see pain?*' In *Fight Club* (David Fincher, 1999), Jack (Edward Norton), the film's depressed protagonist and narrator, takes the advice of his doctor to 'swing by First Methodist Tuesday nights' and 'see the guys with testicular cancer' if he wants to see '*real* pain'. '*I'm in pain!*' A disaffected recall co-ordinator for a major car company and a 'slave to the Ikea nesting instinct' – '*what kind of dining set defines me as a person?*' – Jack feels emasculated by his stiff-collar, bottom-line consumer lifestyle. Sick from despair at his agrypnotic existence, Jack is so 'filled with self-loathing and re-pressed rage [that] he's desperate to get out of his skin and into someone else's'.[1] And at Remaining Men Together, nestled between the post-operative, oestrogen swollen 'bitch tits' of testicular cancer victim Big Bob, Jack becomes, for a while, the 'little warm centre that the life of the world crowds around'. '*Bob loved me because he thought my testicles were removed too. This was my vocation.*' If not (yet) *inside* someone else's skin, then in the silent oblivion of self *between* someone else's skin, Jack's suffering momentarily evaporates with his tears: '*When people think you're dying, they really listen to you.*'

'*It's universal. It's evolutional. It is anthropological. It's biological. It is animal. WE ARE MEN!*' In *Magnolia* (Paul Thomas Anderson, 1999), there is a scene in which Frank T. J. Mackey (Tom Cruise), the hypermasculine inspirational guru behind the extremely successful

men's sexual self-help programme Seduce and Destroy, is being interviewed by Gwenovier, a journalist and the presenter of the TV show
Profile. The scene, which is actually dispersed across about ninety
minutes of the film's three-hour rhizomorphous structure, is remark-
able for a number of reasons, all of which slowly conspire to recast
Mackey's narcissistic mantra 'Respect the cock, tame the cunt', as
well as his bellicose performance in the 'How to Turn That "Friend"
into Your Sperm Receptacle' seminar, as an expression of a deep
pain. For Gwenovier 'knows' more about his past than either she
initially lets on, or he would want her to – a past in which he was
abandoned by a *paterfamilias* as a child to nurse his cancer-stricken
mother into death. *'Facing the past is a way of not making progress.*
This is something I teach my men over and over and over.' Indeed,
as the interview teasingly gives up its information we come to re-
evaluate Mackey's teachings less as a generational revisiting of past
cruelty – *'Come August, we like to celebrate suck my big fat fucking*
sausage'; *'I am the one who is in charge. I am the one who says: Yes.*
No. Now. Here.' – and more as the hyperbolic articulation of loneliness and suffering. By the end of the film, Frank, declaring that he
is 'not gonna cry' for his dying father yet sobbing uncontrollably at
his bedside, pleads with him: 'don't go away you fucking ass hole,
don't go away', as he listens for the last breath to be expelled from
Earl's pallid cheeks.

Two films. Two narratives of male pain and suffering. Two stories
in which emotionally impaired male agency, unable to reconcile what
one critic has called the 'sensitivities, traumas and burdens' of psychological life with a punitive masculine physicality, turn to self-help
programmes and support groups for succour.[2] Or, more precisely, in
approaching what Ina Rae Hark refers to as 'the dilemma of male
subjectivity', both films negotiate between representing violence and
hostility as the pathology of male suffering, and searching not only
for the sociopolitical cause of that pain but also for ways of resolv-
ing it through nonviolent means, through understanding.[3] Each film,
in its own way, breaks apart the link between punitive agency,
masculinity and American geopolitical history, instead offering
narratives which explore the contingency of male 'ethical dilemmas,
emotional traumas and psychological goals'.[4] That is, each of the
two films mentioned articulates the male psychology not merely as
an internal backdrop to external physical action, as a private alibi
for public violence, but as the scene of narrative inscription and

political drama itself.[5] Thus the male psychology not only frames the politics of the respective films, but also determines how we situate– or choose to read – those films within the global historicity of American politics and culture.

How, then, do we understand the historical emergence of narratives of this sort, and what kinds of critical discourse are at our disposal to negotiate the political demands implicit in their emergence? Because the question of masculinity in film theory has – regular as clockwork – been posed as a feminist question, or at least as a question of gender, the first tool out of the box at this stage is usually the metaphoric crisis – that is, to equate masculinity with the national body politic, and take his temperature as evidence of the sick sociopolitical climate. Using this tactic, we might explore *Fight Club* and *Magnolia* as two more instances of what Jude Davis refers to as movies which 'make explicit links between a historical "American" crisis and a crisis of white masculinity'.[6] Following the inexorable logic of this strategic critical move, it is indeed tempting to try to build an explication of Jack and Frank T. J. Mackey's political ballast as a complementary annex to Susan Jeffords's historical model of post-Vietnam masculinity. Beginning with *The Remasculinization of America*, Jeffords maps the ways in which patriarchal conceptions of nationhood have been variously tattooed across the figure of the male in post-Vietnam American cinema, and how, in that inscription, national regeneration becomes commensurate with masculine renewal.[7] Initially this regeneration was imagined in the hard-bodied, 'hard-fighting, weapon-wielding, independent, muscular and heroic men of the eighties' – the *Rambo*, *Lethal Weapon* and *Die Hard* series being only the most obvious examples.[8] In more recent articles, however, she has suggested that this hypermasculine warrior hero who dominated so much of the Reagan years – a masculine renewal effected through violent spectacles of empowerment – has 'given way to a "kinder, gentler" U.S. manhood, one that is sensitive, generous, caring, perhaps most importantly capable of change'.[9] Given this, it becomes possible to embroider *Fight Club* and *Magnolia* on to Jeffords's sociopolitical matrix: on the one hand continuing the exploration of the internal emotional fabric of male identity, while on the other stitching that psychology back together with a violent and (self-) destructive exterior projection of masculinity as nationhood.

On this view, it becomes difficult not to conclude that both films are another example of the tendency – identified by Carol Clover in

relation to *Falling Down* (Joel Schumacher, 1992) – of angry white
middle-aged men 'carving an interest group' of their own by claiming that they are the victims of a culture which is not only unable to
accommodate their supremacist gender identity but, more complexly,
fails to recognise their political or valuative *presence* at all.[10] Variously referred to as 'everyman movies', 'angry white male films',
'mid-life crisis films', middle-age male trauma movies' and 'male
hormone movies', *Fight Club* and *Magnolia*, in their own way, can
be plotted as two interesting instances of a growing body of cultural
representations, emerging in a range of formal and generic contexts,
in which the universalising codes of omnipotent American WASP
masculinity appear irreconcilable: *Falling Down* (Joel Schumacher,
1992); *Last Action Hero* (John McTiernan, 1993); *Disclosure* (Adrian
Lyne, 1994); *Dead Man* (Jim Jarmusch, 1995); *Strange Days* (Kathryn
Bigelow, 1995); *Leaving Las Vegas* (Mike Figgis, 1995); *Jerry Maguire*
(Cameron Crowe, 1996); *The Game* (David Fincher, 1997); *Happi-
ness* (Todd Solondz, 1998); *American Beauty* (Sam Mendes, 1999);
The Straight Story (David Lynch, 1999); *Being John Malkovich* (Spike
Jones, 1999); *Wonder Boys* (Curtis Hanson, 2000); as well as *Frazier*,
Alley McBeal, *The Simpsons*, and *King of the Hill*.

However, while mapping the 'identity and consciousness' of what
she calls 'the great unmarked or default category of western culture',
the one Richard Dyer has likened to *absence*, to a kind of 'death',[11]
Carol Clover cannot help but include a cautionary note, a disclaimer
to her argument: 'It is not hard to see what's wrong with this picture.
Even Average White Males are better off that their Average White
Wives or than Average Black Males or whatever; hold for class, in
other words they still come out on top.'[12]

While they are in part motivated by the incontestable and observ-
able socioeconomic advantages of being born a heterosexual white
male in American society, such intellectual waivers also perform an
implicit valuative and political function – a function which, in the
end, works not to explain the political questions raised by these films
but, rather, to explain them away. For in the critical discourse of
some contemporary film and cultural criticism, it sometimes seems
as if only the pain and suffering experienced by minority, marginalised or oppressed social groups counts as genuine or valid pain.
Analogously – and not surprisingly – there has been a tendency to
whittle out identity groups and erect evaluative hierarchies on the
basis of putative difference from paradigmatic American citizenship

unproblematically understood as the male WASP. So while, on the one hand, the American Constitution inscribed the sovereignty of the people as a collective singular – 'We the People do ordain and establish this CONSTITUTION' – on the other hand Robert Hughes is on to something when he says: 'never before in human history were so many acronyms pursuing identity' in the name of *multi*culturalism.[13] Emerging in part out of the friction generated between the national 'we' and individual 'I' statements, and in part buttressed by a post-Marxist intellectual Left, it increasingly seems that to write political criticism is to endow every rank and file of genetic, cultural and geographical difference with a theoretical and political identity over and above that of a citizen of a social democracy. This critical exaltation of difference not only seems to me just as dubious as the patriarchal assurance that other forms of humanity are weak compared to the masculine, but depends on a bad inference from the premiss that powerlessness and oppression are an index of worth.

This, together with a heady cocktail of guilt and relief, is perhaps what led a number of prominent (male) critics to dismiss *Fight Club* as at best either 'a laborious and foolish waste of time', 'an insult to intelligent men', 'a witless mishmash of whiny, infantile philosophizing', or at worst, a 'frankly and cheerfully fascist' movie.[14] But perhaps most vituperative of all was Alexander Walker's review in the London *Evening Standard*: 'It is an inadmissible assault on personal decency. And on society itself … It echoes propaganda that gave licence to the brutal activities of the SA and the SS. It resurrects the Führer principle.'[15]

To dismiss *Fight Club* in a whirl of anti-Semitic accusations not only replays another bad inference from the premiss that the free-wheeling nihilism embodied by Jack's *doppelgänger*, Tyler Durden (Brad Pitt), is reducible to or isomorphic with the politics espoused by the film, but – more worryingly – sidesteps precisely the complex articulation of sick male psychology and money-motivated, name-brand American society which both distress Jack and conjure Tyler into being in the first place. In short, it picks politics up by the wrong handle in so far as it rehearses the unhelpful idea of a *sui generis* sense of moral and intellectual obligation to interest-group politics. The result is the creation of a critical vocabulary which is unable to capture the genuine sense of helplessness, anomie and pain which attends Jack's narrative and clearly affected the film's audience.[16]

Michael Lerner has recently made the same point in another context. In reflecting upon his research into the psychodynamics of American society, conducted for the Institute for Labor and Mental Health, Lerner says that the set of assumptions that the researchers, many of whom were from 'progressive communities', brought to the table initially led them to believe that the average middle-income American was 'motivated primarily by money', and that these people were moving to the political Right 'primarily because they *were* racist, sexist, homophobic or xenophobic'. 'Instead,' he continues, 'we discovered that this was occurring because people were in tremendous pain.'[17] As a result, Lerner suggests that the presumed valuative map of the American body politic was, in effect, *produced* by the constraints of the representational discourses which frame it: 'We, the academics, intellectuals, liberals, lefties, the social change people, *we* were coming from a higher place and had a different set of values. That's how we understood why we were making the choices that we were making. But *they* didn't have those values and were motivated only by material self-interest. It was startling for us to discover that this simply wasn't true.'[18] One of the more serious consequences of this critical and political *ipse dixit*, Lerner suggests, is that 'we have succeeded, over the course of the past twenty-five years, in telling middle income people that their concerns are irrelevant.'[19] He continues:

> What the Left and liberals are understood as saying to middle income people is some variant of, 'Listen, stop whining. You've already made it in American society; you have the good life already – it's only these others who are genuinely in pain. *Your* pain is nothing and you're just too self indulgent, selfish and insensitive to know where the real pain is. If you want to be a part of *our* social movements, the first thing you've got to do is acknowledge that your pain is secondary or should be listed to twenty-fourth on our laundry list. The real pain is economic deprivations or political rights deprivations.'[20]

Crucially, however, Lerner diagnoses the cause of this state of affairs not as a deep theoretical or philosophical matter but, rather, as a limitation in the semantic descriptive categories which are routinely called upon to 'talk politics', categories which are no longer 'adequate for hearing or understanding' what is going on.[21] Analogously, I want to suggest that a similarly immutable critical vocabulary accounts for the political indigestion caused by *Fight Club*'s narrative: it appears eccentric, and even dangerous, precisely because its male character(s) fail to fit easily into the pre-programmed answers to the questions we pose. Neither entirely powerful nor weak, cruel nor kind, heterosexual nor homosexual, masculine nor feminine, good nor bad, Jack falls outside our descriptions because we have yet to ask the questions which will enable us to attain sufficient semantic authority over such cultural representations. So we attempt to squeeze our descriptions of him into all those shopworn metaphors of masculinity, the 'crisis' figure simply being the most convenient. But this is the political point: *Fight Club* and *Magnolia* are two recent instances of a proliferating body of cultural representations which are involved in expanding that semantic field – involved in imagining new moral and political identities for men, that is, working out a description of contemporary American masculinity which is more useful and more suited for *coping* with contemporary life.

Three meanings of 'politics' in film theory

It is in this context that I want to take up what some scholars and critics have said about the relationship between film and politics, in the hope of pruning back some of the dead wood propagated by the immediate context of our own professional practices, in order to encourage some fresh growth. Taking the implications of Lerner's work together with my own reading of *Fight Club*, I shall argue that it is time to stop talking about 'ideology', 'hegemony', 'patriarchy', and all those other hangovers from Marxism which dictate the dance we do, and instead to talk about the need, as critics, intellectuals and scholars, to modify our critical practices to account for these new perceptions of what is going on. For it is here, at the level of rhetoric and linguistics, that we confront the philosophical and practical difficulty of political criticism, where the descriptions of social practice and cultural representation too often fail to grasp their complexities. In her discussion of *Fight Club*, Amy Taubin argues that 'one needs a new vocabulary to describe its vertiginous depiction of space and time. Pans and tilts and tracks just won't do.'[22] Likewise, to explain the film's political implications away in a welter of prefabricated jeremiads, or as simply another cultural expression of a white-male mean-spirited tantrum, will not do. The film impels us towards imagining new ways of approaching not only notions of a masculinity which is both 'fragile' and 'frangible' but, more

importantly, its relationship to liberal-democratic politics as well.[23]
For as Lerner cautions, our response to a situation in which our
political criticism is out of step with the world it seeks to understand
'cannot be the recycling or putting forward, in a more articulate
way, of the same old leftist politics because those politics haven't
worked'.[24]

Allow me the luxury of anecdote to gloss this observation further.
Towards the end of a recent seminar on cinema and politics in which
I trail-ran some of the ideas addressed in this chapter, one student
posed a question which has a tendency to provoke nervous tics in the
academics who populate our Humanities faculties: what would you
actually *do* if you achieved *real* political power? Not so long ago,
intellectuals of the Left replied to such questions by diverting their
answers through the philosophical defiles of Marxist theory, suggesting that our first priority is to root out the truth about the deep
underlying forces of oppression orchestrated by bourgeois culture
and sugar-coated by the impossible promises of capitalism. And, of
course, Marxism irradiated the intellectual imagination just in so far
as it provided a quasi-scientific general theory of oppression, and an
eschatological fulcrum which would end injustice and lead to universal emancipation. Moreover, Marxism's neat linkage of theory and
politics also provided the principal means by which the leftist intellectual could reconcile a 'romance for self-creation' with the 'ideals of
democracy and human solidarity', inasmuch as her particular talents
for redescription and recontextualisation are precisely the skills required for unveiling the source of social injustices.[25] The cash value
of this answer is that it allowed us intellectuals to believe that we
could be politically useful, that our professional competences had a
direct social function. As Richard Rorty puts it, a belief in the Marxist
picture of history let us intellectuals 'feel that our special gifts are
good for more than giving ourselves sophisticated private pleasures
– that these gifts have social utility, permit us to function as an avant-
garde in a universal human struggle'.[26] To this extent, I agree with
Paul Willemen's observation that the 'shift of avant-gardism from the
area of art practice to the terrain of cultural theory' during the 1970s
'constituted a very positive development'.[27] He goes on:

> Cultural theory operated a critical return of the avant-garde practices
> ... by combining the theoretical investigation of signification with a
> reassessment of Marxist theory ... The cultural theory associated with
> socialist-feminist cultural politics in particular constituted a new avant-

garde that re-posed the questions of signification in terms of a theory of the ideological, addressing the operation of the ideological in the social.[28]

Indeed, this project – like the broader Leninist project – once looked both interesting and promising. But notwithstanding some short-term results – especially for feminism – it has not panned out, and is now a wet blanket we would do well to wriggle free of. Moreover, this sort of answer no longer washes with students for whom talk of total revolution and the uprising of the redemptive proletariat to topple capitalism, thus freeing us from human misery, seems as implausible and about as useful as crossing our fingers and hoping for the Second Coming. Marxism's failure to imagine a satis-factory alternative to market economics, the concession that currently we can do no *better* than complexly organised, technologically ori-entated societies, has created a generation of students who largely accept what Alan Ryan calls 'a kind of welfare-capitalism-with-a-human-face', which is 'not easy to distinguish from a "socialism" with a big role for private capital and individual entrepreneurs'.[29] So when we intellectuals ask our students about what kinds of ideas and events irradiate their political imaginations, the replies we hear – unsurprisingly – are not about the renationalisation of the means of production, nor about the overthrow of capitalism and the decom-modification of culture, not even about the resentment of the strong and powerful. Rather, we hear a patchwork of untheoretical, non-strategic hopes for the levelling-up of life-chances among local and international communities, and the protection and enhancement of our living environments for both us and our children. As Andrew Feenberg argues, the politics of modern technically organised and administered society is no longer about the distribution of wealth, nor even about structures of authority; rather, it concerns what he refers to as a 'micropolitics' of agency:

> Times have changed. There is a continuity of the themes of contempo-rary political movements ..., but activism today is far more modest in its ambitions. We have come to recognize politics in smaller interven-tions in social life, sometimes called 'micropolitics', a situational poli-tics based on local knowledge and action. Micropolitics has no general strategy and offers no global challenge to society.[30]

Crucially, the rhetorical yarn which stitches this sub-political patch-work together is woven from a modified political vocabulary, one

which ignores the revolutionary fantasies of World History prefer-
ring instead reformist chatter about what sorts of laws, charters,
agreements, agencies and decisions would improve the conditions of
people's lives.[31] The set of terms which we intellectuals traditionally
called upon to talk politics – 'bourgeois ideology', 'the working
class', 'alienation', 'the ruling class', 'commodification' – have now
been trumped by a new set of terms, in particular 'ecological movement', 'identity politics', 'equal opportunities', 'human rights'. While
certain themes live on – greed, selfishness, alleviation of suffering –
they are no longer wrapped around an eschatological dream of
emancipation, nor subsumed into a theoretical stratagem.

For academics who cut their intellectual teeth on radical social
theory, and sharpened their pencils for the task of ferreting out the
work of ideology whenever and wherever they caught a whiff of its
stench, this has been a difficult pill to swallow – not least because it
leaves us at a loss to know how to make ourselves useful to the weak
in their struggle against the strong. Stripped of our role in the
Marxist narrative of political history, we intellectuals are forced to
admit, with some regret, that our answers to the question posed by
my student are likely to be no more 'deep' or 'complex', and certainly
no more underwritten by 'the truth of history', than anyone else's. In
other words, like everybody else, we have no viable model to replace
market economics, no clear sense of how state power *ought* to be
related to economic questions, and no programme for making the
world anew. In short, we cannot imagine an alternative to liberal
democracy, just ways of tinkering about with its institutions and
laws which might better guard against 'degrading conditions of existence' and more effectively equalise the life-opportunities of its
citizens.[32]

The picture of intellectual and political life I have been sketching
is, of course, by no means as straightforward as I have so far suggested, and it is certainly one which I am sure a number of readers
fail to recognise. For, as Robert Hughes notes, while Marxism as a
Big Idea 'is dead', its rotting carcass continues 'to make sounds and
smells, as fluids drain and pockets of gas expand'.[33] Indeed, for some
critics a version of the Marxist political narrative of intervention
from below is still the closest thing to a theory capable of either
predicting or effecting transformation in the social sphere that we
intellectuals have come up with. For these critics, the primary political imperative remains some version of 'to decode [the text's] ideo-

logical messages and effects', or 'unmasking naturalised representations' – that is, diagnosing and overcoming distorted communication by cognitive clarity in the hope of catching a glimpse of the
rotten guts of capitalism.[34] Other critics, taking a different tack, have
watched Marxism pass 'through the fires of its own dissolution',
only to resuscitate it as a 'hero with a thousand faces'.[35] For these
critics, Marxism, purged of its impossible eschatological and universalising dream, is reborn in the names of the individual agents
involved as a politics of identity. In this respect, a watered-down
Marxism attempts to do what religion failed to do – make us better
people. Either way, I agree with Hughes's diagnosis of the endurance
of Marxism in the American academic left which understands the
'effort to save some notionally "pure" essence of Marx's ideas from
their results in the real world' not as evidence for its continued vi-
tality but, rather, as 'a proof of the power of nostalgia'.[36] Very few
intellectuals today have faith in a Marxist conception of the relationship between theory and politics – or, for that matter, between the
academy and social change. Political events have long since ridden
roughshod over such philosophical postulating. The attempt to imagine large theoretical ways of explaining and eradicating injustice
has almost universally been abandoned, and the idea that theory is
a toolkit for political trailblazing has been exposed as the pretty
conceit – or at least intellectual romanticism – that it always was.

The bewilderment left behind by the realisation that liberal democracies are the best gimmick we have come up with for organising
sociopolitical systems, and the guilt caused by the intuition that our
intellectual labour has nothing wholesale – or perhaps even interesting – to contribute to political progress is, I think, one reason why
the academics working in our Humanities faculties now devote more
time to cultural studies, and to what has become known as 'transgressive' and 'subversive' cultural politics, than to promoting the
avant-garde. I agree with Rorty when he says: 'lately we have been
concentrating on cultural politics, and trying to persuade ourselves
that cultural, and especially academic, politics are continuous with
real politics'.[37] Part of the attraction of postmodern theory, I think,
is that it seemed to offer intellectuals a way of plugging ourselves
back into the political circuit just in so far as postmodernism
decentres the metanarrative of world history, fractures *the* political
question into multiple questions of identity and subjectivity, and
seems to capture some of the despair left in the wake of the collapse

of Marxism. And it is precisely the sense that intellectuals can no longer think of themselves as an avant-garde that, it seems to me, lies behind the attempt to reinvent politics as cultural politics, to substitute a politics *manqué*, a politics of difference, for politics 'proper'. For cultural politics, of course, is not coterminous with real politics. Digging around in the dustbins of popular culture for the occasional 'counter-hegemonic' pearl, or exploring the depths of selfhood for more ineffable sublimity, says little about how we can improve the lot of the impoverished. But thanks to the sticky combination of postmodernism and a feeling of helplessness which has washed through our universities recently, this point has become blurred, and at times totally lost from sight. Moreover, in some respects the desperate search for a successor to Marxism has led us to install other terms – in particular 'Difference' and 'Identity' – as a new Logos incarnate.

This slippage from a normative and therapeutic to a nominal use of 'politics' has become extremely widespread among cultural critics and, moreover, is chiefly responsible for confusing private with public political spaces – precisely the confusion which misdirects our readings of *Fight Club* exclusively down the gendered structures of the former to the total exclusion of the latter.[38] More specifically, the 'politics of identity' which informs so much recent writing in film studies is a concept which adds little to our understanding of this crucial distinction, and remains largely irrelevant to political deliberation inasmuch as it conducts its investigations on the private side of that divide. Worse still, it might actually be a way of forestalling political argument by redirecting our attention into such scholastic quibbles about 'otherness' and 'difference' in the name of labelling particular areas of culture – film, literature, philosophy, art – 'progressive' or 'reactionary', depending on which methodology we subscribe to. The implications of this argument are no more, but no less, than keeping open the gap between *real* politics – that is, social and economic initiatives for managing populations in a way that minimises suffering and prevents cruelty – and cultural politics – the sorts of abstract and playful writing we intellectuals have a talent for. It means, as Rorty puts it, 'being content to be concrete and banal' when talking public politics, or 'real politics', 'no matter how abstract, hyperbolic, transgressive and playful we become when we turn, in a mood of relaxation, to cultural politics'.[39] It is to this extent that the remainder of this chapter is an attempt to pose Rorty's question – whether a given bunch of people are using the word 'political' in a way that avoids specific unfortunate consequences – in relation to scholars of film.[40]

So far I have been painting in broad strokes in order to capture, before the light changes, a sense of where the political land meets the intellectual skies. Now I want to tackle the foreground with some finer brushwork – a foreground which frames some of the questions and confusions that obscure and blur the horizon when one discusses politics in relation to cinema and cinema in relation to politics. As I hinted above, it strikes me that film scholars generally want to talk about the relation between cinema and politics as if the two terms necessarily entertain specific, identifiable and socially important relations with each other. Criticism proceeds as if the impress of socio-political relations can be traced in the textuality of film – that is, in the material product of the cinematic social institution. Questions are thus posed, on the one hand, when some films are said to evince a questionable or reactionary politics and, on the other, when some other films are found to contain subversive or transgressive elements, perhaps even a progressive politics. Both tendencies, however, form two sides of the same intellectual coin: the urge to calculate the net result of a film's cultural variables, and thereby 'discover' whether its particular politics accelerate or retard sociohistorical progress. Accordingly, confusions tend to emerge out of the casual and often ill-defined (over)use of the word politics in the professional rhetorics and disciplinary vocabularies of film, media and cultural studies, a process intensified as all three fell into the orbit of the politics of identity based around ideas if 'difference' and 'otherness'. These are the questions and confusions I shall pursue in the remainder if this chapter, in the hope of reconnecting *our* political discourse with the project of social democracy. In providing such an analysis, no mysterious or 'distorted' politics remains for critics to puzzle over. Indeed, once the illusion of depth is removed, politics floats back up to the surface, where it belongs. I shall therefore continue by distinguishing three senses of the term 'politics' as it is deployed in film and cultural theory.

'(P)olitics' is what I have already referred to as 'real' or 'proper' politics, and describes a direct linkage between sociopolitical formations, cinematic institutions, and filmic representations. In this sense it is a capital-'P' politics, and is synonymous with institutional and state structures of power: the power to control, manipulate and coerce, or – their watered-down approbative form – persuade, manage and inform populations. (P)olitics is thus a historical politics precisely inasmuch as it implies a diachronic relationship and causal continuity between a particular system of governance, its social organisation and the kinds, diversity and richness of culture that circulate in its public sphere. Appeals to politics in film criticism are generally framed by three topoi, either singularly or in combination. The first – and perhaps most obvious – of these is propaganda: the instrumental use of cinema to manipulate people in a certain way for predetermined purposes. It asks such questions as 'Who wants to regulate culture and insulate communication?'; 'How is this achieved?'; and 'What sociopolitical ends does it serve?'

The consequences of the relationship between economy, institutions and aesthetics constitute the second principal topos of 'politics'. This is sometimes called 'ownership and control' and sometimes 'political economy'. It is distinct from propaganda to the extent that it seeks to describe not an instrumental means–end relationship between those who govern, culture, and those governed but, rather, the material conditions which structure aesthetic activity. More specifically, its point of departure is the imbrication of the capitalist market economy, industrialised production practices, and cinematic forms, and it considers questions such as how capital investment, hierarchical divisions of labour and the primacy of profit 'affect[s] what you can say and how you can say it'.[41] In short, it focuses on the particular ways in which the economic and institutional relations of cultural production bear upon not only the relative diversity of film form, but also the cultural sluicegates which regulate access to particular sorts of cinematic product.

The third main imperative of political analysis examines the work of self-pronounced politically committed film-makers such as Sergei Eisenstein, Dziga Vertov, and Jean-Luc Godard, and is often tied in with accounts of cinema's key role in the twentieth-century cultural avant-garde. This also provides its link to feminist counter-cinema practices associated with second-wave radical feminism. Specifically in terms of American cinema, which is dealt with quite differently from European cinemas in this respect, critics have tended to privilege particular instances of self-conscious political film-making – the film itself – over individual film-makers' *oeuvres*. So while – to pick an obvious example – Godard's films tend to be written about in terms of the way they speak not merely to each other, but to a broader political agenda, critics of American film seem to want to thrash the political wheat from the generic chaff of a film-maker's work. One has only to consider the different critical approach adopted towards Oliver Stone's *Platoon*, *JFK* and *Nixon* on the one hand, and *Natural Born Killers*, and *U Turn* on the other, to taste the difference in the way these films are chewed over. The former group's overt political agendas have indeed been addressed, but the more indirect politics of the latter have generally been ignored in favour of a merely stylistic focus.

This selective critical procedure is not entirely surprising, however, when one takes into account the difficulty of moving between textual and political interpretations of popular film in the wake of the persuasive yet unhelpful postmodern notion that the mass media have levelled down politics and representation to a simulacrum.[42] So although popular culture in American society has – to an extent unmatched by other Western democracies – historically been thoroughly imbricated in the national body politic, I agree with Timothy Corrigan when he says that 'politics of any sort – and especially the American kind – have [now] been so widely identified with media events that any position on the first can be too easily deflected and often dissipated into the slippery, entertaining gloss of the second'.[43] He continues:

> one of the persistent debates and concerns within studies of postmodernism is the very possibility of a truly political position in a cultural landscape [which] seems to disallow thoughtful engagement, provocation, or social reading itself. The question becomes: if a political film operates with some notion of public effectiveness, how does a film become socially and politically effective when its meaning is always wrapped in its reception as a kind of private distraction or a mere public outing?[44]

So while political analysis was once underpinned by something akin to a critical programme – a set of more or less concrete proposals and ideals about the role of the intellectual in relation to the cultural politic, ideals such as the argument for artistic autonomy and a space outside the capitalist economic system in which a genuine avant-garde could operate – latterly, in the face of an increasingly fragmented mediascape, the realisation of the global market economy, and the de-insulation of the national body politic, it has become increasingly difficult to map cinematic representations on to socio-economic contours of power. The ensuing fuzziness is one reason, I think, that appeals to politics in film studies now tend to be made far less frequently and more cautiously, tending to be centred on films such as *Nixon, JFK, Primary Colors, Schindler's List, Saving Private Ryan* – that is, films which force political consideration through their historical content. And since this species of cinema is relatively rare, it also helps to account for a rapid rise in the share price of ideological politics and identity politics in European and American intellectual markets.

'Politics' is also synonymous with ideology – with, as Terry Eagleton puts it, 'ideas and beliefs which help to legitimate the interests of a ruling group or class by distortion and dissimulation'.[45] In this sense of the term, every film, TV programme, novel, painting, advertisement – in fact, every facet of culture – propagates ideology to a greater or lesser extent. This 'drip, drip, drip of ideology',[46] as Roger Silverstone describes it, is regarded as the primary means by which the strong maintain social, economic and psychic advantage over the weak – by, in Noel Carroll's phrase, 'seizing control over the consciousness of citizens in such a way as they find domination acceptable'.[47] So while Marxism largely evaporated in postmodernism's afterburn, the process left behind ideology, and in particular Althusserian ideology, as its precipitate – thus distilling, at least for some, an even more powerful theoretical brew in the heat of that reaction. For it is no accident that critics who remain dubious about the implosion of Marxism into the post-metaphysical philosophical black hole – about the challenge to precisely the metanarratives of religion, science and history around which we have traditionally spun our political hopes and theories – are also those who most insistently cling to ideology as the *lingua franca* of political analysis.[48] Indeed, so equivocal has the term ideology become that the academic euphemism 'ideological critique' is now used either interchangeably or as a cipher for political critique. More specifically, the cash value of this switch for film scholars is that if one has acquired the correct forensic reading skills, and if one rummages deep enough into any text, 'false beliefs' and 'distorted communication' can be unearthed virtually anywhere.[49] Likewise, in a neat reversal, one can further complicate the matter by then going on to claim that a film's apparent meanings and 'obvious pleasures' can act as a 'cover for dominant ideology' even if they are themselves not 'simply reducible' to it. [50]

This is of a piece with Slavoj Žižek's claim that 'ideology really succeeds when even the facts which at first sight contradict it start to function as arguments in its favour'.[51] Such a double-helix approach is also what gives rise to those other overworked terms 'crisis in representation', 'textual negotiations', 'textual struggles', and 'resistance', in the sense that they provide the conceptual lever for the critic to excavate for 'the fissures, faults and excesses in articulations of dominant ideology'.[52]

One of the most sustained examples of this kind of ideological approach to the analysis of American cinema is Douglas Kellner and Michael Ryan's book *Camera Politica*.[53] In their introduction, the authors state that the book aims to provide a 'diagnostic critique of those ideological strategies' which pacify 'the tensions endemic to an inegalitarian society' and to 'analyze the sources, the morphology, and limitations of conservative and liberal ideological cultural forms and to ferret out the forces and possibilities that ideology seeks to deny, forces that point beyond the society of domination toward a more equal social form'.[54] By writing in such terms, Kellner and Ryan gear up the political stakes of film just inasmuch as it forms 'part of a broader system of cultural representation which operates to create psychological dispositions that result in a particular construction of social reality, a commonly held sense of what the world is and ought to be that sustains social institutions'. They go on to say:

> In our view, ideology needs to be seen as an attempt to placate social tensions and to respond to social forces in such a way that they cease to be dangerous to the social system of inequality. Ideology carries out this task through cultural representations which, like mental representations in relation to the psyche, orient thought and behaviour in a manner that maintains order and establishes boundaries on proper action.
>
> Rather than conceive of ideology as a simple exercise in domination, we suggest that it be conceived of as a response to forces which, if they were not pacified, would tear the social system asunder from inside.[55]

Kellner and Ryan's tactics become clearer when, later on the same page, they graft a quasi-Freudian description of ideology on to their already bellicose political methodology:

> The very necessity of ideology testifies to something amiss within society, since a society that was not threatened would not need

ideological defences. By attempting to pacify, channel, and neutralise the forces that would invert the social system of inequality were they not controlled, ideology testifies to the power of those forces, of the very thing it seeks to deny. By reacting against the structural tensions and potentially disruptive forces of an inegalitarian society, film ideology must also put them on display – just as excessively washed hands testify to offstage guilt.[56]

This gives Kellner and Ryan's book a two-pronged purpose: to rummage around texts, rooting out the ideological bogeyman which guards the gateway to a more egalitarian society; and to let out those radical or subversive forces which are hidden away in the basement of texts, and are apparently imperceptible to the untrained eye through the glare of their shop-window displays.[57]

However, the 'it's all ideology' argument has always struck me as pretty weak for a host of reasons, but here I want to mention briefly just two. First, such arguments overwhelmingly tend either to resist any positive evaluation of the social-democratic, liberal state in the first place, or to crush the positive aspects between an eschatological upper millstone – the *a fortiori* desire to make the world anew – and a romantic nether millstone – that the radical intellectual might help to turn the tables of power held by the few in favour of the many. In other words, *Ideologiekritik* accounts of film, and American film in particular, betray staggering myopia to the extent that the picture they paint of American culture filters out precisely the economic and institutional elements that have resulted in more social freedom and the progressive alleviation of 'degrading conditions of human existence'. On the evidence of books like Kellner and Ryan's, one could be forgiven for thinking that suffering and misery had not decreased considerably, nor that citizens' scope for adopting their own 'lifestyle' had correspondingly increased during the past three hundred years of American history. My point is that this sort of description of our contemporary situation seems to me to misrepresent the narrative of gradual social and political progress that characterises the rich bourgeois social democracies of the West, a narrative which tells how we have moved in the direction of more freedom, more diversity and more tolerance.[58]

My second main concern is more academic, in both senses of the term, and is to do with the way so-called ideological diagnostics of popular culture proceed from the deployment of the term 'ideology' as a non-controversial lemma: in other words, passed off not as an *explanans* – for deconstruction usually fills those shoes – but as the *explanandum*. On this view, the existence of ideology is not only a given but, still more essentially, the source of distorted meaning and false beliefs – precisely the intermediary object between thought and reality which, if excoriated, would bring about historical progress and human emancipation. As the logic runs, conscious experiences, including those of the ruling class, are intrinsically informed by ideology. Nobody would doubt the plausibility of all this, of course, if they could just climb outside their minds for a minute and glimpse the truth of their psychological and economic domination. However, once one sees that phrases such as 'militarist, racist, patriarchal and capitalist ideologies in post 1977 Hollywood films', 'the western's ideological construction of a mythic American past', as well as 'crisis in ideological confidence' and the 'socially critical and oppositional moments within all ideological texts' are incantations rather than explanations (because we have no test for the presence of ideology distinct from our descriptions of it), it seems probable that ideology's political edge is blunted.[59] Or – to put it another way – you can no more be sure that an ideological diagnosis is itself free of ideological contamination than you can step outside your own skin. For critics are surely attempting to have their theoretical cake and eat it if they claim, on the one hand, that ideology goes all the way down, while on the other hand they continue to pass off their own beliefs as coterminous with the way things look once ideology is stripped way. In short, the only criterion available to the critic for applying the word 'ideology' to culture is itself culturally grounded, and subject to precisely the same ideological charges. The only empirical basis it rests on seems to be that if a critic skilled in the professional protocols of deconstructing film looks hard and long enough, she will be able to unmask the ideological contraband of any text. But this is not only an intellectual closed circuit inasmuch as it allows critics freely to project a political picture on to cinema, where it is then 'read' as evidence; more importantly, it has the effect of short-circuiting political insight by diverting analysis into a procedural attribution of 'reactionary', 'conservative', 'hegemonic' and – less often – 'progressive', 'subversive' and 'transgressive' labels to film, forgetting Paul Willemen's caution that, depending on one's intentions, films 'can be pulled into more or less any ideological space'.[60]

Something, therefore, has to give. Critics who wish to continue to deconstruct film in order to unmask ideology must modify their conceptions of ideology; reconsider the relationship between ideology and politics; or admit that ideology cannot be squared with a post-metaphysical picture of the world, and that criticism of cinema in terms of this or that ideology is beside the political point. Since the third option rules ideology out of the game, most critics employ a combination of the first two. Kellner and Ryan's response to such criticisms, for instance – a response pretty much mirrored by critics who insist on retaining ideology as their political *foci imaginarius* – is to offer a seemingly more plausible and fine-toothed conception of the relationship between ideology, society and politics, one which uses some convenient threads of psychology and psychoanalysis to stitch itself back together. And by supplementing ideological critique with metonymic and psychoanalytic readings of film, they do indeed give us such a 'refined' conception, but the increased fineness of tooth seems to me to serve little political purpose, and in fact gives us grounds for suspecting that the theoretical boosters one has to invent to make the fighting weight are at the expense of both its intellectual punch and its utility to social practice. Kellner and Ryan, therefore, must either concede the point that ideology is an idea without content, or else give us further *desiderata* for detecting ideology independently of our descriptions of it. I am not sure what such *desiderata* would resemble, but without them proponents of ideology have to admit that political analysis rooted in unmasking the scurrilous work of ideology is hard to integrate with a post-Marxist description of the world to the extent that it always begs the question of verification – a space outside ideology from which we can observe its operations objectively. But addressing the problem in this way, by casting about for philosophical paper to plug the theoretical holes, seems to me to be a case of explaining the abstract by the ridiculous. Besides, once critics start quarrelling about which term to graft on to ideology to reactivate it, they may have abandoned cultural significance to professional rigour. It is to the extent that Kellner and Ryan's book gives us excellent reasons to think that ideology is a stubborn hangover of Marxism that we cannot usefully separate a heuristic ideological critique from a Marxist eschatology – reasons, moreover, to think that these, together with the problems of 'unmaking hegemony' and 'false beliefs', are part of a package deal that we would do well to avoid. For what is so easily lost at the vertiginous level of abstraction required to justify the cost of such a package – the level where all politics are mapped on to the same ideological continuum – is precisely everything that makes it possible to draw critically interesting and politically useful distinctions between different films. In short, once its putative empirical guts are revealed to be tautological, ideology becomes little more than make-believe. And, of course, the only people who profit from sustaining this make-believe game are the academics who play it.

The third model of 'Politics' is a puzzling grab bag of opaque theory and idiosyncratic esotericism. It is what one encounters when, with increasing frequency, one comes across phrases such as 'politics of identity', 'politics of difference', or 'politics of the self'. Identity in this context means something like the aleatoric bundle of biology, genes and beliefs which conspire to produce individual psychology, and which we string into an account of personhood through the stories we tell ourselves about those factors in relation to our experiences. In this respect, Nick Couldry argues that the politics of self-hood is 'a question of insisting that particular selves – with all their uncertainties and contradictions – should be recognised, listened to and accounted for in the types of claim we make about culture and cultural experience'.[61] In thinking through the self – or, more accurately, 'thinking the social through self', to use Elspeth Probyn's phrase – identity politics turns inwards: that is to say, it delves into the drama of subjectivity instead of going public.[62] This partly explains why identity politics has progressively become a dragnet description for both various social movements and theories of subjectivity, of self-exploration. It is a newfangled politics in so far as it skims the poststructural cream off European philosophy, particularly that of Foucault and Derrida, as well as Freudian psychoanalysis, for descriptions of 'self', 'difference', and 'otherness', in order to weave a 'connoisseurship for cultural diversity' together with a narrative of psychological and political autonomy. Indeed, it is no accident that the rise in stock price of identity politics coincides with the eclipse of pragmatism in American intellectual markets by a breed of Anglo-American analytical philosophy which refurbished itself in the poststructural image of European thought. In replacing society and epistemology with 'self' as the centre of political gravity, political theory becomes less concerned with eschatology and more preoccupied with a *rapport à soi* – a search for private autonomy, a quest for self-creation. Charmed by the poststructuralist rhetoric of difference, identity politics ironises selfhood to the extent that personhood becomes a contingency of self-description – that is, no longer a biological or social given, but a series of mutable linguistic and cultural performances.

Shoving concern for solidarity aside, the concept of self which emerges from the politics of difference is chimera-like, 'contradictory, incoherent and multiple'.[63] Identity, as Judith Butler argues in relation to gender, is thus understood as a 'complexity whose totality is permanently deferred, never fully what it is at any given junction in time'. Butler goes on to say that such conceptions of selfhood as an 'open coalition' 'will affirm identities that are alternately instituted and relinquished according to the purpose at hand; it will be an open assemblage that permits of multiple convergences and divergences without obedience to a normative *telos* of definitional closure.'[64] And it is precisely this absence of a normative *telos* which allows Couldry to reformulate the political question as matter of social degree instead of the once-and-for-all historical matter Marxism takes it to be when he asks: 'how can we live with difference and analyse the realm of the intersubjective?'[65] It is also what allows Davis and Smith to argue that the 'bourgeois ideal' has given way, in the political discourse of many recent Hollywood films, to a dissociated identity which is 'increasingly represented in terms of individuated ethnicity, gender or sexuality, according to models drawn from some elements of the traditions of identity politics'.[66] Here, Davis, like many other critics, uses 'politics' in conjunction with 'identity', 'difference', or 'self' as a name for a new kind of political intervention which entails a new kind of critical focus. Yeatman, for instance, argues that this 'new wave of theorizing' actually 'creates a space for those who have been "othered" in discourse'.[67]

The phenomenon to which these critics are pointing clearly exists, but 'politics' seems to me to be the wrong name for it. Indeed, my hunch is that the emergence of identity-based politics owes very little to political tactics and everything to our own community's theoretical prognostications, to the esoteric turn inward in the wake of a collapse of confidence in metanarratives of historical progress. In this respect, the ambiguous and multiple self is the payoff for the disappointment of a decentred world – making our*selves* anew is the most radical act left open to us; claiming our difference is the only assertion of our autonomy.

The linkage of identity to politics would work, of course, if a detailed picture of what Couldry calls 'the self's reflexive life' were the sort of thing that could 'provide a workable and shared basis for a political conception of justice in a democratic society'.[68] But are idiosyncratic beliefs and esoteric desires likely to congeal to form the basis of what Rawls has referred to as the 'overlapping consensus' required to accommodate conflicting and often incommensurate 'doctrines of diversity' fairly into a workable conception of democracy?[69] Why do private hopes for self-creation need to be sequestered into the political sphere? Why should it matter if I am a man, a woman, heterosexual, homosexual or bisexual, black, white, an environmentalist, or even a bigot when it comes to achieving a consensual social organisation which best equalises the life-chances of its citizens? In other words, are theories of identity usefully explicated by the addition of the term 'politics'? For if identity politics means something like acknowledging 'the intersecting, contradictory and cross-category functioning of US culture', then it is merely a descriptive remark about the success of liberal bourgeois democracies in seeing 'more and more differences among people as morally irrelevant to the possibility of cooperating with them for mutual benefit'.[70] In other words, while the dig for ever deeper levels of identity has produced the warp and weft of a new intellectual vocabulary, to claim than it does any more that add some finer brushwork to the political picture already sketched out in the democratic ideals of liberal pluralism is misleading.

We have no need for the idea that there are two kinds of politics: a banal one for working out how best to configure the political institutions of a liberal democracy, and a sophisticated one for embossing the thorough contingency of selfhood into that picture. Indeed, at its most playful, identity politics flirts intimately with meaninglessness – dancing with ethereal concepts kept aloft only by the forward propulsion of their internal motion, mining theoretical seams which make little difference to social practice. I thus see identity politics not as imagining some radically new world, or even as offering ideas for social reform, but simply as further fleshing out John Stuart Mill's notion of liberty as 'doing as we like' subject to not harming others. At this point, the distinction between private subjectivity and public politics can be glossed as the distinction between the exploration and satisfaction of narcissistic and idiosyncratic individuated needs and the satisfaction of common needs that are widely shared and freely agreed upon. In fact, if we attend to the success of realising the latter needs then the former are taken care of in so far as the institutions of a liberal democracy 'equalise opportunities for self-creation and then leave people alone to use, or neglect, their opportunities'.[71] In this way, since the politics of identity can contribute little to the discussion of public affairs, I think there is probably no such politics, or at least little in such work which is relevant to designing social policies for improving our conditions of social existence.

So much for my overall account of the uses of 'politics' in cultural criticism. But why have I been nit-picking at such length about the ways we intellectuals use words like 'politics', 'ideology' and 'identity' in our critical rhetorics? First, because film and cultural scholars have often – explicitly or unwittingly – used these three senses of 'politics' interchangeably, moving from a philosophical investigation of politics to a social critique of politics through the rhetorical defiles associated with personal politics. More recently, the problems of achieving an 'ideal' politics are situated as an impediment to the development of the politics of identity, while ideologically determined politics continues to mediate pretty much all discussions about the relative political merits of individual films, where ideology acts as the intermediary term between things like narrative, visual style and aesthetics on the one hand, and our symptomatic interpretation of those elements along the reactionary–radical continuum on the other.

In the end, however, this is really only a symptom of my main worry, which is to do with the ineffectuality of our current critical discourses for addressing the political questions posed by the films I mentioned above. For precisely the technical and scholastic nature of those discourses constitutes in itself grounds for suspecting that that they are not tied very tightly into our social practices, into observation. Their esoterism, moreover, makes those critical rhetorics susceptible to the charge that they actually *produce* the representational politics of the films they seek to describe, by retrofitting their already formulated criteria for determining the *desirability* for social change to whatever cinematic or cultural sites fall within a particular research programme instead of remaining content to work out, in a piecemeal fashion, how those sites might themselves be politically operational. I think the fact that *Fight Club* could be interpreted symptomatically in reference to some well trodden and reliable conceptions of masculine identity in American cinema explains why critics tended to privilege the textual cues which could be read as evidence for subjectivity while relegating the social dimension of (male) agency to the narrative backdrop for the private drama. In other words, *Fight Club*'s schizophrenic narrative mirrors precisely the argument I made a little way back that private desires and fantasies – represented here by Jack's *alter ego*, Tyler Durden – and public affairs should be kept separate, and thus treated as distinct critical questions. For if we put aside for a moment the critical logics which fix our glare on the question of punitive masculinity in crisis, a logic in which the private is subsumed as a public matter, then we can read Tyler as *merely* the visual projection of Jack's unconscious psychological transactions within the Freudian partitioned self between two 'intellects' with competing sets of desires and beliefs. As such, Tyler is one of the casual network of quasi-persons which populate Jack's inner space, bound by Jack's consciousness and accessible only through introspection. In other words, Jack and Tyler tell two *separate* stories which are alternative extrapolations from a common experience – a sterile, loveless and unfulfilling life. Crucially, however, Tyler's account is only ever Jack's private affair, a interior negotiation, never the public terrorism critics willed it to be. On this account, to criticise the film's violence as *ad hominem* fascism not only attributes to Tyler a corporeal effectivity and volition he does not have, but ultimately ignores the degrading conditions of Jack's existence which generate *Fight Club*'s entire narrative.[72]

This example is intended only to put some meat on the bones of the wider argument I am trying to put forward here, to do with the implications of our own community's critical activities vis-à-vis politics. In sequestering politics into theoretical and professionalised realms, criticism is routed through the operational systems of various interpretative schemata which encourage the critic to delegate the built-in purpose of whatever schema she prefers to the film where it can be 'read' as evidence for both the success of the schema for detecting political communication and the intellectual dexterity of the critic in dragging the schema into ever more cultural contexts. In effect, this reduces cinematic representation to the protocols of interpretative logics: instead of using films to generate political criticism, criticism is used to generate the politics of films.

I have nothing against the fervour for theory, the penchant for tinkering with abstraction, the desire for grinding cultural grist through our theoretical millstones. But such activities tend to be fruitless quibbles when it comes to the question of practical politics. Indeed, the career of Marxism in the political vocabularies of the intellectual Left should by now have taught us that the attempt to build a general theory of emancipatory politics by ascending to the theoretical heavens produces only vacuous slogans or impractical platitudes. There is nothing general or universal to be said about the relationship between cinema and politics. Nor is there any 'correct' methodology for unearthing the political work of film, nor any 'proper' conceptual tools with which to engage in political debates. What I am suggesting is that political progress – the act of getting from the here-and-now to a better future – is too unpredictable, and too dependent on chance and luck, to be explicated by a priori theoretical frameworks or predicted by a meta-politic. The process, in other words, cannot be described as gradually working our way down a neat metaphysical flow chart, for political criticism requires no extra-political grounding. While there are theoretically interesting things we can say about 'ideology', 'identity', *'différence'*, 'subjectivity', and so on, there is little which is of any political use hidden deep within those terms which is not already taken care of by the ideals of a liberal democracy. I think film studies will get along better, politically speaking, once we shrug off our theoretical prefaces to politics and concentrate on small-scale concrete questions – that is, the questions which emerge out of the films themselves, not out of our theoretical prognostications.

The perspective from which I can say that the latter, de-philosophised, piecemeal approach might be both more convenient and *useful* is that of the pragmatist. There is neither the space nor the necessity to delve into the philosophy of pragmatism here, beyond quoting Rorty's Deweyan dictum: 'Pragmatists think that that if something makes no difference to practice, it should make no difference to philosophy.'[73] Translated into the context of cultural criticism, *mutatis mutandis* this conviction would mean that we intellectuals disengaged scholastic quarrels about identity from social policy, stopped trying to adjudicate between competing versions of ideology, and started asking how, when we talk politics, we might be useful to a liberal democracy. For political criticism of film is now rarely useful in the pragmatist sense of the term precisely in so far as, in supplanting the question of democracy with such epiphenomena as ideology and subjectivity, it fails to confront the practical aspects of modern political processes. A quasi-political realm is thus produced somewhere between personal sublimity and universal emancipation by confusing the sophisticated vocabulary of high-minded theory with the simple-minded vocabulary of democratic politics; a quasi-politics that is ill-suited to public purposes, of no political use *qua* politics. In this way, once we become good pragmatists, ideology, subjectivity and identity become theoretical cogs which have no useful function in any political mechanism. One can sum up this idea by saying that if you are sceptical about the circularity of veridical ideological criticism, and frustrated by the ineffability of identity and subjectivity, such a pragmatic reconception of the relationship between film and politics provides good reasons for believing that for the purposes of writing politically minded film criticism, you can safely *ignore* both.

But if we cannot drill for deep underlying answers to the way politics works, and how its course might be manipulated to do some good, what *can* we do? A first step would be to adjust our self-image as intellectuals from political architects to the underlabourers of democratic society. In other words, the politically minded critic might – to paraphrase Rorty – function as something like the professionalised conscience of democratic society.[74] In this way, critics should see themselves as working at the interface between the political ideal of a liberal democracy and the ways in which the chances of realising that ideal are blocked, retarded, helped or facilitated though the art and culture of society. Such a therapeutic critical practice can proceed only on an *ad hoc* basis, and will not yield anything more than an elaborate list of the heroes of liberal hope – people like David Fincher and Paul Thomas Anderson, whose films make us sensitive to the life around us. For it is in the images, marks, words and stories of film-makers, artists, poets and novelists, not in the blurry things we academics talk about, that the realm of the possible is extended. All we as intellectuals can ever hope to achieve is to flesh out the self-image of our liberal democracies by trekking back and forth between the critical low ground – where we talk about such things as the relationship between narrative and visual and stylistic elements – and the political high ground on which we hack out our hopes for a better world. Indeed, providing particular accounts of how those hopes are expressed through our cultural products, and separating out the people whose ideas might hasten the winning of those hopes – either by showing what such a world might look like, or by warning us what might happen if we let go of those hopes – is the only way to hook up a relatively minor academic discipline such as film studies with the political sphere. Scholars of film should thus see themselves as involved at one of the softer ends in a long-term attempt to modify the self-image of society in accordance with the ideal of liberal democracy – not by providing new images themselves but, rather, in drawing attention to cultural practice that is useful in imagining that ideal.

This means, of course, that we will have to be on our intellectual toes much more often, and be prepared to get our hands dirty from time to time – to be willing, that is, to address film less in terms of our pre-programmed theories and more in terms of sentiments: the ways film can alert us to the suffering and pain of humiliation, and how it can provide glimpses of the good life. In other words, it means that when it comes to politics, we need to be aware of what Berkeley called the need to 'speak with the vulgar and think with the learned'.[75] It also means that we will have to be content with our political analyses as a ground-clearing activity instead of the ground-breaking enterprise we so wish they could be.

In another context John Rawls cautioned philosophers to 'stay on the surface, philosophically speaking'.[76] Politically speaking, film scholars would do well to do the same.

Part 2

'Ask not what America
can do for you...'
Views from the White House

Hollywood in elections and elections in Hollywood

Philip John Davies

The film industry never seemed far away at the 2000 Democratic National Convention, held at the Staples Center in Los Angeles, but Democratic vice-presidential nominee Joe Lieberman thought that at least some of the filmic analysis should have been directed elsewhere. Referring to the intensively orchestrated Republican Convention, held in the east coast 'City of Brotherly Love' a couple of weeks earlier, he said: 'We may be near Hollywood here, but not since Tom Hanks won an Oscar has there been that much acting in Philadelphia.'[1]

In 2000, the Republican convention to nominate George W. Bush as that party's presidential candidate was a high-value, skilfully directed marvel of media production, nominated by one (admittedly Democrat) observer as 'Bush's perfectly scripted Republican convention'.[2] TV journalist Ted Koppel, who walked out of the 1996 convention on the grounds that it was so scripted there was no room for news, did not even bother to turn up this year, and the main TV networks planned to restrict coverage of the convention to news broadcasts and occasional highlights, leaving gavel-to-gavel live coverage to current affairs cable channels CNN and C-SPAN.

Instead of following the tradition of filling up one night with a full roll-call vote of all the state delegations for the presidential nomination, the Republicans divided this exercise into nightly episodes of a few states presented in alphabetical order, each brief enough to maintain some attention in a viewing population with a decreasing average attention span. Traditional (and often uninspiring) afternoon sessions disappeared, and the more media- and viewer-friendly convention was scheduled to open at 7.30 p.m., planned to the minute thereafter, and packed with entertainment. In the words of CNN analyst Stuart Rothenberg: 'This is a show. This is a Hollywood extravaganza, a Broadway production … where you try to convey to the voters you care, you're sensitive, you understand their feelings.[3]

'Compassionate conservatism' was indicated from the start by showcasing a series of speakers of colour. Asian Americans, Hispanic Americans and African Americans did their performances on stage, creating, according to one attending journalist, 'the Republicans' Cotton Club convention – lots of blacks on the stage, none in the audience'. According to one speaker in Los Angeles: 'The Republicans pretended they were tolerant, pretended they were moderates … Let's face it, they pretended they were Democrats.'[4] Reporting for the ABC network, Cokie Roberts made a similar analysis: '[The Republicans are] basically turning the Republican convention into a Democratic one, and that seems to work for Republicans.'[5] Bill Clinton's former Secretary of Labor, Robert Reich, put it differently, noting that the Republican convention 'embodied all the traditional images of a Democratic one – a kaleidoscope of ethnic groups; an address by the sole avowedly gay Republican member of Congress; the gentle rhetoric of tolerance and inclusion…', but also that in prosperous times it 'gave America exactly what it wanted – the least political convention in American history, filled with cotton-candy images of tolerance and prosperity, patriotic drivel and sentimental fluff'.[6] In a cinema season when *The Patriot* (Roland Emmerich, 2000) remodelled the American War of Independence in the shape of a colonial yeoman forced to abandon his pacifism, and to embrace an egalitarianism very unlikely in eighteenth-century North America because of the excesses of a British military prone to Nazi-style tactics, and *U571* (Jonathan Mostow, 2000) rewrote an entirely British World War II naval and intelligence operation as entirely American, in order to maximise the patriotic appeal of these films in the US market, the Republican convention could well have come out of a similar school of production.

In 2000 the Democrats chose southern California as the location for President Bill Clinton to pass the torch of party leadership to Al Gore. Ronald Reagan had, decades previously, shifted gradually from a film career to the White House, passing through stages as a Hollywood union leader, Goldwater supporter, partisan political activist, and two-term Governor of California. Reagan's term in the presidency, from 1981 to 1989, had been hailed as an administration imbued with powerful cinema technique. The 'Morning Again in America' campaign for re-election in 1984 had brought into campaign advertising some of the highest production values ever seen in the elections industry.

All this having been said, twenty years after Reagan's election, it was Bill Clinton, approaching the end of his eight years in office, who, for all the scandal and personal crisis that had dogged his administration, seemed to many observers both to bring a Hollywood quality to Washington politics, and to maintain the most successful practical links with Hollywood of any recent president.

With this much star quality, passing the torch cleanly became difficult. According to screenwriter Joe Eszterhas (*Jagged Edge* (Richard Marquand, 1985), *Sliver* (Phillip Noyce, 1993), *Basic Instinct* (Paul Verhoeven, 1991)), the parallels between the film and politics businesses are becoming increasingly clear. '[A] star's career is a lifelong political campaign', and on the other side of this coin, Bill Clinton was America's 'first rock'n'roll president'. Eszterhas goes on: 'the inner dynamics of Hollywood are like politics. Say you give a script to a group of executives – they all sit around, afraid to voice an opinion, saying nothing, waiting to know what the consensus is. Just like focus groups, opinion polls or a cabinet. Meanwhile, politics is about getting a candidate in front of the public as a star, politics as rock'n'roll, politics as a movie.'[7] Eszterhas's thinking is rather unstructured, but his conclusions illuminate a broader analytical perception of – and often a concern about – the convergence of some elements of politics and entertainment.

The Democratic convention did not appear to adjust as much as the Republican one to video demands. In substantial part this was a matter of time zones – a mid-evening 8 p.m. appearance in Los Angeles is simultaneously a fairly late 11 p.m. broadcast in New York City. There were still afternoon sessions when lists of minor party dignitaries and supporters each had a carefully timed spot to speak with as much sincerity and energy as they could muster for an almost empty stadium, and for their home TV stations. Nevertheless, there was a script, and major scenes to put together.

Clinton's valedictory was scheduled for the Monday night. His entrance was one of powerfully contrived drama. It was Ronald Reagan's executive team that knocked out walls and remodelled the White House so that the President would no longer enter press conferences by a side door. Instead they created an imposing hallway behind the podium, which could be revealed when needed so that the President could stride directly towards the audience and towards the camera, using the opening seconds of the encounter to impose his status on the proceedings before he even said a word. Bill Clinton's entrance on the first night of the 2000 Democratic convention in Los Angeles took this trick and built on it to a daring extent. In a very lengthy sequence, '[a] camera showed him alone and without entourage, walking through the corridors and stairwells of the convention centre, before emerging through a tunnel and on to the stage: he looked like Russell Crowe in *Gladiator*' (Ridley Scott, 2000), said Jonathan Freedland. 'It is hard to think of a more charismatic performer in any field, music or the arts or sport, anywhere in the world.'[8] The TV networks took their direction and their feed from the party's convention camera for this sequence, controlled by Hollywood producer Gary Smith, who instructed his staff in the backstage corridors to 'Get everybody out – they want it empty.' As Tom Brokaw, NBC's top-flight reporter, told his viewers: 'This is President as rock star.'[9]

Star quality, nostalgia, emotion and the symbols of a liberal heritage were brought to the second night of the 2000 Democratic convention, in particular by the appearance on the stage of a series of Kennedys. The Kennedys almost have the power of a genre within American politics. Such is the audience familiarity with the highs and lows of many Kennedy life-scripts that their appearance immediately engages even relatively uninformed viewers in a comprehensible language of political and cultural messages that do not have to be spelled out in detail. Edward M. Kennedy, US Senator from Massachusetts since 1962, once himself a presidential hopeful, inevitably brings to his audience memories of his assassinated brothers Senator Robert F. Kennedy and President John F. Kennedy. Both these politicians had links with Hollywood, and both were fully aware of the significance of celebrity, and of visual drama, in their careers. In Congress Bobby stepped into the limelight as the forceful adversary of Teamster Union president Jimmy Hoffa, a confrontation to appear later in Danny De Vito's film (*Hoffa*, 1992). In 1960 the campaign of John F. Kennedy invited Frank Sinatra to produce the new President's inaugural party.[10] The other southern California memories they inspired were mixed. Bobby Kennedy was shot dead in Los Angeles in 1968 during celebrations of his victory in that year's California presidential primary. President Kennedy was nominated as his party's presidential candidate in Los Angeles in 1960.

Ted Kennedy, staunchly liberal throughout the party political swings of the late twentieth century, also served as a living emblem of the liberal element in the Democrat political alliance. Kathleen Kennedy Townsend, daughter of Bobby and Lieutenant Governor of Maryland, and her brother Robert Kennedy Jr were also there to speak in support of Al Gore's presidential ambitions.[11] But most interest was sparked by Caroline Kennedy Schlossberg, daughter of President Kennedy, and, since her brother's death in a 1999 air crash, 'the last child of Camelot',[12] making a rare political appearance to endorse the Democratic ticket. Few have more credibility than the daughter and niece of assassinated political heroes to seize the controversial issue of gun control from the moral high ground and stamp it firmly on the campaign: 'If we believe that we have seen enough gun violence in our land and in our lifetimes, that guns should no longer take the lives of those we love, then it is up to us … to elect Al Gore and Joe Lieberman.'[13]

Patrick Kennedy, Member of Congress from Connecticut's First District, a powerful fund-raiser for the Democrats, and son of Senator Ted Kennedy called this series of family appearances 'surreal': 'This is not the real world here, politics is not about the kind of charisma that my father [has] and uncle had; it is about hard work, everyday hard work.'[14] Worthy though these thoughts may be, in delivering an electoral message the parties' directors increasingly rely on celebrity, whether directly political or not. In this case the generic attachments of the Kennedys could have a powerful effect. 'Four decades on, the name Kennedy represented the liberal ideals that Clinton is thought, by the party's left, to have abandoned, or at least sidelined, and which now lodged their claim … with his successor.'[15] This heritage had never been so fulsomely handed to President Clinton, and the largesse of this family, and its ideological endorsement, served in part to blur the image of the gladiatorial incumbent.

The Democrats proved less easy to direct than the Republicans: 'They knew the game plan; they read the schedule; they just could not help themselves. Speeches went over time; and the old party divisions – left and right, blacks and Jews, union bosses and gay activists – crackled with occasional life.'[16] That having been said, the scripting could be fairly comprehensive at times. Peter Preston reported: 'When Hadassah Lieberman, wife of the man who may be America's next vice-president, came on stage … I had her pre-distributed script in front of me. I knew what her first word would be … "Wow!" she said. And then she ad-libbed. "Wow!" she said again. Modern American conventions are all canned. "Wow!" Nothing happens by accident.'[17] The script for her husband, Joe Lieberman, was probably harder to compose. If Bill Clinton had developed an especially strong rapport with Hollywood, the Gores and the Liebermans were perhaps the Democrats most likely to test that link. Al's wife, Tipper, was 'a pioneer of music censorship',[18] having earlier in her career as a political wife led the movement against entertainment products containing offensive lyrics; and Joe Lieberman, one of the first among Democrats to condemn Clinton for his liaison with Monica Lewinsky, had shown a tendency towards a similar crusading approach to the film industry.

In the wake of the 2000 Democratic convention, *Variety*, the journal of the film industry, contained a full-page advertisement paid for by Joe Eszterhas, urging 'No more Hollywood money for Al Gore'. Accusing Joe Lieberman of avoiding the issue of film and entertainment censorship, Eszterhas suggested to his fellow Hollywood political donors: 'Let's make Joe Lieberman accountable for his rhetoric. Not a penny more until he "clarifies" his position to the satisfaction of our creative freedom.'[19] Election campaigners are always trying to reduce the uncertainties and risk factors in their productions, to be as sure as possible of a satisfactory conclusion. Election managers have increasingly run campaigns in the manner of Hollywood productions – both in the details of the convention, TV debates, and TV advertising, and in the attention to the staging, plot and audience response to the whole event. In so far as Hollywood is a source of experts with media advice, and celebrities with potential opinion influence, it plays a part. But especially as far as the Democrats are concerned, film is also a major industry with large amounts of money controlled by relatively few individuals who have in recent years shown generally more sympathy to Democratic candidates, and therefore a potential source of that most particular electoral resource, campaign finance.

Republican Ronald Reagan may have been the first movie actor to become the nation's president, but his roles, and his politics, harked back to a nostalgic vision of an America that was calmer and more comfortable than late-twentieth-century America had become. Reagan the politician was out of touch with Hollywood politics, and the Republicans have perceived more electoral mileage in attacking contemporary movies as liberal weapons in the erosion of American values. A 1996 Bob Dole presidential campaign leaflet was quite explicit: 'Hollywood once represented the best of America and its values with John Wayne, Shirley Temple and Bob Hope ... Hollywood now sells for profit the messages of random violence, casual sex and even the degradation of religion ... while these may be Hollywood's values, they are certainly not the values embraced by most Americans.'[20] This is one area where the Republicans apparently do not cleave to the virtue of the market, since the leaflet goes on: 'Doing what's profitable has too often become more important than doing what's right.' The film stars cited in the leaflet for their virtuous contributions have all been active Republican supporters, but are of a different generation to the film-makers singled out for opprobrium – those involved with *Natural Born Killers* (Oliver Stone, 1994), *sex, lies and videotape* (Steven Soderbergh, 1989) and *The Last Temptation of Christ* (Martin Scorsese, 1988).

Senator John McCain, the Republican presidential hopeful who gave George W. Bush some trouble in the 2000 primary season, had the previous year sponsored the Media Violence Labelling bill in the US Congress. The bill aimed to create a warning system on media violence in the wake of speculation about connections between media influences and the Columbine High School murders. The legislation stood little chance of passage, but no American industry views with equanimity the threat of regulating parts of its product out of existence. In case the debate became heated, Hollywood marshalled its evidence denying links between film and public acts of violence. It also noted that McCain's Democratic co-sponsor of this legislation was Connecticut's Senator Joe Lieberman, whose press secretary commented: 'If the [film] industry is going to continue to act as it does and not even acknowledge that it has responsibilities, we think legislation is a very reasonable alternative.'[21]

It was reported that during the Democratic convention in Los Angeles, Joe Lieberman 'moved decisively to mend fences with the ... entertainment industry ... [and] made a priority of attending a Beverly Hills reception hosted by film producer David Salzman. The visit was part of an effort to calm Hollywood fears that Mr Lieberman would continue his high-profile anti-obscenity campaign against the entertainment industry if elected.'[22] The Gores had gone through a similar exercise eight years earlier, when Bill Clinton had chosen the then Senator from Tennessee as his running mate. In 2000, Gore indicated a special relationship with Hollywood when his former college room-mate and Oscar-winning actor, Tommy Lee Jones (*The Fugitive*; Andrew Davis, 1993), gave a speech nominating Gore that stressed his warmth, his reliability, and his habit of watching *Star Trek*. But some felt that Los Angeles was still 'an odd place for a Gore–Lieberman festival. Gore has long been estranged from Hollywood. Lieberman has made a career partly out of bashing the movie industry's marketing of sex and violence.'[23] The drive to gather political cash was used as an indicator of this uneasy fit.

Ignoring the notion that fund-raising done under the cover of the nominating convention should be for the direct benefit of the party and its nominee, major fund-raisers were also held to benefit Bill and Hillary Clinton. The 'Hollywood Gala Salute to the Clintons' ($1,000 per person to attend, $25,000 per couple to stay for dinner) raised a million dollars for Hillary Clinton's New York Senate race. A $15,000-per-person brunch hosted by Barbra Streisand diverted more Hollywood money into the fund for a Clinton presidential library. The founders of the DreamWorks SKG studio, Steven Spielberg, Jeffrey Katzenberg and David Geffen, have been particularly supportive of the Clintons. Barbra Streisand, for years an indefatigable fund-raiser on behalf of Democratic candidates and causes, also featured in a convention celebration that raised $5 million for the Democratic Party.[24] In 2000, Hollywood continued to be generous to the Democrats, regardless of any concerns about the Gore–Lieberman ticket and responsive to the candidates' efforts to smooth over any difficulties. A spokesman for Mrs Clinton argued that their fund-raising presented no conflict of interest, since 'Thanks to the very strong economy created under the Gore–Clinton Administration, there is more than enough to go around'.[25] But the particularly golden response to the Clintons gives credibility to Ben Macintyre's argument that 'The affair between Hollywood and Clinton ... was love. Clinton made the neurotic folk of Hollywood feel special. He went to their parties, he tucked them up in the Lincoln Bedroom and he gave them a storyline to die for: by turns mushy, uplifting and obscene ... Even at its lowest points, his presidency was performance art.'[26]

Bill Clinton had been assiduous in his cultivation of networks of friends, the so-called 'Friends of Bill' (FOBs). There was a Southern California contingent of FOBs, among whose early members were TV producers Harry Thomason and Norman Lear, former Columbia Pictures chief Dawn Steel, Mike Medavoy of TriStar, Barbra Streisand and Richard Dreyfuss. The Hollywood contingent was fully aware of Clinton's presidential ambitions well before his 1992 run for the executive office, and they may well have had an intimation of the factors potentially limiting a bid for the White House. Some of them had been in Arkansas on 15 July 1987, whence they had been invited to be present for the launch of a Clinton campaign for the 1988 Democratic nomination. On 14 July he told his friends he would not be running, citing his family as the main reason. Betsey Wright, a trusted adviser, suggested that there was more to this. She claims to have confronted him with a list of women with whom he was rumoured to have had affairs, 'demanding he tell her the truth, and then assess whether the women would keep silence'.[27] Leading Democratic contender Senator Gary Hart had been forced from the presidential race in May 1987, when he was photographed with model Donna Rice, relaxing on a friend's boat, *The Monkey Business*. It did not seem, therefore, in the run-up to the 1988 election, to be the time to test the public's views on personal infidelity and political electability, but by the time Clinton was on the presidential campaign trail, this context – as well as other matters surrounding the Clintons – paralleled emerging themes in Hollywood treatments of the electoral process.

The Clinton years coincided with a rich period of Hollywood movies featuring elections as at least part of their subject matter. Donors to election campaigns in the USA regularly claim that they are not buying legislative influence, merely ensuring that they can have enough access to make an opinion heard in the corridors of power. Furthermore, the argument goes, it is wise, in an expensive system, to help those who share one's opinions, especially if their past actions indicate this, with a kind of retrospective recognition of positions held in common. The movie and related entertainments industry produces a small, wealthy population, highly concentrated geographically. The fact that they are highly sought after for commendation and support may well serve to increase their self consciousness about having political clout. Naturally, a proportion of this population is drawn to causes, and some in the business will be ideologically sympathetic to particular candidates and political parties, but the politically aware in the industry also understand the worth of making contributions to keep the channels of communication accessible. There is a huge spectrum of interpretation of the money relationship in US elections. Some see it as an essential element in the freedom of speech guaranteed in the First Amendment to the Constitution of the United States. Others claim that it is a deeply corrupting foundation on which to perch the world's most powerful democracy. Intimately involved with the funding, delivery and ideals of election campaigns as Hollywood is, it would be surprising if the portrayals of elections in the movies did not reflect the ambivalences of these experiences of American participatory politics.

Elections are rarely a generic context for the unequivocally good and positive in the movies, even where they form only a modest element of the overall plot. *In the Line of Fire* (Wolfgang Petersen, 1993) has a president on the campaign trail, and 12 per cent behind in the polls, and therefore quite unable to deviate from his campaign strategy even if the threat of assassination seems more than usually real. As the assassination threat becomes clearer, and is located in California, the polling gap has reduced to 5 per cent, and the need to fulfil campaign and fund-raising obligations in this key state overrides considerations of danger. The potential assassin – a former CIA agent, trained to kill by the American government, and now disillusioned and amoral, with 'no cause left worth fighting for' – gains access to the President at a fund-raising banquet after contributing to the campaign. None the less, US democracy is, at the last, upheld. Agent Frank Corrigan (Clint Eastwood), still suffering from his failure to save Kennedy when on presidential protection duty in 1963, this time shows himself willing to take the bullet, saves the President, and orchestrates the death of the failed assassin. The film is true to the myths of American democracy. Early in the film Corrigan's landlady uses the well-worn, almost invariably incorrect, but deeply ideological phrase 'only in America', referring to the ability of the public to visit the White House. The movie begins with warm, sun-bathed shots of scenes in the national capital, and ends in equally good weather on the steps of the Lincoln Memorial. Flaws may have been exposed, but the right of the public to vote for its leaders has been protected

Eastwood again draws on political memory in *Absolute Power* (Clint Eastwood, 1997), when his character, Luther Whitney, an unusually skilled and sensitive thief, breaks into a house and accidentally sees President Alan Richmond's violent sexual encounter with his mistress result in the woman being shot to death by security guards. The executive cover-up is reminiscent of the Watergate scandal, and a visual reference is made when we discover that Gloria Russell, the security chief heading the cover-up, lives in the Watergate complex. The murdered woman is Christine Sullivan, whose wealthy husband has bankrolled the President's electoral career. Murder and cover-up close to the White House were hot topics in Clinton's Washington DC, when right-wing groups attempted to spin the suicide of Clinton friend and appointee Vince Foster up to scandal proportions. But the phrases used by Sullivan in this film resonated strongly in the second Clinton administration, when he seems to presage the position of many in the electorate: 'I gave him the presidency ... I knew he was a philanderer – but didn't think he'd betray me.' The question of how far presidential character should be an element of electoral choice is not tested any further in this film. Sullivan kills the President; this is presented to the public as a suicide, and faith in the institution is maintained at the expense of openness.

Murder at 1600 (Dwight Little, 1997) takes death right into the White House. In the film's opening shots, images of the flag, the Washington Monument and other national icons are placed against the background of a Gothic thunderstorm. Obsessive polishing and cleaning are going on in the White House. Portraits of Washington and Jefferson oversee the sexual couplings of a man and a White House Office of Protocol employee. This capital seems deranged, and possibly insane. The woman, a niece of a major presidential campaign contributor who has achieved the post with the help of her contacts, is found murdered, with suspicions moving towards the President's son. The murder investigation sets up a clash between the black, street-smart local Detective Regis, preoccupied with his fight to stop his home being turned into a car park by the federal government; and the white, educated, Iowa-raised National Security Agent Nina Chance. This combative relationship turns to alliance as they realise they both have a common enemy, and have to tease out who it is. The key lies in the next election. The President's inaction in the face of an ongoing North Korean hostage crisis gives an indication of his tense relationship with his national security and military advisers, and his hawkish Vice-President. With just over two years of his term served, resignation by a scandalised or demoralised president would leave the Vice-President to accede to office for the rest of the term, and still be eligible to stand, with all the electoral advantages of an incumbent, for two full terms of his own. With skilful management, the conspirators might take the White House for almost a full decade. The conspiracy is broken when Regis and Chance use the White House tunnels (a favourite location for tense chase scenes in these films) to reach the President. Confronted with the challenging, honest words of the common man, as opposed to the confined, reinforcing wisdoms of a small coterie of advisers, President Neil takes his first decisive act of the movie, ordering the arrest of his own National Security Adviser. In the resulting fracas, Nina takes the bullet to save the President, and again the heroism and self-sacrifice of a few honest guardians mean that the people will be allowed to make their own electoral decision at the proper time. At the same time Regis, now negotiating with his new contacts in government to save his building from the federal bulldozer, points out that 'it's not what you know, it's who you know'.

The potential mass wisdom aggregated by elections is not served very well by the dynamics of the movies. Film is a medium used to serving individual heroes better than it honours groups. It should perhaps not be surprising, therefore, that elections often serve as a location in which to display such unpleasant human motivations as overweening ambition, self-aggrandisement and lust for power, backed up by huge exchanges of funds between the forces of politics and those of American capitalism in its business, industrial and criminal forms. The public are often portrayed as the dupes of this system – usually not so much ignorant as kept too far away from the truth, and so manipulated by the media as to have no more than a niggling sense that something is wrong in the state of representative democracy. In such a vision, heroes are needed to break through the barriers and maintain the value of electoral forms. In *Batman Returns* (Tim Burton, 1992) it takes a mighty effort by the flawed costumed hero to save Gotham from a mayoralty dominated by the Penguin and his evil allies. While other election films do not rely on comic-based superheroes, they tend to applaud individual and personal rather than aggregate and electoral virtues. Sometimes the individual appears to represent the electorate more clearly than others.

In *Dave* (Ivan Reitman, 1993) an election has already provided the nation with a womanising president whose wife, interested in social policies, stays on board only to maintain a last ditch effort to ensure some high-level backing for these policies. When President Bill Mitchell suffers a severe stroke, his double, Dave Kovic, big-hearted owner of a small employment agency, and part-time comic imper-sonator, is persuaded to stand in temporarily, unwittingly providing the cover for a conspiracy led by Bob Alexander, the White House

Chief of Staff. Alexander plots to frame the Vice-President with responsibility for financial scandals that should actually lie at his own and Mitchell's doors, have himself appointed Vice-President under the terms of the 25th Amendment to the US Constitution, and thereafter to accelerate the death of the comatose Mitchell, and leave himself as incumbent president coming into the next election. Kovic, whose name immediately identifies him as different from those running this White House, begins to adapt well to the role he has taken, and in confrontation with his handlers he calls in an old friend from his home town. These representatives of the aspiring US middle class start combing through the national accounts, and confirm what many others like them in the audience already suspect: 'I've been over this stuff a bunch of times and it just doesn't add. Who does these books? If I ran my business this way – I'd be out of business.' Dave finds other 'common man' allies in his search for a way to beat the conspirators. The President's estranged wife accompanies Kovic on an incognito trip into Washington DC, and proves her credentials in a comic routine on the sidewalk of the city to avoid police detection. On meeting Vice-President Gary Nance, who has been sent on a series of foreign tours to keep him out of the way, giving credence to the reputed judgement of Franklin Roosevelt's Vice-President John Nance Garner that the office was about 'as exciting as a bucket of warm spit', Kovic finds him to be an honest man with much of the Harry Truman about him – formerly a shoe salesman who started out by standing for city council. Turning the conspiracy on its head, Dave manages to re-establish the constitutional process of succession and election, leaving a cleared Vice-President Nance to take over from the incapacitated and dying President Mitchell until the next election, launching the conspirators towards investigation and prison, and slipping back into his normal life. But if the electoral process has been saved from fraud by Dave, he too has undergone a political epiphany, for he has seen that honest, common citizens can aspire to become president, and that the political system depends on the engagement of the citizenry. In the closing scene, his home-town friends, neighbours, and the late President Mitchell's wife are working together to elect Dave to the city council.

This redemptive quality also enters films that are not generally so warmly romantic as *Dave*. *City Hall* (Harold Becker, 1996) is a darker vision of the compromises made to run the city, and to win electoral advancement. It is the run-up to the presidential election year, and Mayor John Pappas wants his party's National Convention to be held in his city. He wants the honour of giving a major, network-covered speech at the convention. And he looks forward to the combination of political contacts and public exposure projecting him to higher things – the Governorship of New York, and perhaps then to national office. This carefully constructed edifice of ambition and progression begins to crumble after a gun fight leaves dead a cop, a criminal, and a black child. The criminal, Tino Zappati, was on probation instead of in prison, and the fear in the Pappas camp is that 'the way Willie Horton sunk Dukakis, Tino Zappatti could sink us'. As Kevin Calhoun, loyal and admiring aide to Pappas, investigates the case, he realises that Zappati's freedom to roam the streets was engineered by the Mayor as a favour to the Zappati family, a force in the city with whom he felt he needed to compromise in order to further his urban development plans. The attempted cover-up – organised by this criminal family, and with which the Mayor can plausibly deny direct involvement – is accomplished through a string of deaths. The Mayor, when confronted, uses the Machiavellian excuse 'What good are you to the people without power?' There is no rosy vision of the Augean stables cleaned and sweet-smelling at the end of this film, but it is not presented as a forlorn hope that Kevin Calhoun ends the movie running against the political machine for a seat on the city council.

The US elections in Hollywood's movies commonly contain elements showing avarice, greed, unsavoury links between monied interests and politicians, the damaging and undemocratic effects of unfettered individual political ambition. Elections regularly provide a context in which unscrupulous forces seek to ignore the national interest, and to bend national resources to serve their own narrow interests. While this sceptical and often cynical vision of the electoral process is common, most of the films do offer a redemptive process. Individuals heroically save the day and return the system to its democratic path. Often these individuals are very common people – Detective Regis and Dave Kovic are two examples. In *Striptease* (Andrew Bergman, 1996) it is an exotic dancer, her coterie of fellow strippers, a club bouncer, and one honest cop who finally bring down a chronically bizarre, abusive, deranged Member of Congress who is being kept in his seat by corrupt, featherbedded and exploitative sugar plantation money – another group of very common people managing to return some kind of authority back to the electorate.

There is a battle to maintain electoral democracy in these visions of America. It is a battle in which Hollywood often seems to judge that the electorate is failing to play its part, and average voter turnout rates dipping under 50 per cent in presidential elections, and well under 40 per cent in congressional elections, would suggest that there is *prima facie* evidence for this perception. But it is still a battle that seems worth fighting, as though these movies agreed with Winston Churchill that 'democracy is the worst form of Government except all those other forms that have been tried from time to time'.[28]

Other healing scenarios conclude with characters of established quality undergoing significant change in office, or standing for election in order to bring change, as in *Dave*, and *City Hall*. In *The Distinguished Gentleman* (Jonathan Lynn, 1992) Eddie Murphy's streetwise and opportunist victor, in a seat left vacant by another philandering politician, demonstrates clearly that an amoral confidence trickster fits most successfully into Congress. The shocks of exposure to a child constituent with cancer, and to some politicians and lobbyists with a serious commitment to positive social and environmental policy, provide the stimulus, experience and opportunity to change, and to challenge the electoral corruption of leading politicians and their power industry bankrollers. Geena Davis's committed and policy-directed campaign speechwriter in *Speechless* (Ron Underwood, 1994) mirrors the true-life relationship between Democrat and Clinton campaign manager James Carville and Republican and Bush strategist Mary Matalin when she forms a love match with her opposite number in the opposing campaign. But the outcome is different when – in the aftermath of a campaign again cynically manipulated by the candidates and the interested – she moves on to campaign for office herself, with her partner deserting his former party to work for a candidate with true belief in the virtue of politics and policy. Even in *Storyville* (Mark Frost, 1992), a film which takes a young Louisiana congressional candidate through a dark journey of deception, fraud, murder and almost Gothic family secrets, election night is one of transformation. The falseness of the past has been overturned, love for the loyalty of an adopted parent is affirmed against the demands of a corrupted blood line, an inter-racial alliance has been formed where no prospect of one seemed to exist, and the scion of a rich family who was standing for office with no clear understanding of why has discovered the value of standing up for justice even in the face of countervailing self-interest.

Some movies give less indication that the electorate has a defence against the apparently endemic corruption of elections. In *Bob Roberts* (Tim Robbins, 1992), a country-singing capitalist piles up one campaign trick after another *en route* to victory. Running for the US Senate on the slogan 'I have had enough', Roberts (Tim Robbins) campaigns against the heritage of the 1960s, singing from a right-wing song book modelled with wicked humour on the works of Bob Dylan. He favours prayer in schools, and a war on drugs, promoting his own Broken Dove Clinic as part of the response to the decay in American life. His unashamed commitment to being rich is exemplified by the campaign bus, which is wired and staffed for international stock trading, and a willingness to go into rapid attack on combative interviewers, labelling them communists, and journalism in general as 'yellow'. He smears his opponent, the lugubrious and decent incumbent Brinkley Paiste (Gore Vidal), first elected in the Kennedy presidential year of 1960, with a teen sex rumour, and combats Paiste's Kennedy-like appeals to the electorate's sense of social contribution and personal sacrifice with the rhetoric of personal wealth enhancement and tax cuts. Vicious negative advertising skilfully weaves welfare, affirmative action, and a congressional pay rise into a personal attack on Paiste. Campaigning from church, Roberts portrays his own 'rebel's path to Washington DC' as equivalent to a religious battle. The film builds on the 1980 elections, when campaigns underwritten by the National Conservative Political Action Committee and other conservative groups helped to unseat a clutch of stalwart liberal Democrat Senators, and gave Reaganaut Republicans control of Senate. It mirrors the skills of Lee Atwater, guiding hand behind George Bush Sr's extraordinary 1988 attack campaign against Democrat Michael Dukakis. It parallels Pat Buchanan's 1992 Republican National Convention speech declaring that there was a religious war under way in America, one that Republican Christians had to win. And it is a precursor to the 1994 successes of Republican candidates and their Contract With America in gaining control of the House of Representatives and the US Senate. There are many direct references to contemporary politics – for example, to the Savings and Loan scandals that touched many politicians in the Reagan years, as part of which Broken Dove comes under investigation. When Roberts is shot, a radical journalist, Bugs Raplin (like Dukakis, 'a card-carrying member of the ACLU'), is suspected, although using a broad brush, the Roberts camp claims that the attack is 'caused by a liberal agenda'. But in this world of make-believe – film, campaign, self-invention – no truths are reliable. Raplin says that the bullets were fired into the ground; Roberts' backer and former Iran/Contra link Lucas Hart III (Alan Rickman) says 'it would be a miracle if he ever walked again'; and Roberts's latest song, coincidentally titled 'I Want to Live', hits the number one spot. Roberts, the comatose hero, wins the election, and though he emerges later in a wheelchair, it seems that he is tapping his crippled feet to the beat. Raplin – who knows 'There are no Mr Smiths in Washington', and who is the one figure determined to reach behind the manipulation of the self-interested politicians and campaigners, and dig further than the corporate media dare, or wish, to go – is killed, news that gets a rapturous reception from a Roberts-loving crowd. Only the British crew making a documentary on Roberts are left feeling a distant shock at the way things have developed. There is little redemptive or hopeful in the US elections process of *Bob Roberts*, where skilled media and political operatives trade in public emotions and urgent contemporary issues with the same facility that they trade in international stock, and where a system that could at one time put a Kennedyesque patrician in office for a generation, when the time comes to replace him, allows demagogue and mob to meet in the choice of a Bob Roberts.

Another fairly bleak scenario is the stuff of *Wag the Dog* (Barry Levinson, 1997). If the rumour and reality around the Clintons had in some way encouraged film-makers increasingly to tackle topics such as presidential sexual scandal and campaign spin-doctoring, this movie helped to complete the circle. The film's president, in the late stages of his re-election campaign, faces allegations of sexual impropriety from a young woman, and a campaign team moves into top gear to spin the candidate away from the electoral danger. The movie opened in America's film theatres just as the world was beginning to hear of the real President Clinton's sexual liaison with Monica Lewinsky. In the film, senior campaign troubleshooter Conrad Brean calls on Hollywood producer Stanley Motss to develop, produce and project a storyline to the American electorate that will protect the President in the final days of the campaign. The Motss team, to a man and woman, have all the trappings of the most flaky of media people – their lives appear to revolve around swimming pools, sun loungers, drugs and drink, and none of them votes. None the less, there is considerable awareness of the more cinematic of political events, with references to the bombing of the US Embassy in Beirut, the invasion of Grenada, the manipulated image of the planting of the US flag at Iwo Jima, the Gulf War, and current campaign advertisements punctuating the movie backdrop. The production team create a series of diversions, sending journalists into a feeding frenzy by laying a trail of interrelated false stories on defence contracts, the threat of terrorism from Albania shifting into the posturings of war, and the rescue and death of a heroic American soldier. The team operates at arm's length from the White House and the official campaign, but is in constant contact through Winifred Ames, a White House aide on the production team who spends most of the movie on the cellular phone. The diurnal pattern of day and night is irrelevant to this team as campaign time – full alertness and readiness to respond every second, to provide plot alterations, create special effects, write and record lyrics and music, make up props and put them into place – takes over their lives. Producing, says Motss, is 'like being a plumber' – do your job right and nobody notices. However, like the White House plumbers of the Watergate era, Motss begins to find the requisite self-effacement difficult. As the President cruises to re-election victory, Motss is incensed that the creators of the campaign advertisements – those usually accused of media wizardry and manipulating the public mind – will be credited with that victory. He knows that their productions are tawdry, small and unconvincing: 'I am the producer of this program ... [it] is a complete fucking fraud and it looks one hundred per cent real. It's the best work I have ever done – because it is so honest.' Stanley's conviction that the beauty of his work should be recognised proves his undoing, and he disappears quietly into custody on his way to being disappeared into an early death. The campaign fixers appear to have won. The electorate, and the film audience, were distracted from ever pinning down the truth by the flak of false stories and lachrymose, sentimental nationalism. The relentless – if often slapstick – comic action of this movie ultimately turns coldly ruthless in a very dark vision of electoral democracy undermined.

Darkly comic too is the action of *Bulworth* (Warren Beatty, 1998), which opens with Senator Jay Bulworth watching, rewinding and rewatching his own banal campaign advertisements, full of 'third way' rhetoric decorating nit-picking conservatism as core values and opportunity 'at the doorstep of a new millennium'. Apparently deeply depressed, emotionally lost, physically exhausted and tearful, Bulworth is contracting his own assassination in a way that will remove him from all this, while leaving a vast pool of insurance money up for his heirs. The insurance, with a tinge of revenge, is a fringe benefit extracted from those special interests which have simultaneously kept him in office and undermined his idealism over the years. In this heightened mental state, Bulworth undergoes an epiphany when, speaking to the congregation of an African-American church, he discovers the exhilarating liberty that comes with deciding to tell the truth about campaigns and power. Authority lies with contributors, he tells a black neighbourhood audience: 'You haven't really contributed any money to my campaign – do you have any idea how much these insurance companies come up with – they depend on me to bottle up and kill bills.' And viable political strength has to be based on credible electoral blocs: 'If you don't put down your malt liquor and chicken wings and get behind somebody other than a running back who stabs his wife you're never going to rid of somebody like me.' Bulworth's behaviour becomes increasingly unorthodox, driving his campaign aides to distraction. He acquires an entourage of young black women, and begins to find wisdom in the idioms, rap and clothes of black urban America. The wisdoms are not all new or revelatory – rather, these adopted contexts are allowing his own original liberalism to rise to the surface, emerging through the long-acquired carapace of political convention, and allowing him to hear and comprehend again the underlying truth and analytical value of the economic and social theories of the 1960s. Rapping, smoking dope and dancing his way closer to political awareness, Bulworth continues to make startling public appearances, interpreted by the media as a skilful shift in image campaigning, and climaxing in a TV debate in which his vivid directness is received by the media as the innovativeness of a powerful candidate. Escaping from the clutches of the campaign, he hides out in the family home of his new young black friend, Nina. In the ghetto he confronts equally the lazy racism of the police and the businesslike street terrorism of the drug pushers and racketeers before returning to the TV studio to give another virtuoso performance. Back with Nina's family, Bulworth sleeps, unwakeable for two days, while somewhere else in California the campaign ends, the election takes place, and he takes 71 per cent of the vote. When Bulworth rises from his deep sleep he emerges besuited, but after some hesitation his transformation is validated by Nina's kiss, and her acknowledgement 'you're my nigger'. The process has been transformational, even though the events have often been stereotyped, as mental and physical stress, confrontational experience, fear and love have taken Bulworth to an altered emotional and philosophical state, and presented him with the context to bring observers and electorate on some part of the same journey. But at the last, the transformation is threatened by an assassin's bullet, apparently directed at Bulworth at the behest of the insurance interests that had so long been his mainstay. The film ends with a shot of the hospital, ambivalent as to whether even a spirit as mystical as that which has entered Bulworth and his electorate can ultimately live and triumph.

The most direct evocation of the Clinton years in film was in *Primary Colors* (Mike Nichols, 1998), based on the novel by Joe Klein, a *Newsweek* presidential election journalist. Jack Stanton, the southern governor candidate with sincere charm, a weakness for and attraction to women, a firm grasp of policy, genuinely multiracial and class-conscious empathy and appeal – in a marriage that is sometimes shaken to the roots, to a directed and politically astute woman who can call him a 'feckless, thoughtless, disorganised shit', but a marriage which rides each threat on its political and emotional strength – going through a campaign that acts out some of the reports and rumours of the 1990s White House races, cannot help but invite the audience to look for seams between Clintonesque political reality and Hollywood elaboration. Stanton is no angel, but those around him are ready to control the damage from his acknowledged personal failings because of their faith in the morality of his political and social vision. It is when Stanton and his wife appear ready to abandon their campaigning standards, and use smear tactics to destabilise the main opponent, that a campaign aide prone to depression feels her years of previously immovable faith in Stanton so undermined that she commits suicide. This film, like Oliver Cromwell's portraitist, includes at least some of the candidate's warts, and depicts a challenger for office who can claim to be in some degree extraordinary and worthy, even while he is failing to live all the elements of the American Dream. Not that this indicates a sea-change. The opponent's links to a homosexual cocaine dealer now dying of AIDS, even though they are the distant relics of an exuberant youth, are still enough to take him out of contention. Stanton, like Gary Hart, would

surely not have stood up to the investigative criteria of a 1980s campaign, but he can be a successful candidate in the 1990s.

At the beginning of the new century more than ever, the successful presidential candidate has to have a sense of the cinematic.
George W. Bush fitted easily into an unchallenging 'good old boy'
clubbability that harked back to Reagan's own image, and appealed
to many voters. Gore needed something more stirring to overcome
the ghost of his predecessor, and to bring himself to life for the
viewers. The most cinematic moment of the 2000 Democratic Convention appeared to be unscripted. At the end of an acceptance
speech that had been well delivered and well received, Al Gore turned
to greet his wife Tipper on to the podium, then drew her into a
prolonged and breathless kiss. The slight clumsiness and evident
commitment drew the audience's attention to the Gores in surprise,
some embarrassment, and ultimately a sense of pleased belief in the
couple, and in the candidate. Voters knew that Clinton was perhaps
slightly threateningly sexy, and George W. Bush had gone to some
lengths to acknowledge (or perhaps establish) that he has a 'bad boy'
past, but the Gores were going for passionate and wholesome simultaneously. Gore's poll results, having trailed those of Bush throughout the campaign, surged him into contention for the first time in
the aftermath of the convention, and many poll respondents
identified 'The Kiss' as having loosened up their attitude to the Vice-
President. 'The Kiss' even wiped out memories of Bill Clinton's
'Gladiator'.

'The Kiss' embodied family values and heroic vibrancy both at
the same time. A long-drawn-out moment of filmed passion, it may
have contributed something to ensure the subsequent long-drawn-
out election process. It helped to establish Gore's genuine potential
as a candidate, even with those in Hollywood whose Clinton loyalties
were strained by the Gore–Lieberman ticket. On 20 September 2000
at a Beverly Hills dinner, the Democratic candidates came out – in
Joe Lieberman's words – as 'fans of the products of the entertainment industry'. 'It's true,' he continued, 'from time to time we have
been, will be, critics but ... We will nudge you, but will never become
censors.' Al Gore still warned his audience: 'We feel strongly about
the responsibility that the entertainment industries need to take when
it comes to marketing inappropriate material to children ... we're
going to fight to change that.'[29] Few audiences could justify the at-
tendance of both the presidential and vice-presidential candidates of

either ticket so close to Election Day. Over dinner the Democratic candidates picked up $3 million in support for their campaign, and the Hollywood link with the US elections process clearly remained alive and well.

Oliver Stone's presidential films

Albert Auster

The noise had a power. The dark had a power.

Don DeLillo, *Libra*

In spring of 1947, two first-term congressmen were invited by a local civic group in McKeesport, Pennsylvania to debate the Taft–Hartley law. This was the first meeting of two politicians irrevocably linked in American history – John F. Kennedy and Richard M. Nixon. These two men, later the 35th and the 37th presidents respectively, were subsequently bound by many other cords of memory and emotion, and even after their deaths by two separate yet complementary myths – the first, originated by Kennedy's widow, Jacqueline Kennedy Onassis, which would forever link the one thousand days of John F. Kennedy's assassination-shortened presidency with the legendary 'Camelot', the other, initiated by Senator Bob Dole at Richard Nixon's funeral in 1994, proclaiming the last half of the twentieth century the 'Age of Nixon'.

It was probably inevitable that the lives and presidencies of these two men should inspire Hollywood – the source of so much of our contemporary cultural mythology – to produce films about them. No one, however, could have imagined that the two films that were produced by award-winning writer/director Oliver Stone, *JFK* (1991) and *Nixon* (1995), would have stirred up as much controversy, even outrage, as they did.

The initial reception accorded both films by the American media was hardly what one might call either restrained or polite. Even before film critics had had their say, journalists, political commentators, and assorted literati weighed in with denunciations and critiques of the films. Tom Wicker, former op-ed columnist of *The New York*

Times, called *JFK*, 'paranoid and fantastic, filled with wild assertions, that if widely accepted would be contemptuous of the very
constitutional government Stone proports to uphold'.[1] Syndicated
political pundit George Will anathemised *JFK* as an 'act of execrable
history and contemptible citizenship, by a man of technical skill,
scant education, and negligible conscience'.[2] The Nixon family comment on *Nixon* was the less eloquent, but certainly more succinct:
'character assassination'.[3]

Stone, however, was hardly without his defenders. In an article in
The Atlantic, political and cultural critic Garry Wills referred to
Stone's body of work, saying that 'great novels are being written
with the camera – at least when Stone is behind the camera'.[4]
Norman Mailer, no stranger to the pungent metaphor, said that
Stone 'has the integrity of a brute',[5] and in an especially insightful
afterthought commented that *JFK* 'should be seen not as history but
myth, the story of a huge and hideous act in which the gods warred
and a god fell'.[6]

Stone would readily have concurred with at least part of Mailer's
estimate. In interview after interview following the release of *JFK*, he
consistently argued: 'I'm presenting what I call a countermyth to the
myth of the Warren commission.'[7] Chastened by the reception of
JFK and the many charges of inaccuracy that dogged it following its
release, Stone issued a 500-plus-page text to accompany *Nixon*[8]
which supported his film's major facts and interpretations, but, attempting to have it both ways, asserted that it was a director's privilege to interpret history through his own prism, and that 'This thing
is in flux; history is not agreed upon.'[9]

The storm over the historical accuracy of Stone's presidential
films, notwithstanding the essential emotional and aesthetic power
of both, was acknowledged by a number of important film critics.
For example, *New York* magazine film critic David Denby described
JFK as 'appalling and fascinating, unreliable, no doubt, but an
amazing visual and spiritual experience, nonetheless'.[10] It was a
judgement that was repeated in reviews of *Nixon*, of which *New
York Times* film critic Janet Maslin wrote: 'Reckless, bullying and
naggingly unreliable, this mercurial *Nixon* is also finally as gutsy
and overpowering as it means to be.'[11]

What, however, seemed lacking in most appraisals of the films
were any references to connections between them besides the obvious
historical links, such as the frequent references to Jack Kennedy in

Nixon and the failed Bay of Pigs invasion in both. Nevertheless, there were two very essential links between these two films. The first was that in an important sense they were both mysteries – or, more precisely, one was a murder mystery (*JFK*), the other a moral mystery (*Nixon*). The second is that, taken together they presented Oliver Stone's mythic interpretation of America history and politics since the 1960s.

JFK's status as a murder mystery is most clearly evoked by New Orleans DA Jim Garrison (Kevin Costner) in his summation to the jury (one that in fact Garrison never delivered) in the Clay Shaw trial, in which he referred to the Kennedy assassination as 'the murder at the heart of the American dream'. Underscoring this murder-mystery aspect of the film is the fact that throughout it Garrison's whole purpose is to find out the truth about the Kennedy assassination. Needless to say, the image of DA Jim Garrison walking the mean streets of New Orleans in pursuit of the real Kennedy assassins is the one that gave critics of the film the most pause – especially when even die-hard conspiracy theorists considered Garrison's investigation and subsequent indictments a 'grotesque misdirected shambles'.[12] Others, perceiving even more sinister motives, saw it as a smokescreen to hide the New Orleans Trifficante–Morello Mafia families' connection to the assassination.[13]

To Stone, however, Garrison's record as a thrice-elected New Orleans DA, his over-twenty-year service in the military, and his later career as an appellate court judge marked him as a patriot and a Capraesque uncommon common man. Equally significant for Stone was the fact that Garrison was the only American law-enforcement official ever to bring indictments in the Kennedy assassination. This permitted Stone to enter the surreal world of the Warren Commission Report, and gave him the opportunity to present a grand unified conspiracy theory of his own.

In *JFK*, Garrison's suspicions are initially aroused by the summer Lee Harvey Oswald (Gary Oldman) spent in New Orleans, presumably working on behalf of the 'Fair Play for Cuba Committee', just before the Kennedy assasssination. Garrison's doubts are also increased by the black holes he finds in the Warren Commission Report, with which, much to the consternation of his wife Liz (Sissy Spacek), he becomes obsessed. The combination of these things results in Garrison's decision to open his own probe into the Kennedy assassination.

Thus begins Garrison's descent into the lower depths of New Orleans society, and his initial encounters with the dark side of the American dream. Among the delta city's demimonde he meets gay defrocked priest, self-proclaimed cancer researcher and anti-Castro freelance pilot David Ferrie (Joe Pesci), and former homosexual prostitute and prison inmate Willie O'Keefe (Kevin Bacon). This latter encounter contains just a hint of what Garrison is up against. Besides providing Garrison with information about the charmingly sinister presumed mastermind of the assassination plot, Clay Shaw, aka Clay Bertrand (Tommie Lee Jones), and regaling him with his Aryan Nation philosophy, O'Keefe pronounces Garrison 'a handsome man', and then, when both his sexual and ideological overtures are greeted with indifference by Garrison, berates him with the comment: 'Hell, Mr Garrison, you don't know what the world is like, cause you ain't never been fucked in the ass.'

The overt libidinous suggestion in O'Keefe's remark aside, the implication is also that Garrison's life of bourgeois respectability (which Stone presents in cloying detail in the frequent domestic scenes between Garrison and his nagging wife and clamorous children) and his commitment to the rule of law have left him unprepared to confront the dark side of American life. None the less, Garrison's persistence brings him more and more into conflict with the immense power of that side of American life, especially its political economic incarnation – the military–industrial complex.

At the very beginning of the film, Stone refers to this colossus in newsreel footage of President Dwight D. Eisenhower's farewell address warning of its power. However, not until Garrison's meeting with the former Black Ops agent, the shadowy Colonel X (Donald Sutherland), in Washington DC does he really begin to understand the full dimensions of the forces he is confronting. As Colonel X says: 'Don't ask the how and the who. Those questions merely divert us from the real question. Who had the most to gain from Kennedy out of the way?' Colonel X then proceeds to fill Garrison in with his descripton of the machinations of the military–industrial complex, the CIA, and Lyndon B. Johnson in the Kennedy assassination; an event he labels a *'coup d'etat'*.

With Colonel X as his Virgil, Stone also reveals the political subtext of his film. Thus, according to Stone's historical scenario, Kennedy was killed because he wanted to end the Cold War and begin withdrawing American troops from Vietnam. Indeed, in Stone's view, had Kennedy lived, we would have been spared the trauma of Vietnam. Therefore, for Stone, Kennedy's assassination not only resulted in the loss of a beloved prince, but embodied an end of American innocence and idealism.

Stone's mythic historical scenario was based on two very real but ultimately ambiguous statements and actions which took place during Kennedy's last months as president. The first was his speech in June 1963 at the American University in which, in lyrical terms, he held out an olive branch to the Soviets saying,

> In the final analysis our most common basic link is that we all inhabit this small planet. We all breathe the same air. We all cherish our children's future. And we are all mortal ... World peace like community peace, does not require that each man love his neighbor – it requires only that they live together in mutual tolerance, submitting their disputes to a just and peaceful settlement ... Our problems are man-made – therefore, they can be resolved by man. And man can be as big as he wants.[14]

The other basis for Stone's claim is a National Security Memorandum which Kennedy signed in the last days of his administration, ordering a reduction of troops in Vietnam. Of course, what Kennedy would have done or not done about Vietnam had he lived remains one of the great counterfactual historical issues of the Cold War era. Nevertheless, enough competing evidence has emerged since Kennedy's death to render Stone's assertions dubious at best. For one thing, at the very same time as Kennedy was indulging in such idyllic rhetoric at American University, he and his brother were waging a war of subversion against Fidel Castro which prompted Lyndon B. Johnson to call it a 'virtual murder incorporated in the Caribbean'.[15] As a matter of fact, at the very same moment as he was arguing for the peaceful settlement of disputes, contingency plans were being developed to bomb China's nuclear production sites. And finally, on the very day he was assassinated, Kennedy was to deliver a speech at the Dallas Trade Mart which contained the following statement about Vietnam: 'Our assistance to these nations can be painful, risky and costly, as is true in South East Asia today. But we dare not weary of this task ... We in this country, in this generation are by destiny rather than choice – the watchman on the walls of freedom.'[16]

Needless to say, these days, when we know that Kennedy turned parts of the White House into a veritable Plato's Retreat, while he himself shared a mistress with a mafioso *capo de tutti capo*, when he and his brother acquiesced to the bugging of Dr Martin Luther King, Jr and cheerfully plotted to kill Fidel Castro (or, at the very least, make his beard fall out) with exploding cigars, poisoned scuba-diving suits and other assorted 'katzenjammer kid' devices, it seems hard to believe that Stone can still maintain his faith in the essential idealism of President Kennedy.

However, this historical cognitive dissonance is shared by Stone and, to a greater or lesser extent, by many Americans. Reinforced by an endless loop of media images, the Kennedy presidency has become an overdetermined Gatsbyesque 'golden moment' associated by Americans (especially of the baby-boom generation), with their own youth, innocence and idealism. As a result, no amount of revisionism can really shake the faith in what has become for many a primal nostalgic myth, for to do so would be somehow to deny the existence/ fantasy of America's – and, implicitly, of their own – 'better self'.

As a result, after his indictment of Clay Shaw, Garrison is asked to justify his prosecution, and announces his credo 'Let justice be done, though the heavens fall' (*Fiat Justica, Ruat Caelum*). Indeed, for Stone the only way of atoning for the loss of that idealism, and perhaps regaining it, is somehow to solve the murder mystery 'at the heart of the American dream', whatever the consequences.

This loss of idealism so central to *JFK* is also referred to time and again in *Nixon*. Idealism, however, is, of course, the last thing one associates with Richard M. Nixon. Yet Stone's Nixon is a complex figure, at once as Machiavellian and filled with hubris as he was equally paranoid, self-pitying, and guilt-ridden. The mystery that Stone tries to solve in *Nixon* is the question of what were the personal and moral sources of such a tragic and complicated character. Here Stone was magnificently aided and abetted by actor Anthony Hopkins, who, though bearing scant physical resemblance to Nixon, none the less expertly re-created his physical awkwardness, light-switch smile, and – most important of all – his combination of machismo and mawkishness.

Just as significant as Hopkins's contribution to *Nixon* was Stone's frequent visual references to *Citizen Kane* (Orson Welles, 1941). Stone's appropriation of this classic film as a central metaphor was quite possibly for both its epic nature and its efforts to penetrate the mysteries of character. Indeed, this time, instead of one 'rosebud' there are a host of possible rosebuds which are offered as clues to the enigma that was Richard Milhous Nixon. *Citizen Kane* was also a quintessential critique of American political aspiration, achievement and corruption, and clearly serves as a structural – and, indeed, ethical – influence on *Nixon*.[17]

First and foremost of these rosebuds is Nixon's mother, Hannah (Mary Steenburgen), whom he described as a 'saint', but whose quiet reprimands, rigid self-righteous demands, and unintentional rejections would have eviscerated the soul even of a more self-confident child than little Dick Nixon, who once referred to himself in a letter to her as 'your good dog'.[18]

Stone also offers other tantalising clues, such as the 'four deaths' that Nixon refers to as stepping stones to his presidency. These included most prominently the deaths of John and Robert Kennedy, and more personally the deaths of Nixon's two brothers (Arthur and Harold), the latter enabling him to attend law school.

Similarly, Stone also allows us to ponder whether or not it could have been petty-bougeois resentment that motivated Nixon. As John Ehrlichman (J. T. Walsh) says to H. R. Haldeman (James Woods): 'You've got people dying because he didn't make the varsity football team. You got the Constitution hanging by a thread because the old man went to Whittier and not to Yale.' Finally, there is Henry Kissinger's (Paul Sorvino) portentous judgement: 'Imagine, if this man had been loved.'

Whatever the source, the consequences as depicted in *Nixon* result in a character marked by at once hubris and maudlin self-pity. Thus, while watching scenes of the Kennedy funeral, Nixon remarks sombrely to his wife Pat (Joan Allen): 'They never would have killed me.' Counterbalancing this was a self-pity so massive that it caused the despairing outburst 'Why do they hate me so?' during the Watergate crisis. In addition, Stone presents Nixon as a man who feels a sense of profound guilt over what he considers was his responsibility for the assassination of President Kennedy. Indeed, as Nixon sees it, he, as Vice-President, was the moving force in the Eisenhower administration's covert plans to assassinate Fidel Castro and the ill-fated 'Bay of Pigs' landings, and as such initiated the series of events that ultimately resulted in Kennedy's assassination.

Indeed, it is Kennedy, like Banquo's ghost, who hovers about all of Nixon's personal relations and political acts. For example, as the pressures of his presidency mount, Nixon plans a getaway to Key Biscayne with his friend Bebe Rebozo. Pat Nixon tries to get him to take her along. When he objects, she makes a sexual overture, which Nixon brutally rejects with the comment: 'I don't need that, I'm not Jack Kennedy.'

This obvious reference to the Kennedy concupisence is only a hint of the troubling spectre that Kennedy presents in *Nixon*. Thus, on the night of Nixon's quixotic trip to the Lincoln Memorial to talk to student protesters during the Cambodian crisis, the subject of Kennedy comes up when the insomniac Nixon asks his valet Manolo if he admired the dead President. After a moment's hesitation Manolo says: 'Yes', and then, when asked why, replies: 'He made me see the stars.'

It is Nixon himself, however, who most clearly states the difference between himself and Kennedy. Alone in the White House, maddened by grief and anguish as the Watergate scandal engulfs his presidency, Nixon addresses the portraits of the dead presidents. Stopping at Kennedy's picture, he provides the film's defining comment on the contrast between them: 'When they see you, they see what they want to be. When they see me, they see what they are.'

Ultimately, in Stone's vision the death of Kennedy propelled us into an era of political demoralisation, where cynicism and corruption reigned. Stone's Nixon is the Machiavellian embodiment of that loss of innocence and idealism. Nevertheless, Stone's Nixon is no mere demonic figure. Although he is emotionally inauthentic and obsessively driven by ambition, he is none the less still possessed of a brilliant political mind, the love of his family, and the professional respect – even devotion – of a coterie of political officials. As a matter of fact, upon viewing the film, one lifelong Nixon hater was moved to comment: 'Having grown up in Southern California, assured by my working-class parents that homeboy Nixon was the incarnation of evil, and learning nothing in my adult life to disprove that, I thought it impossible that I could feel the slightest tug of sympathy for the man. But by the end of Stone's meticulous and surprisingly fair-handed film an uncomfortable knot of ambivalence had formed at my throat.'[19]

That knot of emotional ambivalence was undoubtedly aroused by such heart-tugging scenes as Nixon's teary-eyed departure from the White House in August 1974. It is also aided by Stone's intellectual rationale for some – albeit not all – of Nixon's political failings. Thus, by the time of *Nixon*, the cancer that Stone had diagnosed in *JFK* as composed of the military–industrial complex and the CIA had metastatised into an invincible all-powerful hidden government, an almost metaphysical creature Stone refers to as 'the Beast'.

The moment at which 'the Beast' is finally revealed is during Nixon's memorable meeting with students at the Lincoln Memorial in the wee hours before the Cambodian invasion demonstrations of 1970. Starting the conversation with small talk about the Syracuse football team, Nixon sees the dialogue quickly escalate into a debate about the Vietnam War. When the President states his desire to end the war too, one frustrated young woman confronts him with the comment: 'What's the point of being president? You're powerless.' To which Nixon replies defensively: 'I'm not powerless. Because I understand the system. I believe I can control it. Maybe not control it totally, but tame it to make it do some good.' When the young woman surprises Nixon with the thought 'It sounds as if you're talking about a wild animal,' he can only respond meekly, 'Maybe I am.' Then, as Nixon is hustled off by his palace guard, he says to H. R. Haldeman, 'She's got it. She understands something it's taken me twenty-five fucking years in politics to understand. The CIA, the Mafia, the Wall Street bastards...'

The power of the Beast, that hidden government at which Nixon only hints, is the penultimate metaphor in Stone's vision of American politics embodied in *JFK* and *Nixon*. This is quite simply that, had Kennedy lived, he would have withdrawn from Vietnam and ended the Cold War. However, the threat of that caused such consternation in that lethal Leviathan/Beast – the military–industrial–CIA–Mafia–Wall Street complex – that they passed a death sentence upon him. And in the wake of his death there occurred a period of political demoralisation, of which Richard Nixon, with his combination of relentless political ambition, ruthless pragmatism and self-destructive vindictiveness, was the tragic culmination.

Of course, Stone's vision leaves out the last twenty-five years of American politics – not to mention the last twenty years of Richard Nixon's life, when he underwent his final transformation from pariah to the statesman/sage of Saddle River. This, notwithstanding the strength of Stone's presidential films, is a testament to their ambivalence about historical accuracy (despite Stone's voluminous arguments to the contrary) and the promotion of their mythic elements. Indeed, he has created in his presidential films the only full-blown mythic version of American politics since 1960. Thus, for better or for worse, he fulfils Ernest Renan's profound advice that an essential ingredient for any nation was to get one's history wrong. In this Stone may have succeeded far beyond his own expectations. As a matter of fact, he has created historical myths that may not be as elegant or grandiloquent as the myths of Camelot and the Age of Nixon, but which none the less attach new meaning to the presidencies of John F. Kennedy and Richard M. Nixon.

Part 3

'In order to form a
more perfect union...'
Some manifest destinies

Gender and family values in the Clinton presidency and 1990s Hollywood film

Carol R. Smith

[The family] has continued to play a central role in American culture, as an organising social institution, a lived experience, and a powerful metaphor.[1]

If you don't get married, you're abnormal.

If you get married but don't have children, you're a selfish yuppie.

If you get married and have children but then go outside the home to work, you're a bad mother.

If you get married and have children but stay home, you've wasted your education.

And if you don't get married but have children and work outside the home as a fictional newscaster, you get in trouble with the Vice President.[2]

The more pointed of these quotations, dating from 1992, is a classic feminist diagnosis of the negative impact on available female life-choices created by the 'family values' policies and rhetoric of the Reagan and Bush presidencies. It typifies critiques of the conservative Republican/Moral Majority/Christian Right construction of hetero-sexual marriage, as threatening the lives of individuals and the nation.[3] More particularly, the openness of attack and the humorously demeaning swipe at Dan Quayle (who had famously criticised fictional newscaster Murphy Brown's decision to have a baby out of wedlock) marks this speech as an attempt to contest the domination of 'family values' over political and presidential elections. The future First Lady finished by exhorting the Class of '92 'to transcend and forge an identity that is uniquely your own'. At the same time, her husband promised an equally radical shift in national rhetoric and policy. 'Family values', replaced by 'it's the economy stupid', related reforms in healthcare, education, and welfare, and a pledge to repeal the ban on gay Americans in the military.

Feminist critiques of the naturalness of heterosexual marriage and gender relations were also evident in Clinton-era films and their critical reception. The early 1990s saw two films which in very different ways, echoed Hillary Rodham Clinton's speech: *Pretty Woman* (Garry Marshall, 1990), and *Thelma and Louise* (Ridley Scott, 1991). Despite their generic differences, this romantic comedy and road movie/Western were perceived as radical reinterpretations of the romance/marriage narrative that marked a shift away from an unquestioning acceptance of the social and economic policy of Reagan/Bush.

Hence, in a reading of *Pretty Woman* Hilary Radner[4] focuses on the reworking of the traditional marriage plot, which, she argues, had been historically repressive of female sexuality in enforcing virginity until marriage. Radner argues that this plot is radically transformed as the heroine, Vivien, is shown to attain liberation, selfhood and romance through sexual knowledge. This is in part because feminism, with its reworking of gender relations, has allowed sex to be enjoyed and valued by females. Elsewhere, the reworking of this romance narrative has been read as 'playing out certain anxieties to do with masculinity and Reaganite economics'.[5] Similarly, *Thelma and Louise* has been read by Sharon Willis, Yvonne Tasker and others as contesting traditional gender stereotypes through its reworking of the road movie/Western. The drive into the canyon at the end of the film resonates as a refusal of heterosexual patriarchy.[6]

Thus, when the Democrat Bill Clinton was elected President in 1992, the political and cinematic culture of America did seem to be marked by similar shifts. The reworking of traditionally androcentric cinematic forms was paralleled by the election of a very different First Family (one for two), whose concepts of 'family values' and public policies promised tolerance and inclusion rather than demonisation and exclusion. Yet what were the American people watching during the election campaign of a president pledged to lift the ban on gays in the military and whose wife, a working woman, made overtly feminist speeches attacking the Republican 'family values' agenda? Arguably, this is a faithful remake of *Father of the Bride* (Vincente Minnelli, 1950), but it clearly resists Minnelli's implied critique of the family, and his concerns about the emasculation of the father figure.

In contrast to the incorporation of feminist ideas in movies such as *Pretty Woman* and *Thelma and Louise*, this remake is a faithful, almost shot-by-shot reproduction of the Spencer/Taylor original of 1950. As such, it reinforces the original's adherence to heterosexual and patriarchal gender norms. (Though it does register the impact of such films tokenistically through the inclusion of a 'gay' wedding organiser.) This nostalgic remake and other romantic comedies which centre on weddings were among the most successful of the Clinton Presidency. What should we make of this disjuncture – or conjuncture?

This chapter is an attempt to trace some of the connections be-tween Clinton's political rhetoric and these cinematic (re)turns to the romantic comedy. I want to suggest that 1990s reinterpretations of the romantic wedding comedy can be seen to be typically Clintonian in their depiction and engagement with ideas of family and gender. Such films contrast with the cinema associated with the Reagan and Bush presidencies. There, the popularity of the Vietnam War movie and blockbusters has been read as a sign of the success of simplistic and conservative policies regarding gender which act for 'the re-generation of the interests, values and projects of patriarchy'.[7] The 1990s romantic comedies offer no such simplistic or nostalgic over-arching narrative of American identity, but are related to politics in more complex and uneven ways. In this, they are no different from their generic precursors, as Frank Krutnick has described them: ro-mantic comedies 'never spring magically from their cultural context but they represent instead much more complex activities of *negotia-tion*, addressing cultural transformations in a highly compromised and displaced manner.'[8] It will be the compromises and displace-ments that this chapter will follow, in particular how the hetero-sexual marriage movies in the 1990s needed and deployed male homosexuality – as long as it was racially white – to alter and stretch the conception of American identity.

In what follows, then, I will discuss three romantic comedies as negotiating with Clinton's political trajectory as president from a variety of positions. *The Birdcage* (Mike Nichols, 1996) emerges as a critical assessment of the figuration of the family in American politics, and a sign of Clinton's inability to change this figuration. *My Best Friend's Wedding* (P. J. Hogan, 1997), less directly engaged with political discourses of the family, exemplifies a nostalgic return to and partial reworking of traditional gender forms in the face of shifts in feminist agendas. Finally, *In and Out* (Frank Oz, 1997) is seen as a direct analogue of Clinton's compromise policy on gays in the military, expanding the logic of 'Don't ask, don't tell' into an inclusive vision of American society, but one which remains fundamentally and problematically formed in the shape of white, male, heterosexual privilege.

The feminising of America: the Quayle-ing of Clinton

Of course, it could be argued, from the perspective of the end of Clinton's two terms, that these wedding comedies might be read as Clintonesque because his presidency failed to break properly with the family-values policies and rhetoric of Reagan and Bush. The failure to fulfil pre-election pledges on healthcare reform (the end of which also signalled the end of Hillary's role as 'co-president' and return to the more traditional role of First Lady), the shift in budget priorities from education and jobs to crime and prisons, welfare capping and the fudge over the gay ban in the military, could be said to mark him as unsuccessful. The romantic comedies discussed below do echo this loss of political power, a feminising of the white heterosexual male and the presidency. But much more than this, their complex negotiations of gender, sexuality and marriage reproduce in cinematic form the achievements, shifts and compromises of Clinton's trajectory.

In 1992, when Quayle and the Republicans blamed the failure of the economy on African-American single mothers and a lack of 'family values',[9] Clinton attempted to shift the discourse back to the economy. In contrast, by 1994, in the midst of legislative failure, Clinton echoed Quayle on the sources of and remedies for the ills of America:

> What [the Democrats] cannot accept is that government proposals have failed. It is the family that can rebuild America. The dissolution of the family, and in particular, the absence of fathers in the lives of America's children is the single most critical threat [to our future].[10]

> That is a disaster. It is wrong. And someone has to say again, 'It is simply not right. You shouldn't have a baby before you're ready, and you shouldn't have a baby when you're not married.'[11]

Rather than focusing on actual economic realities or legislative change, which had marked his election speeches, Clinton here followed Quayle in resorting to the language and debates of 'family values'. Moralistic rhetoric replaced legislation in a presidency which had been noted for its distancing from the Republican debate, and its careful and contained communication strategies.[12] Such a shift has been read by social commentators as symptomatic of Clinton's two terms, and of the political climate generally. Judith Stacey highlights the danger of this political consensus across party lines for the long-term viability of the health of the American nation:

> Addressing emotional, rather than rational, frequencies, family values discourse offers politicians and populace a brilliant defense mechanism with which to displace anxieties over race, gender, sexual, and class antagonisms that were unleashed as the modern family regime collapsed.[13]

It is in this political climate, where presidents and previously ridiculed ex-vice-presidents invoke marriage as the panacea for the nation's ills, that *The Birdcage* must be read. The film both draws attention to and satirises the use of marriage as a political defence mechanism, while never totally undermining the institution. Thus the film can be read as working through, in Krutnick's terms, displaced anxieties over family values and politicians, and linking them to the question of white male identity.

The Birdcage is a remake of the French film *La Cage aux Folles* (Édouard Molinaro, France, 1979). Largely set in Miami, it follows the meeting of two families: those of prospective groom Val (Dan Futterman) and bride Barbara (Calista Flockhart). The comedy is generated by the clash of two very different modern conceptions of families and values. Barbara is the daughter of ultra-conservative US Senator Keeley (Gene Hackman) and wife Dianne Wiest. Val's father, Armand (Robin Williams), owns a 'wild Miami Beach nightclub' and is in a long-term relationship with Albert (Nathan Lane), who is the club's main drag act. Val has told the Keeleys that his parents are heterosexual Christians, and that Armand is a diplomat. Barbara's father, a co-founder of the Coalition for Moral Order, is at first against the marriage. When, however, his co-founder is found dead in bed with an underage (female) African-American prostitute, he is persuaded of the desirability of a marriage in terms reminiscent of the terms employed by Quayle and Clinton in September 1995. As Mrs Keeley puts it:

> What about a wedding, a big white wedding? It would restore your image. A wedding is hope, a white wedding is family and morality and tradition, and it would be such a special marriage, and to a cultural

attaché's son. It would be love and optimism versus cynicism and sex. It would be an affirmation.

The Birdcage thus begins by openly satirising the deployment of the discourse of family values by white male politicians for political expediency. The major focus of its comedy, however, is the simulation of heterosexuality undertaken by the Armand–Albert household when the Keeleys visit in order to plan the wedding. Hence two allied discourses of compulsory heterosexuality, the specifically politicised one of 'family values' and the normative one of conventional family life, are thrown into relief.

This simulation of heterosexuality involves wholesale redecoration of the Armand–Albert family home (situated beside the club), while Albert the drag queen attempts – and fails – the challenge of passing as a straight man. While this could have been played in ways that affirmed a right-wing notion of homosexuality as aberrant, the mode of transformation itself comically foregrounds the constructed nature of heterosexuality as the mainstream. Thus, for example, when the flat is redecorated, a camp, stereotypically gay interior design, overloaded with explicit phallic imagery, is supplanted by symbols of straight male sexuality such as a moose head and a copy of *Playboy*. (When this is queried by Val, a helpful drag queen replies: 'That's what *they* read.') The obvious excessiveness of these symbols prompts Val to caution 'Don't add – just subtract'. Of course, the invocation to subtract might again reinforce the position of heterosexuality as the norm or centre to which gayness is added and unwanted excess. Yet the magazine and the moose head position heterosexual masculinity as both excessive and inadequate, in the sense of needing overt representation. This ironisation is pushed still further when the moose head is eventually subtracted, only to be replaced by a giant cross.

This satire on the symbolism of male heterosexuality is complemented by Albert's attempts to emulate the performance of male heterosexuality. Satisfaction at his ability to emulate John Wayne's swaying walk is soon dissipated when Armand and Albert alike recognise a campness that was there all along. Again, paradigms of male heterosexuality are revealed as both excessive and performative rather than neutral and essential.

Female heterosexuality comes in for similar treatment when, as a last resort, Albert drags up to play Val's 'mother'. Keeley falls for the décor, Christian cross and all, and for this figure, who bears a perhaps unintentional resemblance to Barbara Bush, and voices opinions from the Pat Buchanan/Rush Limbaugh school of gender values. Since it is Keeley's reliance on strict norms of gender and sexuality that largely contributes to his gullibility, the episode comically exposes both their inaccuracy and their distorting effects. This ludic satire is brought to a close, however, with the unexpected arrival of Val's birth mother, which prompts the revelation that Armand and Albert are a gay couple who own a night club and are Jewish. The moment of outing is played, as before, to comically undercut the Senator's position. He is shown to be unable to grasp that Albert is male. Even when Mrs Keeley explains, he is reduced to repeating 'They're Jewish?' The comic form knowingly exposes how his anxiety over the fluidity of gender roles is displaced on to a religious/ethnic identity marker.

Thus the film again comically questions the conception of mainstream American identity as, by default, WASP and heterosexual. The gay couple are presented as possessing real family values, mutual admiration and respect for one another, and are so full of parental love as to go to these extreme lengths for their son. By contrast, the straight couple's closeting of the sex scandal from Val and his parents, while advocating marriage for political expediency, reveals them as hypocritically hiding behind a façade of family values. Hence the critique of a traditional view of 'family values' and those politicians who invoke and hide behind them is but one thrust of *The Birdcage*. At the same time, the film strategically deploys the marriage narrative to normalise gay American identity.

The film ends with the final feminisation of the Senator as he leaves the nightclub in drag in order to dodge the press and potential scandal. Ironically, he escapes not by embracing family values of whatever sort, but through impersonating a female. Then, as the credits go up, the elaborate white wedding of the son and daughter is shown. At the wedding, a series of identities previously presented as irreconcilably different are paired off together. Openly heterosexual and gay guests are shown, and the ceremony is officiated by a Christian minister and a rabbi. The marriage form offers a narrative closure that openly signals difference in positive terms. This inclusion of sexual difference, though, is exemplified only within white racial identities. Black drag queens are shown, but are marginal, and negative stereotyping of gay masculinity is concentrated in the portrayal of Armand's Latino cleaner. While the marriage narrative can and does represent an inclusion or opening up of some alternative identities – here gender and sexuality – the ethnic limit remains conservative. There is also a conservative limit to the kind and function of gay identity. Sex, gay or straight, is not represented, and the gay coupling is affirmed arguably because it mirrors monogamous and economically successful heterosexuality. *The Birdcage*, then, offers a critique but no radical dismantling of the link between the family, marriage and identity.

If you don't get married you're abnormal

My Best Friend's Wedding is at first glance less obviously related to Clintonian politics. Julia Roberts plays Julianne, a white, heterosexual, feminist, twenty-seven-year-old unmarried successful restaurant critic whose male best friend, Michael (Dermont Mulroney), is getting married. They had been involved in the past, and have made a pact that, should neither be married by twenty-eight they will marry each other. That twenty-seven should be the sell-by date for matrimony is never problematised. On being told that Michael is marrying someone else, Kimmy (Cameron Diaz), Roberts decides that she really loves him and, in a rather perverse replaying of her *Pretty Woman* role, tries to get the man by making him break up with his true love. In a series of ever more absurd and slapstick manoeuvres she tries to discredit the bride, get him sacked, and latterly make him jealous by making her openly gay editor George (Rupert Everett) pose as her fiancé. The marriage of Michael and Kimmy takes place, and the suitably repentant Roberts is left unmarried with her compensatory gay friend.

Roberts's behaviour, her refusal to get married before the 'old age' of twenty-eight, her focus on her career, her duplicity with the innocent bride, her pretended engagement and attempts to get Michael sacked, are all indiscriminately labelled as aberrant and played as the source of comedy. Her deferral of marriage and focus on her career mirror the material and hard-fought reality of contemporary women, but a consciousness of this connection is absent from the film. Instead, its comic dismissing of such connections is, of course, what positions it ideologically. The consolidation of the gains of second-wave feminism in forging new identities for American women – of the kind hoped for by Hillary Rodham Clinton in 1992 – is clearly not rewarded, or even imagined here.

The use of the marriage narrative as a conservative and containing strategy against feminism is widely acknowledged. Its place in the discourse of 'family values' is also connected to the backlash from both Right and Left against any past or further calls from American women for equal rights.[14] A similar deployment of the marriage narrative in movies has a long history, going back to the films of D. W. Griffith, where – as Virginia Wright Wexman has shown – 'Marriage and the family are here judged as being far more significant than the choices that were then opening up to them [women] to participate in larger political processes.'[15] In a discussion of *My Best Friend's Wedding*, Chrys Ingraham exposes similar ideological imperatives: 'by providing images and messages that construct romantic love and the heterogendered division of labor as the "natural order" of things, the continuation of marriage and of patriarchal relations of production that subordinate women's interests to men's power is secure.'[16]

The film reproduces this economy of natural order in a number of ways. The main strategy is through the comparison of the Roberts and Diaz characters by the use of some traditional stereotypes of the feminine. Hence Roberts is dark-haired, works, refuses to kiss in public, drinks and smokes – all, especially the smoking, negative shorthand for the feminist and against the heterogendered division of labour. In comparison, Diaz is blonde, is giving up on College to follow Michael in his peripatetic job as sports writer, sings love songs to him in public, and is peppy (she is called Kimmy). Faced with the choice between 1950s femininity and 1990s career woman, Michael picks the 1950s and true love.

In case the audience is left in any doubt about Michael's choice, a further strategy is employed to discredit the Roberts character and cement its negative status as a stereotype of femininity. At the pre-ceremony dinner, while Roberts and Everett are pretending to be an engaged heterosexual couple, they are asked to explain how they met. Everett claims that they met in a mental asylum, and how as soon as he saw Julianne he fell in love. To Julianne's obvious discomfort, he then goes on to give a stirring rendition of the Diana King classic 'I Say a Little Prayer', in which the whole restaurant joins in, waving their lobster bibs and napkins (it is a themed restaurant, highlighting the farcical tone of the scene). So, as in *The Birdcage*, the comic effect comes from the audience's awareness that a character is playing against normative gender types. Here, however, the excessive performance of King's hymn to heterosexual love by a gay man to a potential groom-stealer emphasises the duplicitous and dangerous nature of Julianne's actions. Building on the comparison with Diaz discussed above, the film encourages a questioning of Roberts's motives, even her sanity, and reaffirms the natural order of the romance and marriage of Kimmy and Michael.

The film closes with Julianne at the wedding reception in a dance with George, who promises her 'no sex, no marriage but dancing'. The heterosexual career woman's compensation for forgoing marriage is to dance with a gay man. This is an unusual ending for a romantic comedy. Not only does the main female character not get married, but companionship of the right kind can be given only by a gay man. Such an ending could be seen as foregrounding the inadequacy of the traditional marriage narrative for contemporary women. Nevertheless, it is still unmarried or unmarriageable femininity that is configured as 'the problem' – a problem resolved narratively only by the coming together of two individuals (Kimmy and Michael) in heterosexual love.

A more positive reading of the film is suggested by reference to *The Birdcage*. Perhaps the partnership of Roberts and Everett offers a long-term sustaining relationship, rather than just a convenient narrative closure. Maybe the lack of sexual engagement offers a combination of emotional support with sexual freedom. Such a reading would be consonant with the 1990s (post-) feminism articulated in television shows such as *Sex in the City*. Yet, as with *The Birdcage*, the image of a suitable man remains constrained by traditionally dominant assumptions about race and ethnicity. In the almost uniformly white world of the film (the only evidence of a multiracial America is in a crowd scene at a baseball match), Rupert Everett's whiteness is unmarked. Nevertheless, the lack of any non-white speaking parts ensures the purity of the film's economy of gender. In this economy, white femininity occupies the position of the 'problem' in a way that may displace fears of the other other – blackness.[17]

Don't ask, don't tell

The narrative of marriage as necessary for female self-actualisation at whatever age is handled in another film of 1997, *In and Out*. Here Kevin Kline plays Howard Brackett, a High School English teacher in Greenleaf, Indiana. Four days before the date set for his wedding,

Howard is outed on national television. At the Oscar ceremony, watched expectantly by the whole town, an ex-student wins Best Actor for a portrayal of a gay soldier and, in his acceptance speech, outs Kline/Brackett as gay.

What follows is an 'is he or isn't he gay?' narrative, with some obvious yet well-handled stereotypes of male gay behaviour mostly centered on knowledge of Barbra Streisand. Pressurised by his parents (who declare his sexuality more or less irrelevant to their own desires for a wedding) and his headmaster (who suggests that marriage is essential if he is to keep his job), Brackett decides to go through with the wedding, but announces that he is gay at the altar.

If *My Best Friend's Wedding* seemed at first remote from the politics of Clinton's presidency, the narrative of *In and Out* could hardly reflect more directly the compounded politics of revelation and sexual identity around the issue of gays in public life. The conditions faced by Brackett through most of the film directly reflect the pre-Clinton conditions for military service, in that he is called upon to demonstrate his heterosexuality in order to satisfy his employers.

Clinton's pledge to repeal the ban on gays serving in the military was widely regarded as one of his most anti-'family' policies. As has been documented, after lobbying by the Joint Chiefs of Staff, a compromise policy was adopted, commonly known as 'Don't ask, don't tell'.[18] In response to this albeit limited reform, and to the State of Hawaii's legitimisation of same-sex marriage under the Equal Rights Amendment in 1996, the Defense of Marriage Act was introduced into Congress by Jesse Helms. In proposing the act, Helms argued that it 'will safeguard the sacred institutions of marriage and the family from those who seek to destroy them and who are willing to tear apart America's moral fabric in the process'.[19] In delivering even this limited reform, while also signing into law the Defense of Marriage Act, Clinton seemed to be taking up two contradictory positions. The complexity of this political climate is mirrored by *In and Out*'s complex negotiations over sexuality and marriage.

The climactic scene of the film takes the form of the High School graduation ceremony. In a parallel to his televised outing, when Brackett's sacking is made clear, the assembled student body and assorted townspeople leap to his defence, proclaiming his usefulness as a teacher, his membership of the volunteer fire brigade, his aesthetic advice to the bridal shop, and his filial qualities. When these vows prove insufficient in themselves, various students and townspeople declare one after the other that if Howard Brackett is gay, then 'I'm gay'. The last to do so is Brackett's mother, played by 1950s icon of heterosexuality Debbie Reynolds.

This is a marriage of sorts – a public affirmation of identity, inclusion and place in the community. By this ritualistic affirmation, the town as family is shown to be flexible enough to incorporate a gay man. Brackett remains silent throughout this sequence; and his silence is perhaps the price of inclusion. He is never questioned directly on his sexuality, and nor does he bear witness to his experience or identity. In other words, he is not asked, and does not tell.

This form of inclusion is an opening out of the small-town community which maintains its basic terms. The film narrative reiterates this, ending, after all, with a more traditional marriage, in the form of a ceremony at which the Bracketts renew their vows. At the ensuing reception everyone couples off, though not necessarily as heterosexual pairings. All these scenes adapt the form of the wedding in order to preserve its centrality, in much the same way as 'Don't ask, don't tell' operates as a policy. In both, a potentially disruptive sexuality is domesticated, to the extent to which it can fit within – or, more precisely, mimic – the institutions and manners of heterosexuality.

As with homosexuality in *The Birdcage* and career femininity in *My Best Friend's Wedding*, Brackett's difference can be assimilated here because it is singular. All of these films portray a world which is almost exclusively white, and while this could be considered to be contingent, their very coincidence suggests, rather, that a uniform racial background is an ideological precondition for the satisfactory incorporation of these other forms of difference.

As 'Don't ask, don't tell' exemplifies, a certain shift in desirable forms of citizenship was discernible as Clinton's second term drew to a close and Bush Jr's began. Inclusion within the circle of privilege is no longer dependent on being able to approximate a white, male norm. The films under discussion here suggest that so long as you act married, help someone else act married, or participate in a public ceremony which is as near as you can get to marriage, you can be part of the American family. Whatever the immediate results of Clinton's negotiations over family values, at least political and cinematic discourses of the family have begun to incorporate some of the diverse material realities of the family in contemporary America.

Part 4

'And crown thy good with brotherhood, from sea to shining sea...' Crossing boundaries

New York City in American film

Leonard Quart

In the waning days of November 1997, a gunman sprayed bullets at a group of young men playing football on a grassy field in a southeast Bronx housing project. The gunfire killed two of the young men and wounded a number of other players. The reasons for the violence at first remained unclear, though the newspapers casually mentioned that it was probably the result of a gang- and drug-related dispute. A while later, however, there was a news story reporting that an imprisoned gang leader in North Carolina ordered the shooting to prevent one of the men from testifying against him.

Despite the radical reduction of violent crime in Giuliani's New York, the burst of sudden violence was not a unique event in a Bronx neighbourhood where assaults, street robberies, drug-dealing, and livery cab stick-ups remain an integral part of daily life. However, in this chaotic world of limited options and opportunities, of social isolation and class marginalisation, most people in inner-city neighbourhoods still try to do other things than deal drugs, assault, rob and murder. Obviously, social pathology is a significant aspect of inner-city life, and affects most people who live there, but it is not all-encompassing. Some inner-city inhabitants are able to escape to social worlds that offer greater possibility for serenity and mobility; a small number, who have choices, remain and struggle to make neighbourhood life incrementally better; and many more get low-paying, sometimes marginal jobs (supermarket cashiers, security guards) and just scuffle hard to survive. Nevertheless, it is usually the most convulsive, destructive and self-destructive inner-city lives that Hollywood tends to dramatise. It is what fits best into the un-complicated conventions of action melodrama, where all the internal

pressures and conflicts people live with are externalised and simpli-
fied into violent confrontations and extreme behaviour. There is not
much of a market for films that deal with the complex lives of the
many inner-city inhabitants who just endure without succumbing to
ruinous behaviour. Movie audiences seem to be uninterested in everyday lives that can be touched with a mixture of happiness and quiet
despair, and are devoid of melodrama. What they like is a great deal
of murderous, often gratuitous violence to involve and entertain them
– behaviour that conveys little emotional nuance or sense of dailiness.
These films may depict a great deal of horrific behaviour, but the
sheer weight and excess of it begins to inure an audience to the
moral outrage and anguish they should elicit.

Consequently, the inner city of the popular imagination is dominated by boarded-up, burnt-out, graffiti-scarred houses, monolithic,
concrete housing projects, abandoned, garbage-strewn lots and cars,
feral drug-dealers, wasted addicts, tattered homeless men, wailing
police sirens, and constant violence and danger. Those physical images have permeated inner-city films even when abandoned slices of
the South Bronx and Brooklyn have seen their desolation filled with
standardised private homes with picket fences built by non-profit
and church groups. These are some of the images that can still dominate New York-based films like Martin Scorsese's *Bringing Out the
Dead* (1999), whose Manhattan is a degraded world of predators and
victims, and also crime-ridden police shows like *NYPD Blue* (a police show, of course, cannot sustain itself without having people
murdered), even when life in its inner-city neighbourhoods began to
change incrementally for the better in the mid-1990s. Film after film
in the 1990s, like Mario Van Peebles' commercially successful *New
Jack City* (1991) and *Juice* (Ernest Dickerson, 1992), made use of
these oppressive and murderous images to depict inner-city New
York. The Los Angeles-based *ghettocentric* films (a term coined by
film historian Ed Guerrero), like John Singleton's *Boyz N' the Hood*
(1991) and the Hughes Brothers' *Menace II Society*, portrayed the
same pernicious reality, except that the greener, more spacious,
lighter, detached private house and postage-stamp-sized lawn, and
car-dominated world, gave the illusion of a more intact and prosperous social environment (though the ominous whir of police helicopters constantly hovers over their lives).

The Los Angeles-based films were, obviously, not of a piece. Singleton's film veered from genre violence – epitomised in drive-by

shootings, and fluid cross-cutting to build tension – to Afrocentric and patriarchal speechifying about the need for responsible fathers raising their sons to become politically conscious, enterprising young black men. The prodigal sons would ideally be capable of both rejecting the pernicious seductions of street culture, and fending off dominant white society's supposedly conspiratorial desire to destroy blacks. The Hughes Brothers claimed that their frightening and cold *Menace II Society* was an attempt to portray inner-city Los Angeles as a concrete Vietnam that did not glorify violence and tried to avoid giving an audience an adrenaline rush. However, the film's casual drug-dealing, ripping people off and killing, and the boys' brutal victimisation of women, elicited cheers and catcalls from inner-city and suburban adolescent audiences. *Menace II Society* includes an authoritative black teacher who talks to the young men, without preaching, about responsibility and community, and a few other characters struggling to get out of the inner city (through playing football or becoming a Muslim), but it is the directionless lives and gratuitous violence – the casual and unexpected nature of the brutality, accompanied by the heavy rap score – that dominate the film.

There were other 1990s inner-city films that broke more sharply from the conventions of the action melodrama: films like Nick Gomez's *Laws of Gravity* (1992), Darnell Martin's *I Like It Like That* (1994) and Spike Lee's *Clockers* (1995) conveyed the respective ethos of New York working-class white, Puerto Rican, and Afro-American worlds. Each film projected a different angle on inner-city life; with all three eschewing tight narratives, non-stop action, and conventional box-office formulae for an auteurist perspective.

Nick Gomez's low-budget film *Laws of Gravity* (filmed in 12 days for $38,000, and borrowing heavily from Scorsese's 1973 *Mean Streets*) deals with petty thieves in Brooklyn's Greenpoint. Gomez drops the neighbourhood's stable Polish immigrant and second-generation population from the film, and by doing this he creates an edgier, more volatile world, devoid of families and populated by a narrow group of marginal young white men and women who hustle, shoplift, loan-shark, hijack, sell guns, and hang out in a neighbourhood bar. It is a seedy world; the characters live in squalid, claustrophobic railroad flats, but it is not quite a slum. The real slum in their minds is the adjoining more desperate Puerto Rican part of Williamsburg, with its abandoned buildings and garbage-filled lots. The film is *Mean Streets* without the stylisation and literary flourishes, or the intense semi-anthropological examination of neighbourhood codes and rituals. It is a film that does not use establishing shots, so we have little sense of place, or of the physical structure of the neighbourhood. It is also an episodic work without a true narrative, fading constantly to black, and depending primarily on a hand-held camera that nervously tracks after the characters as they go about their aimless, drifty lives. This vertiginous camera adds a great deal to the all-pervasive anxiety and energy of a film that sacrifices social context for the fragments of lives.

Just as in *Mean Streets*, the film's focus is on a bond between two male friends – an older, soft-voiced, tattooed ex-convict, Jimmy (Peter Greene), drawn to the bravado of his dimmer, self-destructive and anarchic friend Jon (Adam Trese). Jimmy has a genuine friendship with a tough, smart barmaid, Denise (Edie Falco, before her success as Carmela in *The Sopranos*) to whom he is married. She is one of the few characters in the film who seems to work and is ready for a normal life. Jon, for his part, has an abusive relationship with his attractive, flirtatious, masochistic wife. Jon breaks the neighbourhood code by publicly beating her – something that seems acceptable only in private. Jimmy, more settled and controlled than the manic Jon, is totally committed to and utterly protective of him. He continually tries – and fails – to act as mediator between Jon and his wife, and Jon and the world.

The film takes place in the existential present. We learn nothing about the characters' pasts, or what shapes their behaviour. Gomez offers no social or economic explanations for the world he evokes; behaviour is all. What we get is a great deal of semi-improvised, naturalistic, inarticulate talking. The characters constantly talk over each other, tossing off a Babel of profanity, and there is much irrational shouting, fighting, and mercurial shifting of mood. Although the male characters have known each other a long time, and project a generalised feeling of camaraderie, everybody is so volatile that they are ready to come to blows over a chance remark or put-down.

Despite the film's predictable close – the meaningless murder of Jon by a supposed pal – it constructs a dead-end, brutal world where anything apocalyptic rarely occurs (the murder of Jon is not the norm in this neighbourhood). There are no shoot-outs, car chases, melodrama – just a taut, tense, awkward, everyday portrait of marginal whites engaging in minor hustles to survive. *Laws of Gravity* focuses on these marginal whites, who have more economic opportunities than Afro-Americans and Hispanics, but choose hustling rather than hard labour as a way of life. The film makes no excuses for them, avoiding projecting any sort of explanation or rationalisation for their behaviour. In that way it feels similar to Gary Oldman's more psychologically relentless film *Nil By Mouth* (1998), about underclass white South Londoners. Gomez just feels that it is sufficient for an audience to observe them going about their tedious, melancholy daily routines, and making their own judgements about what they observe on the screen.

I Like It Like That is Darnell Martin's first film. Martin grew up in a Puerto Rican neighbourhood in the Bronx, though she went to private and boarding schools; she is the progeny of a mixed marriage – black father/white mother – and has worked as an assistant to Spike Lee. Her film centres on vibrant, fiesty Lisette, who is trapped with three children in a marriage to dim, macho, self-centred, but loving and sweet-natured Chino, a bicycle messenger. Martin's film is more a feminist fable, shot in a cartoon-like, high-decibel style, than an attempt to convey the social texture of Bronx life. In an opening scene shaped by rapid cuts, between Lisette (the animated Lauren Valez) and Chino (Jon Seda) having sex with music booming and their children banging on the door, a downstairs neighbour thumping on the ceiling with a broom, and Chino's friends hanging out on the stoops gossiping about what is going on upstairs – Chino is trying to break a record for how long he can hold an erection without coming – a loud hyberbolic vision of South Bronx life is evoked. We do not get much more of a public world than a large graffiti-covered mural memorialising a dead cop, kids playing street games, and sidewalks filled with intrusive people and sound (rap, salsa, boogoloo, and rhythm and blues). Martin looks with a clear, unsentimental eye at the strutting stupidity and narrow resentment of Chino's friends, who spread destructive rumours about Lisette's relationship with her yuppie boss. There is also a neighbourhood sexpot, Magdalena, who beds everybody on the street, and Lisette's parents, her West Indian father and her acquiescent Hispanic mother, who brutalise her campy, empathetic, transsexual brother, Alexis.

Still, it is not the murderous milieu of *Menace II Society*, though theft, numbers, and drug-dealing are part of the film's depiction of Bronx daily life, and Lisette's eight-year-old son, Chino Jnr, feels that he must become a hood to prove his masculinity. However, Martin provides a relatively benign and comic coloration to the desperation (for example, buying diapers with food stamps, the difficult search to find some privacy in the overcrowded apartment's toilet) that informs much of Lisette's world, the film focusing much less on social pain and pathology than on how constricting to the individual (especially in terms of gender identity) the milieu can be. When Chino is arrested, Lisette is forced financially to keep the family together. Almost too patly, she becomes the self-possessed talented assistant to a record and music video producer specialising in Hispanic artists. She finds life in the larger world and its economy liberating, achieving for the first time a sense of identity and self-esteem which the neighbourhood never offers her. Martin's film conveys neither a sentimental attachment to the Bronx, nor any overview of the Puerto Rican social and political situation there. The focus is on Lisette, a less sophisticated, more fettered variation of herself who is able to transcend the sexism and desperation of the Bronx and forge a career in the larger world. Martin, however, wants it both ways – Lisette as feminist heroine, and as loving wife. The film's concluding images show Lisette filming a music video, and walking on a beach hand in hand with Chino, with Coney Island's Wonder Wheel intrusively present in the background. Martin is obviously unwilling to follow the harsh logic of the film's narrative and vision, which would lead Lisette to leave Chino and the South Bronx behind. However, in the way of more conventional films, it wills that their love should transcend their real, seemingly insurmountable differences.

The most socially critical and evocative of the three films is Spike Lee's *Clockers*. The quality of Lee's work has fluctuated radically. The ethos of the inner city has been the subject of a number of his films, including arguably his best film, *Do the Right Thing* (1989), and more recently, the uneven basketball drama *He Got Game* (1998). *Do the Right Thing* is a formally dynamic and intellectually serious and balanced film that deals with a number of issues facing a Brooklyn black community – police brutality, white racism, the jiving irresponsibility and empty race rhetoric of black men, and their resulting black resentment of Asian and white storeowners' relative success.

The film may be flawed by too many film-school tics like unnecessary tilts and tight close-ups, the sanitising and sweetening of some of the more destructive aspects of black inner-city street life, like drug abuse and crime, and the sexist strain that turns the film's main female character into a nagging sex object. Still, Lee successfully fused realism and stylisation into a rich evocation of the ethos of a Brooklyn inner-city street during one summer heat wave. It is not only Lee's mastery of street vernacular, rapid panning, jump cuts, point-of-view shots, deep focus, artificial light, characters who skirt the edge of being cartoons, and other distantiation devices like the disc jockey, Love Daddy, and the Greek chorus of three unemployed street-corner philosophers, all of them providing commentary on the action; but also his capacity to make Sal (Danny Aiello), the white owner of the neighbourhood pizzeria, the film's most complex character. Sal has an amicable relationship with his customers, whom he treats, despite a paternalistic undercurrent, as individuals. However, Sal is also a product of a working-class subculture where the use of racist epithets like 'nigger' is not unusual. Enraged by being angrily and noisily confronted by the glowering, threatening Radio Raheem and the manic 'race man', Buggin' Out, Sal spews out racist invective, but Lee never calcifies him as a bigot. He sees him as a sympathetic, decent man placed in a frightening situation, whose complex social dimensions he does not understand, responding the only way he knows how.

What is more, one is struck by the genuine sense of political ambiguity the film projects. *Do the Right Thing* avoids being polemical by asserting that there are many political choices, and offers Malcolm X and Martin Luther King as two alternative political visions and strategies. The choice made by Lee's conflicted, underachieving protagonist, Mookie (Lee himself), to fling a garbage can through Sal's pizzeria window in the midst of a riot is depicted not as a heroic act, but as one that leaves Mookie perplexed and saddened. The film's conclusion carries with it no facile answer as to what it means to 'do the right thing', and only poses more questions.

Clockers is a very different sort of film from *Do the Right Thing*. On a superficial level it looks like a 'hood' or *ghettocentric* film, and was marketed as a film about gangbangers. However, despite the film focusing on clockers – minor drug-dealers in a Brooklyn housing project – it is a powerful lament against the violence and pathology of inner-city life. The narrative of *Clockers* does focus on the murder of a black dealer, and there is a driven, white homicide detective, Rocco Klein (Harvey Keitel), who attempts to get to the bottom of it. Typically, Lee is not interested in carefully shaping the film's narrative, or in the heightening of its tensions, or in the violence. In fact, this is all too brief and graphic to offer the audience much that might exhilarate them. Rather, *Clockers* is a meditation on its protagonist, Strike (Mekhi Phifer), a young black man who, with his adolescent cohorts, spends his life on the project benches dealing crack.

Strike himself is no abstract symbol of inner-city pathology or victimisation. He is an ulcer-ridden, solitary dreamer, obsessed with model trains, and caught in a criminal ethos that demands that he hide his tender side. Strike craves a father, but the only paternal figure he is linked to is his insidious employer in the drug business, Rodney (Delroy Lindo), a manipulative, quietly ominous figure who offers nothing but crime and money – 'the green' – that derives from it. The absence of fathers (on one level the film deals with the cycle of destruction set by fathers, whom novelist John Wiedman calls 'empty-handed ghosts'), general family breakdown, white racism, unemployment, and a world of thwarted possibilities constitute the urban fabric of the film, but Lee does not allow any of these factors to absolve his characters of responsibility for their own actions. Lee is repelled by the blacks attempting to coerce other blacks' acquiescence in criminal activity through the mobilisation of race identity and social disadvantage. He conveys only sympathy for Strike's upright, hard-working brother, Victor, a man who breaks emotionally because he cannot withstand the daily economic and social pressures of the inner city. Victor is attacked by an angry black drug-dealer and dubbed an Uncle Tom for just doing his job as a security guard protecting an Asian-owned store.

Lee's opening montage – which moves from brilliantly reconstructed police file photos of bloody corpses, including close-ups of entry wounds, to brightly coloured murals of dead adolescents, to tabloid headlines crying 'Toy Gun, Real Bullets' – quickly establishes the film's perspective. What Lee wants us to see is that the inner city is so permeated with internecine violence and blood that the greatest immediate danger to blacks comes from other blacks. Death rates due to homicides have ranged between six or seven times that of whites during the past fifty years, and most black criminals victimise other blacks, not whites. Lee reinforces this vision by intercutting music videos, malt liquor advertisements, video games, 'gangsta' rap, slasher movie images, and sounds that exalt the mindless violence and macho posturing of Strike's world, though Lee never makes the media into the film's villain.

Lee's critique is moral, not political or economic, in nature. He exhorts black adolescents to purge their lives of guns, drugs and violence, and to reject the seductions of easy money and the glamour of becoming a dealer. He also pleads for them to stay in school, and avoid listening to peers who make fun of learning. Nothing intellectually new here – and if there is a political commitment, it is to voluntarism, not socialism – but great imagist power: for example, *noir*-style night scenes that capture the heart of the spiritual emptiness and oppression of inner-city life, and seamlessly cut daylight scenes skilfully evoking the waste of intelligence that goes into the clockers' elaborate and efficient drug-dealing manoeuvres. The film is also so free of cant about race (no anti-white polemics) that its moral message is delivered by Rocco Klein, the emotionally exhausted, cynical, but thoroughly professional white detective. He is also one father figure who offers – in his relentless pursuit of justice – a glimmer of hope to Strike and his young protégé, Tyrone.

The police are corrupt, casually racist ('nubians' and 'yos' are what they contemptuously call Afro-Americans), and so utterly jaded that a murder – 'a stain on the sidewalk' – is viewed as serving the community, because in their terms it is like a 'self-cleaning oven' in a 'world of shit'. Their notion of a social solution does not go beyond dynamiting the projects 'to Timbuktu'. Still, Lee is never facilely and reflexively anti-police. They may be brutal, corrupt and detached (they toss their garbage into the street without a moment's hesitation), and though they are of little help to the community, operating as an occupying army and often reinforcing its poisonousness, Lee does not simplify the situation by turning them into the neighbourhood destroyers.

Clockers provides an overview of the neighbourhood that does include a few characters who have not succumbed to the drug culture. Men and wmen who go to church, hold down jobs (for example, Andre, the angry and upright Afro-American housing cop, who sets up a gym for the neighbourhood kids), and those who try to raise families; though their choices do not define the communal life conveyed in *Clockers*. Lee's vision of the inner city is greater than the sum of the individuals who inhabit it, though he usually stays bound to Strike's or the police's point of view. He may not have a politically sophisticated overview which embraces and delineates all the variables that shape the culture – the legacy of slavery; racism; the absence of positive role models; the reduction of social services; inadequate parenting, and so on – but *Clockers* projects a vision of inner-city entrapment that exposes the nihilism and potentially self-destructive aspects of Afro-American experience. It is a threat posed by the profound sense of rage, self-hatred, social despair, and impotence that envelops segments of Afro-American society, and makes both communal and familial life so difficult to sustain. In addition, without explicitly underlining what unemployment does to people in the inner city – in both *Clockers* and *Do the Right Thing*, few characters have real jobs to go to, and have too much aimless time on their hands – the films' evocations of unemployment and underemployment show their virulent consequences. What should be noted is that in Lee's most recent film, *Summer of Sam* (1999), his Bronx Italo-American working-class characters may not suffer economically or socially, but they are as trapped by their claustrophobic sexist and racist ethos as the clockers are by their own impoverished, nihilistic milieu. For Lee, no one ethnic or racial group has a monopoly on being or feeling entrapped, though his deepest sympathies are extended to his black characters.

The critique, however, has power not because of its intellectual elegance or complexity, but as a result of Lee's gift for getting at the emotional heart of his characters' pernicious behaviour without oversensationalising or sentimentalising it. He does not allow the clockers to make excuses – for they often make daily life impossible for so many ordinary people who share their neighbourhood, and spread their poison to the next generation of boys growing up in the projects. These are the boys who care little for the feelings and lives of other people, and lack any consciousness of the role historical and social forces play in shaping their own lives. The film's co-scriptwriter, Richard Price, upon whose novel the film is based, notes: 'the reality is that these kids don't give a fuck about stuff like preying on your own people. They don't think of themselves as political or sociological. They are thinking about how to get visible. Plus, they are teenagers, and teenagers think of nothing but themselves, not whether they are black or white or rich or poor'.[1]

Lee condemns the clockers' actions, but at the same time he avoids stereotyping them. He is able to construct an empathetic, nuanced portrait of his destructive central figure in Strike, rather than turn him into a swaggering, frightening ghetto tough in a rap video. In *Clockers*, Lee combines a gritty realism – a sharp eye and ear for the detail of street behaviour, colloquial speech, and the physical geography of the projects – with his usual stylistic virtuosity. There have been other films that dealt with New York street life, but in a different spirit. Larry Clark's raw, unsentimental and tightly structured *Kids* (1995) is but one example. Clark's film uses quasi-*cinéma vérité* techniques to provide an authentic, richly detailed portrait of adolescent boys and girls – white, black and Hispanic – discussing and having sex, smoking dope, drinking, night-clubbing, and brutally stomping somebody who offends them unconscious. It takes place in Washington Square Park and Manhattan apartments and streets, without the director offering any sort of explanation for the behaviour it observes. Almost all the adolescents are morally vacant and nihilistic: kids without any goals or direction except for the next sensation. The film feels true, but lacking in a clarifying moral vision beyond the director's voyeurism.

Despite films like *Kids*, the New York of the second half of the 1990s was no longer the same city that existed in the first half of the decade. The streets were less anarchic – drug-dealers, prostitutes, squee-gee men, panhandlers, and threatening adolescents were less visible. Traffic deaths were down sharply, violent crime continued to fall even more in inner-city neighbourhoods than in upper-class ones; tourism and hotel occupancy boomed; there was little vacant office space; unemployment dropped to 5.5 per cent by April 2000, down from 6.4 per cent the year before; while the city added 16,000 more jobs.[2] The average price for a Manhattan condo is a stratospheric $700,000;[3] Times Square is filled with movieplexes, new office buildings, theatres, a number of new hotels, even a branch of Madame Tussaud's, and a milling, unthreatening, tourist-dominated crowd. In Harlem, derelict brownstones are being renovated by black upper-middle-class professionals, and its main thoroughfare, 125th Street, now includes movie theatres, giant supermarkets and national retailers like Nike and Starbucks.

The city still has intractable problems, from homelessness and drug-dealing to gridlocked traffic and a public education system whose buildings are crumbling, where student standardised test scores have shown little change, and graduation rates are the lowest in the State. There is also the continuing tension between the police and minorities, exacerbated by a couple of police killings of innocent black men, and New York Mayor Giuliani's brutal and tone-deaf response to them. And despite all the glamour and glitter, we still have a dual city where luxury co-ops on Central Park West can sell for millions, while one in four New Yorkers continue to live below the poverty line.

However, although social pain and criminal violence still exist – drive-by shootings and sexual assaults still proliferate – the city – and that includes the inner city – looks better, and is more coherent and controlled than it has been in decades. Still, there have been few recent films that deal directly with the city or inner city's changed climate. No film of note has touched on the end of the crack epidemic or the strengthening of the inner-city economy. In fact, few of the African-American films made in the mid- to late 1990s have dealt with the inner city. Given the booming economy, which has meant gains in black employment and home ownership, the kinds of films that seem to appeal to black audiences have been romantic comedies. They range from *Waiting to Exhale* (Forest Whitaker, 1995) to Malcolm Lee's *The Best Man* (1999), all of them depicting mobile middle-class black characters rather than entrapped inner-city thugs.[4]

But if the films do not explicitly deal with the social and economic factors that have made the city more buoyant and seductive, there are films like the frothy, forgettable *You've Got Mail* (Nora Ephron, 1998), which recently turned New York's Upper West Side into an urban paradise just as Woody Allen did in a more difficult decade for the Upper East Side's streets in *Manhattan* (1978). What one remembers after watching this film are the affluent, smart-looking people sitting in cafés; the montage of distinctive, beautiful small stores opening on a sunlit morning; and side streets filled with handsome brownstones and blossoming trees. There are no homeless people camped on the sidewalks, just a glistening, pedestrian-filled, brightly coloured urban neighbourhood that anybody in the audience who likes cities would want to live in.

A film like *You've Got Mail* goes back to Hollywood's version of New York as a dream city, evoked in musicals like *On the Town* (Stanley Donen and Gene Kelly, 1949) and *The Band Wagon* (Vincente Minnelli, 1953), whose artfully designed sets evoke a vital, glamorous place that often provokes the most giddy and exultant of responses from its characters. Films like the latter two musicals and others like Vincente Minnelli's *The Clock* (1945) – a wartime city symphony with Judy Garland that conjured up a romance between two wide-eyed Middle Americans amid New York's volatility, cacophony and massiveness – had no interest in depicting the manifold realities of city life. Of course, the city was more serene in the 1940s and 1950s, so it was easier to sanitise and turn into an urban idyll. Nevertheless, constructing New York as dream city is less of an act of will or a selective vision in the late 1990s than when Woody Allen was creating it in the dark days of the late 1970s. There are enough radiant surfaces and genuine urban beauty to focus on in New York – so the dream city does not have to seem utterly fabulistic.

Of course, American films, even those that focus on the city's social reality, rarely provide an institutional or historical context for the nature of urban life. We are more apt in films to personalise a social and political dynamic or issue, or make it secondary to the conventions of the genre, rather than explore its structural basis. A film like Howard Becker's *City Hall* (1995), which deals with New York politics and the mayoralty, suggests that most political decisions in New York are not simply right or wrong but grey; in fact, that making political choices usually demands mediation between varied economic, racial, ethnic and ideological interest groups so that the city can function. *City Hall*, however, fails to build on that perception, and make the kind of film that depicts a mayor who is a complex individual facing social issues and problems like police brutality, corporate demands for tax abatement, the failures of the school system, racial demagoguery and rioting, and trims his notion of the common good to achieve some semblance of it. Instead, it is an uneasy hybrid. Its perceptive evocation of urban political manoeuvrings and power-mongering – dealings with machine bosses and real-estate interests – is subsumed by a pedestrian and confusing political thriller that involves mob killings and the melodramatic search for the person who made the phone call that got a sentence fixed.

In Hollywood films, if it is Vietnam we might typically get a *The Deer Hunter* (Michael Cimino, 1978), where the emphasis is on an indomitable working-class superman, Michael Vronsky (Robert De Niro), who destroys the 'evil' Vietnamese, even if we might also get intelligent films like *A Civil Action* (Stephen Zaillian, 1998) and *The Insider* (Michael Mann, 1999). If corporate poisoning of the environment is the subject, Hollywood gives us *Erin Brockovich* (Steven Soderbergh, 2000), with Julia Roberts playing the spunky, undereducated, single-mother heroine, who, breasts leaping out of her dress, defeats the corporation. Hollywood understands that the mass audience doesn't want politically sophisticated Ken Loach-like explorations of Spanish Civil War ideological conflicts. To make a profit, the narrative must focus on the fate of a sympathetic individual with whom the public identifies, and leave the social and historical forces that helped to shape the world the protagonist must confront in the background.

Of course, there are American independent films like John Sayles's *City of Hope* (1991), which, like Eastern European political films such as Pal Gabor's *Angi Vera* (1978), or one of a number of Andrzej Wajda's films, construct a dialectical relationship between the lives of individual characters and the social and political context they inhabit. Sayles, however, is a rare figure among American directors – a literary film-maker who rarely indulges in the use of genre formulae and action, and is politically committed and sophisticated enough to make social films that eschew sloganeering for an intricate analysis of how racial and ethnic politics function in a small city. For example, one central character in *City of Hope* is an idealistic black councilman, who is committed to social change. However, he must compromise his notion of justice to gain his community's support and serve it more effectively, in essence accepting morally suspect means in order that the community make some gains.

There are innumerable films to be made about inner-city and urban life in general that get at its contradictions, complexities, and constantly shifting nature, films that refuse to romanticise, cynically use, or degrade inner-city lives, and go beyond most of the clichéd media representations that shape public consciousness. There are also other urban subjects that have barely been touched on in film: the respective ethos of New York's diverse ethnic and immigrant groups, and their relationships; the power of the media, Wall Street, real estate interests, and the Mayor to shape the city's present and future; and the gap between wealth and poverty in the city. I hope that the films made about New York that explore these and other themes will do so without becoming mired in gratuitous violence, car chases, and genre conventions. I look for films that devise original and subtle fictional narratives the equal in their social, political, and psychological insight to a Fred Wiseman (for example, *Public Housing*, 1997) *cinema vérité* documentary, and more shapely and concentrated in their art. A city like New York contains infinite narratives, just waiting to be constructed, which eschew the sensational and sentimental for what is intricately genuine.

Dixie's land: cinema of the American South

Ralph Willett

Anything that comes out of the South is going to be called grotesque
by the Northern reader, unless it really is grotesque in which case it is
going to be called realistic.

Flannery O'Connor

... most literature and film about the South are either about poor
white trash or faded Southern aristocracy.

Fannie Flagg

One

In the 1930s, nostalgic portrayals of the Old South – white-pillared
mansions and a stable, genteel, feudal social system – provided
escapism for Depression audiences. Since then, 'The South' has remained an image-bank and a narrative resource manipulated by
Hollywood to answer some of the nation's psychological needs. The
parading of stereotypes and the construction of mythic fantasies have
taken place on the terrain of opposed representations.

The Sunny South myth projects the region as a pastoral version of
Eden, in tune with bounteous nature. A later refinement is the South
as Sunbelt, a region of prosperity and enterprise, though the Sunbelt
is a slippery concept that works better for *nouveaux riches* Southern
cities such as Atlanta and Charlotte than for states. Yet suburban
expansion, shiny new buildings, sunshine of course, and prosperity
based on oil, aerospace, and tourism offer evidence that many parts
of the region have caught up economically with the Northeast and
the West Coast. Also, the evils of the South (racial conflict, violence,
religious fundamentalism) have been reinterpreted as national traits.
It is clearly premature, though, to claim that the bright modern cities

of the South, the region's increasing affluence, and its newly acquired articulate confidence have consigned negative images to the past.

The obverse of the Sunny South is the Visceral South inhabited by rednecks, hillbillies, zealots, Klansmen, and degenerate aristocrats. This image was fostered by national figures such as DuBois and Mencken (himself from Baltimore), and supported by the writings of Southern journalists and literary artists in the 1920s and 1930s. Consequently, the South was perceived as a land of racial injustice, intellectual sterility and religious fanaticism. A psychological version, the Decadent South, was disseminated by the Southern Gothic of Williams, Faulkner, McCullers and O'Connor. The region was regarded as dark, exotic and sexually repressed, a world exemplified by grotesque characters and menacing atmospheres in which physical and emotional violence were latent.

> The South [has been] viewed more recently as a land of rambunctious good old boys, demagogic politicians, corrupt sheriffs, country and western good old girls, nubile cheerleaders, football All Americans with three names, neurotic vixens with affinities for the demon rum, Bible-thumping preachers haunted by God, sugary Miss America candidates of unquestioned patriotism, toothless grizzled 'po' white trash', and military 'lifers' of considerable spit but little polish.[1]

In the 1970s and early 1980s, some of these figures appeared in TV comedy and in movies structured around a basic situation which sets in opposition a representative of law enforcement and a charming, scheming populist with little respect for authority. This plot formula produced either rural comedy in movies exploiting the good old boy persona of Burt Reynolds (*Smokey and the Bandit*, Hal Needham, 1977; *WW and the Dixie Dance Kings*, John G. Avildsen, 1975), or a more dramatic narrative in which the plausible, self-regarding hero clashes with a brutal sheriff or prison officer.

My Cousin Vinnie (Jonathan Lynn, 1992) is one of the more inventive versions of the paradigm. The potential victims are two New York students arrested in Wazhoo, Alabama on a murder charge. In desperation they turn to cousin Vinnie (Vincent Gambini), played by Joe Pesci, for a defence lawyer, although it emerges that he is an ambulance-chaser who has repeatedly failed his bar exams. From the beginning, the film introduces and then inflects – even reverses – accepted regional images. The soundtrack opens with a country rock number, 'Way Down South', which contains the phrase 'just across the border'. Before visiting the convenience store where, after their departure, the killing takes place, the students have been stigmatising the South in terms of incest, corruption, and 'medieval laws'. Road-side signs like 'Dirt for Sale' and 'Free Horse Manure' appear to endorse the prejudices of the cosmopolitan visitors.

My Cousin Vinnie sets up these stereotypes only to demolish them. The Southern judge is a Yale Law School alumnus and a stickler for courtroom propriety; Vinnie, with his casual manner, his ignorance of Alabama law and his smart-aleck, wisecracking confidence – the casting of Pesci and the name Gambini (cf. Gambino) imply a differ-ent kind of 'wise guy' – regularly finds himself in contempt. The glib, affable New South District Attorney exploits Vinnie's ineptness and attempts to sidestep the legal practice of disclosure.

In this comedy, generic considerations determine that justice will be served and the students released. However, Vinnie's success – and, by extension, the revalorisation of Northern values and styles – is not merely a function of the narrative. For his first appearance in court, he dresses in black leather coat, black T-shirt, medallion and cowboy boots. This flamboyance is echoed in the final courtroom scene when Vinnie, by default, wears the costume of a vaudeville artiste and uses his new-found knowledge of grits to destroy a testimony; dressed as a magician, he calls on his verbal skills both to put on a show and to win the case. He is abetted by his ostentatious girlfriend, whose cogent testimony on the subject of US automobiles and their tyres is crucial. Southern formality is made to look fusty and outmoded in the face of Brooklyn flair and personality. For the South to be pushed aside by show business is, in a Hollywood movie, an instance of overdetermination.

Two

Such country music films as *Sweet Dreams* (Karel Reisz, 1985) and *Coal Miner's Daughter* (Michael Apted, 1980) are related to a cul-tural phenomenon of the early 1980s. Described in *The New Republic* as 'Rural Chic', this was manifested in a group of films about rural work and life in the South and Southwest during periods of eco-nomic hardship: *Country* (Richard Pearce), *The River* (Mark Rydell) and *Places in the Heart* – all 1984. Despite being set during the Depression, the last-mentioned, directed by Robert Benton as a hom-age to Waxahatchie, Texas, is the most resonant for its use of racial and religious materials. The movie begins and ends in the local church; at the conclusion, the dead and departed reappear to sit in the pews, underlining the Baptist belief in the 'reconciliation of the spirits'. This counteracts the bigotry which has threatened community values and the survival of the film's main characters: the widow (Sally Field) trying to hang on to her smallholding and the two men who assist her, a black, dispossessed farmer (Danny Glover) and a blind veteran (John Malkovich). These agents of a populist tale are marginal figures, but working for each other, they become the repository of those doctrines that lead to social peace.

An important link is established through the various female stars. Sissy Spacek plays a farmer's wife in *The River*, while Jessica Lange takes a similar role in *Country*. Respectively, they are the country star protagonists in *Coal Miner's Daughter* (Loretta Lynn) and *Sweet Dreams* (Patsy Cline). Ed Harris, Cline's husband in the latter, also appears in *Places in the Heart*. As Duncan Webster has pointed out: 'There is a chain of country connotations which performers bring with them from film to film; memories of other roles provide viewers paradoxically with a sense of authenticity.'[2]

A genuine change in the region's image took place just before the Reagan years, and was generated by the presidency of Southerner Jimmy Carter and the growth of the prosperous Sunbelt. Carter's links with farming, his concern for family values, his religious conversion and his evident decency – all these made him a worthy exemplar of Southern customs. In addition, his prominence focused attention upon the major economic, demographic and social changes taking place in the region. To the extent that such changes included suburbanisation and modernisation, many deplored them (or saw them as illusory): the writer Marshall Frady lamented the transformation of the region into a world of neon cityscapes, pollution and 'styrofoam politicos', while in *Nashville* (1975) Robert Altman exposed the Tennessee town as a plastic country music Disneyland which still fostered extremism.

Certainly country music, with its narratives of love, family and Southern mores, was gaining a national acceptance, but the country music filmic biographies of the 1980s are a complicated response to the culture of the New South. 'Ironically what emerged in the forefront of the nation's consciousness was less this radical transformation of the Southern economy than a sense of the South as representing fundamental American cultural and moral traditions.'[3]

Collectively in recoil from Nashville cosmopolitanism and its cross-over sounds, these films sought to restore the 'tears and tragedy' to the music, and to acknowledge those traditions.

Coal Miner's Daughter, tracing a journey from poverty to wealth, might appear to have sidestepped conflict and misery. In this movie's final credits there is a reprise of characters (parents, DJs, Patsy Cline, etc.) as a summation of Loretta Lynn's life. Included are shots of the Ryman Auditorium and the Lynns' palatial mansion in Tennessee's Hurricane Hills. While Loretta is performing 'I'm a Honky-Tonk Girl', however, her husband is in a Nashville bar looking for one. Romance and marriage underpin Hollywood's discourse of hetero-sexuality, but often produce emotional tension and barriers to personal fulfilment, especially when the belief system of the Southern working-class male is also a determining factor. Compared with Patsy Cline's marriage in *Sweet Dreams*, Loretta Lynn's is relatively idyllic. Cline's husband, Charlie Dick, belongs to the South's gallery of 'lovable losers, no-account boozers'. Lynn's husband Doo (Doolittle), while prone to the vices of the good old boy, remains her capable manager, and it is he, not Cline, who fills the crucial role of the protagonist's friend – the figure in biographies who proclaims the qualities of the star, and whose life is given meaning by their association. Dick, on the other hand, senses himself unmanned by Patsy Cline's success, and explodes in physical rage. Destruction is at the heart of *Sweet Dreams*, with Dick's brutality towards Cline (which, like a loyal Southern woman, she attempts to play down) serving as a premonition of both the car crash which puts her in hospital and the air crash which kills her. These elements in the movie run parallel to the entertainment ideology, with its songs about sweet dreams and faded love.

There is a further romance in these films – a romance with fans and the audience. Democratic scenes of public approbation signify the performer's accomplishment and increasing fame. In country music films this is usually marked by an appearance at the Grand Old Opry, where acceptance by the audience precedes and predicts acceptance by the music industry. Doo's understanding of show-business dynamics, and the need to erase the distance between centre and margin, is portrayed in the scene where he patiently takes a fan's call at 1 a.m.: 'She loves you too,' he insists, 'she'll pray for you.'

Married at thirteen with four babies by the age of seventeen, and a grandmother at twenty-eight, Loretta Lynn is continuously associated with nature. From the beginning of *Coal Miner's Daughter*, when Loretta rides through the wooded hills to the sound of a coal train, and Doo drives his red jeep up a junk heap, the film is structured by the polarities of nature and the machine. In a country song by Dottie West, 'Everything's a Wreck [Since You're Gone]', the wife is unable to start the mower or change a fuse. Although the world of technology, in the film of Lynn's life, is masculine, it tolerates and may need the female artist. On the other hand, it is always liable to frustrate and baffle, as Loretta learns when she tries to learn her lines by tape-recorder. Her naivety disappears in those songs which express assertiveness and a desire for independence, although such attitudes are enlisted in a defence of the marriage partnership. Her most controversial numbers ('The Pill' and a song about divorce, 'Rated X') are passed over in assembling a narrative whose trajectory is positive and progressive.

Loretta's assertiveness is demonstrated by the publicity tour improvised to promote her record of 'Honky-Tonk Girl'. *Coal Miner's Daughter* could have achieved greater precision in describing the singer's professional marginalisation in the early days. Kentucky artists experienced greater difficulty than their counterparts in Georgia, Texas, and Tennessee in achieving mass-media exposure, and were obliged to leave the State to find an audience. As a character in the movie explains: 'You born in the mountains, you got three choices: coal mine, moonshine, or moving on down the line.' The first of these was not an option for women, who were forbidden to work in the mine by law and superstition. It was thought that a mine would explode if a woman entered. The barriers these attitudes represented, and the problems for women miners generally, were addressed in an independent documentary, *Coalmining Women* (Elizabeth Barrett, 1982) produced by the regional media centre Appalshop.

While these biographies are less vulgar and less sanitised than the average Hollywood example, certain absences handicap them as persuasive Southern cultural documents and identify them as commodities for a largely 'country-politan' audience, one which is national rather than regional. They can be considered as part of the Southernisation of America, country music having ceased by this time to be an exclusively Southern phenomenon.

The 'hillbilly' or poor white discourse in American media practice comprises irresponsibility, drunkenness, ignorance, evangelical religion and bestial sexuality. Its visual signifiers are rusting automo-

biles, dilapidated shacks, grizzled faces (mean or bloated), faded
dungarees and cheap print dresses, images largely excluded from or
romanticised in the country music biographies discussed above. In
other genres Hollywood drew upon these characteristics to represent
the Visceral South (see Section One above) located by W. J. Cash in
the Carolina Piedmont and in Appalachia (Virginia and West
Virginia). The film version of James Dickey's *Deliverance* (John Boorman, 1972) perceived Appalachia as a version of hell, destroyed by
civilisation but a nightmare of barbarism and menace nevertheless.
Its 'white trash' inhabitants, like the natives of undeveloped lands
elsewhere, are representatives of a primitive past which the modern
West has discarded; the ancient landscape which enfolds them is
seductive to the bourgeois adventurers, drawn by what Lewis (Burt
Reynolds) describes as 'the last wild, untamed, unpolluted, unfucked-
up river in the South'.

The famous 'Duelling Banjos' contest between the Atlanta busi-
nessman and the retarded musical genius (a Flannery O'Connor
grotesque) provides a temporary point of identification, hinting at a
sympathetic perspective on the life and folk culture of a region. The
film's narrative swiftly suppressed the suggestion, for it is based on
an irreconcilable dualism. Throughout *Deliverance* – which is heavily
masculinist, but arguably a deconstructionist reading of a nightmare
'buddy' movie – relationships between city and rural men are at best
hostile, at worst murderous. The class difference (between middle
and lower) is displaced by a civilised/savage binary division which
demeans and racialises the mountain folk. Thus the 'poor white'
South and its music are still regarded as Other and unassimilable,
beyond recuperation.

Filmed in Florida, Martin Scorsese's *Cape Fear* (1991; a remake of
an earlier 1961 version) takes place in the steamy coastal town of
'New Essex, North Carolina', where a rich upper crust lives in uneasy juxtaposition with a dangerous underclass. Robert De Niro,
covered in ominous biblical tattoos, is Max Cady, an avenging angel
(or devil) in a film which shows the unstable nature of civilised values. The ranting and delirium that verbalise his born-again fundamentalism, along with quotations from Dante and Nietzsche, create
a character worthy of imitation in a 1995 B-movie, *Just Cause* (Arne
Glimcher), where Ed Harris plays Blair Sullivan, a psychopath and
serial killer on Death Row. A more tenacious son of Cady can be
found in Robert Altman's *The Gingerbread Man* (1998), set in a

rain-drenched Savannah that awaits the arrival of Hurricane Geraldo. An overcast sky and thunder create a mood of foreboding on the swampy Georgia coast, justified by the emergence of Dixon Doss, the frenzied, barefoot leader of fundamentalist hoboes.

With frequent references to white trash, a categorisation with definite class, sexual and behavioural implications, *Cape Fear* displays a strangely all-white South which generates the nightmare of the underclass rising up and engaging in violence and violation. The New South family which Cady threatens is itself dysfunctional, so the movie seeks to avoid a rigid morality. Nevertheless this remains an exercise in Southern Gothic, profoundly embedded in the images of the primeval swamp, and constantly reinforced by Bernhard Herrmann's music.

Three

When it appeared in 1988, *Mississippi Burning* (Alan Parker) was regarded as a trailblazer tackling the history of racial violence and the Civil Rights movement in the USA – specifically, in this instance, the Freedom Summer of 1964 and the murder of Goodman, Schwermer and Chaney. The result – unhappily – was in the tradition of films which 'subordinate complex political and social processes to individual heroics and spectacular set pieces'.[4] These set pieces included firebombings, lynching and castration, shot in night-for-night chiaroscuro and placed in the humid atmosphere of the Mississippi small town with its courthouse, storefronts, and – further out – dilapidated farms and shacks strewn with dead animals.

The Civil Rights movement was established through the heroic actions of black Americans in the South. Absurdly, Parker's narrative turns the events of the time into a struggle between white law-enforcement agencies, the emergent (white) heroes being two FBI agents whose temperamental rivalry inevitably overshadows the larger conflict. In reality, it was the Justice Department that brought about desegregation; Hoover's FBI was hostile towards the Civil Rights movement in the South, directing its attentions at protesters rather than at racist killers. Interestingly, the FBI characters are played as self-righteous and arrogant, employing the same ruthless methods as the Klan.

In juxtaposition, the blacks in the film are mere noble victims, as much a part of the background as the soundtrack of Gospel music.

The white discourse organises African Americans within the racial hierarchy, a procedure evident elsewhere – even, for example, in *Mississippi Masala* (Mira Nair, 1992), where the exploration of the theme of Indian/Southern black relations would appear to preclude such an occurrence. But the white presence is evident in the desire of the incoming group of Indians (emigrants from Uganda) not to be associated with the 'lower' American blacks. More closely related to Parker's film is *Ghosts of Mississippi* (Rob Reiner, 1996), based on the murder of Medgar Evers, which similarly uses the Civil Rights movement as a stage on which to play out a white lawman's uncertain quest for justice.

In terms of gender politics, *Mississippi Burning* achieves some degree of balance: Anderson (Gene Hackman) is a dominating figure, an ex-sheriff who insinuates himself into the populace with a folksy manner and racist jokes, but is prepared to act pragmatically and to get down in the sewer to defeat social evil. The moral centre of the film is the beauty shop owner Mrs Pell (Frances McDormand), whose conscience overrides her prejudices: despite the consequences, she gives testimony that indicts her husband: a deputy, a Klansman, a killer.

In 1991, a TV movie, *Carolina Skeletons* (James Erman), also portrayed an attempt to right racial wrongs. A teenage black boy is railroaded into the death cell for the murder of two young white girls. The setting is the segregated South of the Depression years, more precisely Crawfordsville, South Carolina ('Nasty little backwater town, nasty people', recalls Judge Brigstone, who had served as Defence Attorney for the boy, Linus Bragg). What really happened in 1934, and who is responsible for related contemporary killings, is established thirty years later by an uneasy alliance between Green Beret hero James Bragg, the next generation of the family, and the town sheriff, Junior Stoker, whose father had been arresting officer in 1934. Junior is played by Bruce Dern who, for David Thomson (in his *Biographical Dictionary of Film*), usually suggests 'the slightly unbalanced man who believes he has been wronged'. Dern's character here is haunted not by a grievance but by the execution, an event he was forced to witness and the source of recurring nightmares. Junior seeks to exorcise the past by solving the crime; he needs to earn the respect and trust of 'Jimmy' in order to do so. The real murderer is one of Fannie Flagg's 'faded [and depraved] aristocrats', a member of the wealthy Campbell family whose saw mill provided employment

for the town. T. J. Campbell's paedophilia signifies the radical decline of a quasi-Faulknerian dynasty, one which ran the mill like a
plantation, yet provided money for the NAACP (the National Association for the Advancement of Colored People). Despite the faded
wall signs, which recall Walker Evans's photographs, there is no
nostalgia for Crawfordsville, and the comments of present-day locals
on 'gook lovers' and 'uppity niggers' indicate its remoteness from the
liberal political centre.

Media representation of Black America in the 1980s was both
repressed and dominated by *Roots* (1977), a TV series seen at some
stage by 130 million Americans. Its realistic depiction of slavery in
the South was partly accomplished by excessively brutal stereotypes
of whites and, despite the positive stress on black family continuity
and pride, traditional images of blacks as resigned and enduring
were reinforced. The goal in life for the majority of black slaves was
seen as survival by any means, and the slaves' adoption of masks and
personae was open to misinterpretation as character weakness.
Although a sequel took the narrative into the twentieth century, the
effect of this historical saga was to expiate white guilt without confronting the problems of the contemporary South.

Unlike *Roots*, *The Color Purple* (Steven Spielberg, 1985) is one of
those movies which, in Ed Guerrero's words, 'locate the Black community in naive or idyllic, rural settings removed from the containment of the surrounding white community'. The idyll is, of course,
postponed by the cruel behaviour of black men towards their women
(the plural form is relevant). Racism by whites is present in the film,
but it is the image of black men as violent and sexually abusive, and
the not unconnected demonstration of black family instability, that
drew the criticism of stereotyping. In contrast to *Roots* and its piti-
less white overseers, *The Color Purple* introduces a black authority
figure, Mister, who is – iconographically and in his attitude to his
black workers – a parody of the white planter and slave owner. Only
for black women consumers has the combination of male harshness
and female love and bonding offered the gift of recognition, although
the lesbian motif was played down in the film.

The white discourse mentioned above is also a showbiz Hollywood discourse, revealed in the musical element which suffuses this
studio spectacle. Spielberg crosscuts between the blues singing of
Shug in a juke-joint and the spirituals being harmonised in the local
church where Shug's father is the preacher. Reflecting the studio's

mainstream preferences, the church music is allowed dominance, and Shug's reconciliation with her father is pictured as a humiliation. (In Alice Walker's novel, Shug rejects the patriarchy represented by her father and his white god.) So despite the involvement of Quincy Jones, arguably, 'the film's musical form ... is the same old generic, cliché, Eurocentric movie music [and simply] packages Afro-American music for popular consumption'.[5]

Although it is set in 1962, *Eve's Bayou* (1997, written and directed by Kasi Lemmons) overlooks civil rights but provides the psychological depth and cultural authenticity missing from *The Color Purple*. Its narrative is reminiscent less of cinema than of literature – its enclosed black community looking back to Zora Neale Hurston; its revelation of memory evoking Toni Morrison. The opening voice-over by Eve as an adult announces: 'Memory is a selection of images', a definition later modified by the acknowledgement that memory changes according to 'the light' and to desire, and is rewritten by time. As key moments are recalled, they are frozen or turned into computer-enhanced black and white.

Upper-class blacks rarely make appearances in American popular culture. In *Eve's Bayou*, the Batistes, descendants of an earlier African Eve and onetime owner General Jean-Paul Batiste, are a bourgeois family whose sumptuous house (or rather 'home') might have featured in *Southern Living* were it not that the style and content of the film are far removed from the untroubled, idealised domestic surface of the New South projected by that magazine. Its themes of spirituality, sexuality and coming of age situate the movie in the tradition of the 'woman's film', but decorated with Gothic elements of the delta country such as voodoo, snakes slumbering on cypresses, and exotic hanging moss. Eve's Bayou (the place), named after the Batistes' slave ancestor, yields up a past of miscegenation, land inheritance and life-saving witchcraft – one which, as in Faulkner, influences future generations. The white magic is created by Eve's aunt, Mozelle Batiste-Delacroix. 'The soulful essence of Creole culture', she is both community counsellor and spiritual centre of the family world. She provides an emotional anchor for the young Eve, who shares her gift of clairvoyance. Mozelle's goodness and generosity oppose the greed and malice of the white-faced voodoo witch Elzora, who plies her trade at the local market.

Incest as represented by Hollywood is often associated with Southern poor whites, and is used to shock and to demonise the marginalised group. In *Eve's Bayou*, adultery and incest threaten the Batiste family image, but the topics are dealt with in a sophisticated manner. Eve's fairy-tale perspective (the vision of a child) is endowed with the technique of a French New Wave film, and this fractured, layered style renders its thematics ambiguous; characters such as the philandering father, Louis (Samuel L. Jackson, who co-produced the film), and his teenage daughter Cisely, struggling to control her highly charged sexuality, cannot be reduced to heroes and villains. With its Southern setting and its emphasis on the lives of the women in the Batiste family, *Eve's Bayou* challenges the male-defined aesthetic of New Black Cinema: 'Lemmon's portrait of a rural, affluent French-speaking black family [threatens] essentialist notions … of black experience as definitely urban, ghetto-centered and youth-culture dominated.'[6]

Four

Critics of Jon Avnet's 1991 movie *Fried Green Tomatoes at the Whistle Stop Cafe* claimed that its feminism and its treatment of a same-sex relationship were seriously weakened by its narrative method. More explicitly, its racial violence and lesbianism, elements of an aberrant, demonic South, were contained by the framing tale of 'New Woman and 'New South'. In actuality, frame and centre are interwoven to show the resemblance on the level of friendship and female bonding between Idgie and Ruth, who ran the Whistle Stop Cafe and, in the present, Evelyn and Mrs Threadgoode. Moreover, one of the film's achievements is to insert women into the South's oral tradition of tale-tellling where Eudora Welty is their great predecessor, not least through Mrs Threadgoode's overarching narrative.

The contribution of black Southerners to that tradition is diminished in the transition from book to film. Similarly, the efforts of the legendary Railroad Bill, a black man who threw food and coal off the train to 'the coloured people who lived along the tracks', becomes (in the movie) Idgie tossing hams and cans of food to a racially mixed group of people at the local Hooverville. (This is one of many scenes indicating the – sometimes deadly – importance of the railroad in the life of Whistle Stop and the South.) But the film does intensify the brutality inflicted on the black community. Big George, Idgie's 'colored man', is beaten by the KKK *in public* by the railroad tracks, though in reality, especially in the 1930s, the Klan administered their 'justice' in private.

Despite that scene, the black population are presented as docile and contented, a condition maintained by the warmth and friendship which Idgie and Ruth supply. The two women are instrumental in creating a genuine community that resembles a large family engaged in an virtuous process of giving and sharing; this impression is strengthened by depicting Whistle Stop in the Depression with a poignant romanticism: 'a pastoral landscape of dusty lanes, mules, goats, passing trains, and small-town bustle'.[7]

The most important thing in life, says Mrs Threadgoode in the film's final words, is 'friends, best friends', and it is friendly sisterhood that characterises the intimacy Idgie and Ruth share rather than a sexual love, which remains no more than an undercurrent. The bottom line is the unacceptability of a misogynist culture epitomised by Ruth's brutal husband, Frank Bennett. Idgie's tomboy appearance gives rise to a butch image constructed from work boots, waistcoat and rolled-up jeans, and the activities of fishing, smoking, drinking and gambling. Yet Idgie transcends gender categories; her caring, loving side is never suppressed, and she risks her life to ensure that Big George is not indicted for Bennett's murder.

Throughout the film there is an oscillation between 'feminine' and 'masculine'; it is the gentle, skinny black cook, Sipsey, who summons the strength to strike Bennett as he attempts to remove Ruth's baby. The Whistle Stop Cafe, standing for nourishment of various kinds, and the careers of Idgie and Ruth are an inspiration to Evelyn in the 1990s. Like Ruth, she rejects passivity and finds a voice to articulate her feelings and her newly achieved identity. The offer to Mrs Threadgoode of friendship and a home to replace the one destroyed is the logical outcome of the old lady's affection and her role as conduit for the models of the past. *Fried Green Tomatoes at the Whistle Stop Cafe* is a genuinely feminist film that is also rooted in Southern social and family values.

Beth Henley grew up in Jackson, Mississippi, and used her knowledge of the South, especially its women, to create a series of dramatic works, including *Crimes of the Heart* and *The Miss Firecracker Contest*. Although the former is better known both as play (Pulitzer Prize) and movie (1986) it has adhered, in the Bruce Beresford film, more to its origins as a work for the stage. The relevant descriptive phrase is 'Theatre of the Absurd', for at the centre are three colourful sisters, the MaGraths, whose mother hanged not only herself but also the family cat. Henley's offbeat trio are grown women, one of whom, following an affair with a fifteen-year-old black boy, has just shot her husband in the liver. But their daily lives as sisters, playing childhood games, hiding and giggling in the corners and niches of their sprawling Southern mansion, suggest the antics of adolescents, linking the work with Thomas Schlamme's film *Miss Firecracker* (1989). Although bizarre, they are not prisoners of fantasy: their histories encompass a variety of life-changing scandals, so the giggling swells into hysteria.

With its cupolas, gazebos, screened-in porches, chintzy bedrooms and staircases, the MaGrath clapboard home is as quaint and fascinating as its inhabitants, whose faded gentility it mirrors. The style is black humour emerging as the sisters reel from one crisis or surprise to another, yet this remains a feminist film, since the Gothic elements are softened by the sisters' warmth and affection for each other. Their mutual support brings them to the point where they can unsentimentally look to the future with a measure of hope.

Miss Firecracker, based on Henley's play *The Miss Firecracker Contest*, is a self-consciously Southern meditation on beauty, female personality and the power of the past; filmed publicly in Yazoo City, Mississippi, its authenticity was underlined by Southern actresses (Holly Hunter, Mary Steenburgen) in the lead roles. Here, as in *Crimes of the Heart*, Henley analyses the condition of Southern women, tensed between established standards of feminine behaviour and the impulse to rebel and follow the imperatives of the self. The vehicle for this analysis is the beauty pageant combining the populist pleasures of small-town spectacle with the aristocratic trappings of the Southern belle – conspicuously so in the rendition by a contestant of one of Scarlett O'Hara's best-known speeches. The concern in *Miss Firecracker* with the subject of beauty finds an echo in Herbert Ross's 1989 film *Steel Magnolias* ('There's no such thing as natural beauty', says Truvy, the much-in-demand hairdresser), though the female bonding which is tested throughout Ross's film (set in Louisiana) is more reminiscent of the MaGraths in *Crimes of the Heart*.

Carnelle Williams's obsessive campaign to become Miss Firecracker on the Fourth of July is energised by the memory of her cousin Elain beaming and waving from her float in 1972. Elain's crowning owed not a little to her blazing red dress, which evokes Bette Davis's Oscar-winning performance in Warner Brothers' *Jezebel* (William Wyler, 1938). It is Carnelle, though, denied the loan of Elain's red dress, who replicates Davis's passion and independence:

up to this point she is best known locally (and carnally) as Miss Hot Tamale ... Orphaned as a child, later adopted, now a catfish-gutter at the local plant, Carnelle attempts to move socially from the margins of the town to its centre. Her defeat and shame prove to be a kind of victory; having confronted her dreams and a need to belong, she can learn from experience and move on. The emotional support from two other outsiders – Mac Sam, a wandering carnival worker and an ex-lover, and Popeye, a young black seamstress – prepares her for new possibilities beyond the façade and shield of surface glamour. Elain, by contrast, has undergone a career which reveals more serious levels of desperation and damage. Carnelle remains an individual, but Elain will remain Miss Firecracker and suffer the consequences: a selfishness that masks a lack of self-esteem and an aloofness from the everyday world. Henley's oddball characters have persuaded some critics to describe *Miss Firecracker* as Southern Gothic, but the abundant night scenes are suffused with an idealising radiance. This balmy lustre is amplified in the final scenes of Independence Day fireworks. As Carnelle reaches for the stars and Popeye embraces the philosophic drifter Delmount (another Williams) while boating on the lake, the connection with the poetic side of Tennessee Williams is confirmed.

Media narratives of the South often focus upon family feuds and revelations arising at meals or homecomings, and the rituals of births, weddings and deaths. *Steel Magnolias* was overtly structured by Easter, Hallowe'en and Christmas as well as birth, marriage and death, and *Cookie's Fortune* (Robert Altman, 1999) takes place over an Easter weekend in a small Mississippi town.

With its integrated police force and its First Presbyterian Church (hot for culture) putting on Oscar Wilde's *Salome* for its Easter pageant, Holly Springs is a microcosm of the South in the 1990s. Yet, as its various historical markers indicate, the town's history continues to resonate; eventually, personal histories, too, will be divulged. A sign in a local liquor store, resembling one of those markers, proclaims: 'On this site in 1897, nothing happened.' That year marked the beginning, in the South, of the long decades of 'separate but equal' segregation (lasting until 1954) which were initiated by the Plessy *v.* Ferguson decision in 1896. The film's racial and social coordinates are announced at the outset: the juke-joint where local blacks gather for blues and booze; the bright new police station and town jail; the church, dominated by the terrifying and deranged Camille Dixon, who directs and has co-written *Salome*; and the run-down antebellum estate of Camille's aunt, Cookie Orcutt, a sweet, pipe-smoking *grande dame*. For her, the loneliness of widowhood is only temporarily assuaged by the companionship of her black live-in handyman, Willis Richland. In a sense, Willis is Cookie's fortune.

Their close friendship suggests (uneasily) a similar – if more formal – relationship in *Driving Miss Daisy* (Bruce Beresford, 1989), but it contributes crucially to Altman's sly humour. *Cookie's Fortune* takes up the themes of Southern society and blood ties, which it considers ironically: the previously unacknowledged, even unwilling racial mixing by earlier generations is normative in the laid-back New South. It is as though, in 1897, nothing happened ...

Altman's dizzy women recall characters in the feminist movies discussed above, but the film's intertextual strategy is not only to evoke but also to put a spin on recognisable roles and situations. After Camille conceals Cookie's suicide, Willis is charged with murder. The investigating officer is a hip black detective whose raffish straw hat conveys his distance from Virgil Tibbs in *In the Heat of the Night* (Norman Jewison, 1967). Audience fears for a black suspect in a Southern cell are allayed by Deputy Sheriff Lester's assertion of Willis's innocence, based on one simple proof: 'I fished with him.' The movie's idiosyncratic characters, embraced by the cosy warmth of Holly Springs and brushed by the good-heartedness of Willis, resist Southern Gothic and its grotesqueries: more Eudora Welty than Flannery O'Connor. The exception is the diabolic Camille, a cross between Blanche duBois and Norma Desmond, whose chilling fate is mellowed by the final image of a fishing party.

Altman's 1999 movie encompasses many of the South's distinctive traits: its emotionalism that provokes violence, its clannishness, its religious observance, its race relations, its storytelling, its musical and literary traditions. If the film takes a sunny view of race in the South, that is a consequence of the director's Renoiresque humanism. At a time when the USA is – in Gavin Essler's words – 'a continent of almost unlimited possibilities and hope for the future, coupled with levels of despair and wickedness unparalleled in any other industrialized country', *Cookie's Fortune*, with its celebration of family life, roots, friendship and racial equality, is a Southern fable that wistfully speaks to American yearnings.[8] Its symbol of simple goodness and dignity is one more marginalised character, a poor middle-aged black man who often takes a drink and who, like Holly Springs, believes in coming together rather than breaking apart.

Part 5

'Into the crucible with you all,
God is making the American...'
Melting-pots and pans

Independent cinema and modern Hollywood: pluralism in American cultural politics?

Brian Neve

Some sense of the significance of 'independent cinema' to the American cultural politics of the last two decades of the twentieth century can be gained by exploring attitudes to what has been the best-known marketplace for such films, the Sundance Film Festival. Robert Redford established the Sundance Film Institute in 1980, but it was five years later that the Institute began its association with an annual festival for independent cinema. Five years into the Reagan presidency, the Festival was not only designed to provide a showcase for alternatives to the Hollywood mainstream; its emphasis on multiculturalism inevitably thrust it into emerging debates about the centrality of culture to American politics.[1] A template was formed early on that saw the independents as playing a political as well as an aesthetic role, broadening the range of representations of contemporary America, and in particular enfranchising those groups and minorities whose voices were largely unheard in mainstream film. It is an index of how Sundance has changed since 1985, however, that the Festival is now attacked if it fails to produce a box-office hit, and now exists alongside, rather than in opposition to, the values and practices of the Hollywood industry.[2]

Notions of independent cinema are notoriously difficult to pin down, but broadly, two lines of argument are often used. One stresses the means of finance, seeing such independent films as those made outside the studios and the traditional Hollywood sources of finance. The other common approach is to deal with the films themselves, and explore the work of directors and other film-makers who are independent of mainstream aesthetic strategies and genres, and express a distinctive vision.[3] The latter notion allows consideration of film-makers who may graduate from low-budget to Hollywood productions, or switch from one form to another. In the latter category are film-makers such as Robert Altman, Spike Lee, and Joel and Ethan Coen.

By the 1980s, the cultural experimentation of 1970s Hollywood was in decline, and the emerging independent cinema took on – at least for some activists – the responsibility of a Gramsci-like struggle against the hegemonic culture. The early 1980s saw mobilisation on the Left against Reagan's tax cuts, increased military spending, and Central American adventures, and for a nuclear 'freeze'. Even in the mainstream arena of studio production, writers have pointed to political debates, with films such as *Rambo* (George Pan Cosmatos, 1985), *Red Dawn* (John Milius, 1984) and *Top Gun* (Tony Scott, 1986) taking militarist and right-wing positions, and being contested by liberal-left perspectives in such films as *Missing* (Costa Gavras, 1981) and *Under Fire* (Roger Spottiswoode, 1983).[4] It was arguably in the lower-budget area, less vulnerable to dominant ideology, that one might expect evidence of such a struggle for an alternative agenda. Making reference to the independent sector, Ryan and Kellner suggest, in their survey of American film in the 1980s, that the 'Left is on the whole more alive outside of Hollywood than inside'.[5]

A cultural ebb and flow is always evident in American politics and culture. Evidence of the subtextual battle between mainstream Cold War culture and the underground (and blacklisted) radical and Popular Front culture of the 1930s and the war years was still evident in the 1950s. The late 1960s and early 1970s saw the breaking through of the cultural and political concerns of the baby-boom generation and the emergence, as part of the struggle over Vietnam, of a new set of political agendas. By the late 1970s and early 1980s, the cycle of culture and interests was again on the turn: the Moral Majority organisation was founded in 1979, while by 1982 attempts to pass an Equal Rights Amendment were finally abandoned. With the Reagan administration came a hostile response to this counter-culture of post-materialist values, with a president giving renewed symbolic legitimacy to traditional sources of authority. By the end of the Reagan–Bush era there was much discussion of what Arthur Schlesinger Jr called the 'disuniting of America', while conservative and liberal activists saw America and its public philosophy through different lenses.[6]

Another end-of-the-century political theme was the growth in cynicism. Roderick Hart writes of the media's complicity in blurring the private and public lives of politicians, while the end of the Cold War and the growth of Washington scandal seemed to construct an image of a corrupt public realm that was beyond the redemptive capacity of any campaign or movement.[7] The black alternative journalist in *Bob Roberts* (Tim Robbins, 1992), whose fate reflects a particularly negative view of the possibilities of real pluralism and democracy, makes reference to the populist politics of Frank Capra when he announces that 'Mr Smith has been bought'. Together with *Wag the Dog* (Barry Levinson, 1977), the independent cinema's view of national politics is not so much cynical as despairing of any possibility of change. The Republican Revolution of 1994, and its attendant Contract with America, saw a rare revolt against incumbency, but did not, in retrospect, offer a viable redemptive politics of the Right. Into Bill Clinton's second term, the year-long saga of the President, Kenneth Starr and Monica Lewinsky further reduced the dramaturgy of the chief national political office to the status – and aesthetic sophistication – of a television soap.

This chapter explores some of these cultural and political conflicts through the imaginative world of American independent cinema, loosely defined. I broadly select my film examples from the list used by Emanuel Levy in his recent survey, *The Cinema of Outsiders*.[8] While I explore the various political strands of this cinema, the intention is to ask questions about the overall cultural impact of a body of work which, by definition, claims to broaden the pluralism of American cultural politics, forcing consideration of aesthetic and social agendas that challenge those of the mainstream. Does this cinema prompt debates on issues such as race, ethnicity, feminism and sexual orientation, which are marginalised in the dominant political culture and mainstream entertainment? Has the moment gone for such a national independent cinema that is distinct from the processes and discourses of the mainstream film industry?

John Pierson has provided an entertaining account of the development of independent film culture in the decade from 1984 to 1994, although the emphasis here is less on any national political debate than on issues of regional and multicultural identity. There was a striking increase in independent production in the second half of the 1980s.[9] There is much on the emergence of Jim Jarmusch as an art-house director, using the new independent film culture of festivals,

agents and specialist distributors, but more politically significant was
Spike Lee's first feature film, *She's Gotta Have It* (1986). Yet Lee and
John Sayles – who also dealt with racial issues in his early *The
Brother from Another Planet* (1984) – are relatively exceptional at
this time in their direct engagement with contemporary political
issues.

As Thomas Schatz argues in his work on the characteristics of the
'New Hollywood', the concentration of resources on blockbusters
has opened up a 'space' for independent and alternative cinema.[10]
He sees the blockbuster mentality establishing itself in the later 1970s,
with the mass appeal of *Jaws* (Steven Spielberg, 1975), *Close Encounters of the Third Kind* (Steven Spielberg, 1977) and *Raiders of
the Lost Ark* (Steven Spielberg, 1981). Such successes demonstrated
the appeal of high concept, plot driven, visceral entertainment based
increasingly on special effects, and targeted at younger audiences.
Into the decade of *Jurassic Park* (Steven Spielberg, 1993) and *Titanic*
(James Cameron, 1997) production and marketing costs for large-
budget 'event' films, given saturation release and marketed in multiple
media, have escalated.[11] By the end of the Clinton era, the majority
of the major studios had became subdivisions of diversified, and
global, media conglomerates. 'Independent' production was now seen
less in terms of a political or aesthetic alternative to this 'New
Hollywood' than as a supplement to it, providing a niche product to
the differentiated audiences reachable within multiplex culture. Certainly the distributors who play a significant role in Pierson's first-
person story of Sundance and the independent film movement are
now, in most cases, divisions of major conglomerates, using the
Festival and other showcases of independent production as sources
of product with the capacity to 'cross over' into mainstream appeal.
Miramax, for example, became part of Disney in 1993, while New
Line is now part of Time-Warner.[12]

Quentin Tarantino's dramatic success with his first two films as
director is indicative of the way independent film is equally susceptible to the laws of celebrity and marketing. Certainly *Reservoir
Dogs* (1992) and *Pulp Fiction* (1994) straddled the boundary between
art film and mass entertainment, while his production company, Band
of Outsiders, was named in homage to Jean-Luc Godard. *Pulp Fiction* cost $9.5 million to make, and grossed $96.1 million worldwide
in 1994. Positive responses refer to the vibrant dialogue, performances and music, and the intertextual play with the cinematic and

literary pulp tradition. According to the French postmodernist theorist Jean Baudrillard, postmodernist culture is a culture of the present made from fragments of the past.[13] The Vincent Vega character (John Travolta) echoes this in the film when he refers to the retro diner where he takes his boss's wife as 'a wax museum with a pulse rate'. It is far from being realist in form, but many of the elements – drugs, crime, gang life, danger on the streets, narcissism and style – are central enough to the life and mythology of contemporary Los Angeles. Unlike many of the traffic cop directors of studio entertainment, Tarantino, although aware that he was part of the selling process, clearly cared about the cinema as a battered twentieth-century metanarrative.

Independents and the public realm

The pride in politics that Almond and Verba revealed in their surveys of public opinion, first published in the early 1960s, has long faded. Public trust in government has declined since the 1960s, with only a partial break in the trend in the early 1980s. The early 1990s saw earnest discussions of the pervasiveness of cynicism, and of the reasons why Americans, in Dionne's words, 'hated' politics.[14] Public cynicism about politics has obviously grown: Goldfarb, for example, sees traditional irony and criticism being replaced by 'a mocking cynicism that does little to address contemporary problems', and particularly infects the realms of politics, journalism and social science. He sees Tom Wolfe's *The Bonfire of the Vanities*, with its 'exaggerated stereotypes', as indicative of a new condition in which this cynicism replaces 'positive democratic and cultural ideals'.[15] Hart has emphasised the way in which presidents and politicians in general are increasingly seen intimately and personally, stripped of any cloak of public authority. This appeal is both part of their electoral strategy at a time of ideological consensus, and also reflects the desire of voters – expressed through their demand for tabloid stories – to know the private as well as the public story of politicians and celebrities of all types. Such a frame not only pervades contemporary American political culture, but has also influenced reassessments of the politics of earlier times.[16] Revisionist accounts of the Kennedy presidency have picked over stories of personal relationships that were unreported at the time; while Oliver Stone's screen biography of Richard Nixon investigates the man in terms of the crucial intertwining of his personal and public life. At the academic level, psychohistory, from being something of a rarity, has become a standard frame for discussions of political power. The protracted melodrama of Bill Clinton, Monica Lewinsky and Kenneth Starr captured the world's headlines and prompted a congressional and constitutional challenge to the President, further confusing the distinction between the personal and the political. As Hart argues, Americans have been led into a relationship of emotional intimacy with their leaders, yet this intimacy has substituted for rather than deepened understanding of the way public office, and the public realm generally, has operated.[17]

In the 1990s, a number of writers and directors themselves had experience, if not as candidates, then as speechwriters, advisers and activists. Oliver Stone (*JFK*, *Nixon*), Tim Robbins (*Bob Roberts*) and Warren Beatty (*Bulworth*) have records of political affiliations and single-issue involvements; while Gary Ross, writer of *Dave* (1993) and writer-director of *Pleasantville* (1998), is a sometime Democratic speechwriter for both Dukakis and Clinton. Robert De Niro, co-star of *Wag the Dog* (1997), involved himself personally in a lobbying effort on Capitol Hill before the impeachment vote against Bill Clinton. Michael Moore, best known for his left populist television shows and for *Roger and Me* (1989), a documentary study of the consequences of the General Motors lay-off in Flint, Michigan, also directed the feature film *Canadian Bacon* (1995). Finally, a number of those involved in the 1998 film production of Joe Klein's best-selling book *Primary Colors*, including director Mike Nichols, were well-documented 'Friends of Bill'. A distinction between mainstream films and those that are defined, in terms of their more specialised audience and more limited finance, as independent productions may be more important than one based on the political leanings of the film-makers. Independent films are less distinctive aesthetically than once was the case, and it is not easy to classify large-budget productions made with considerable personal input by 'auteurist' directors (such as Oliver Stone and Warren Beatty) or low-budget productions (such as *Wag the Dog*) which owe much to mainstream conventions.

A number of personal 1990s film projects suggest the superstructural nature of candidate and presidential politics, and the importance of economic and military forces as structural constraints on political power. In the 1950s, the 'power elite' notion of American politics was marginal to social science and journalistic discourse, but by the 1990s more radical perspectives on political and media power were more widely disseminated. In particular, Noam Chomsky's analysis (often with Edward Herman) of what he calls the 'propaganda model' was fairly widely discussed on campuses, with Chomsky having something of the status of a 'dissident' intellectual through television appearances and the documentary film *Manufacturing Consent* (1992).[18] In *JFK* (Oliver Stone, 1991) a counterhegemonic view of the Kennedy assassination was presented which, paradoxically, burnished the Kennedy legend just as further revelations of the late President's extramarital affairs were contributing to public and scholarly reassessments of his public record. Several years later, Stone returned both to the presidency and to notions of a military–industrial complex in his unexpectedly sympathetic study of Richard Nixon (*Nixon*, 1995). Here again, the President is detached from any aura of presidential power, and viewed as an outsider within the wider national security state. In a more current age, people are less persuaded about the mythologies once constructed by Cold War and other dramaturgies around both the common man and the uncommon leader.

An updated notion of the military–industrial complex is also implicit in *Bob Roberts* (1992), which depicts a right-wing Senate campaign that expropriates the post-1960s counter-culture associated with liberal and left politics. The film-makers are concerned less with presenting the political context in which such an unlikely alliance could emerge, or with psychological realism, than with a particular thesis of political power. Roberts himself may be linked in films about politics to the Andy Griffiths character in *A Face in the Crowd* (1957), and with the use made of Willie Nelson to sell political myths in *Wag the Dog*. What can loosely be called country music – or that element of it that straddles left and right cultural politics – is seen as having a continued populist resonance with American political culture. The use made of Woody Guthrie's anthem in *Bob Roberts* highlights what is presented as the enlistment of a left-wing populist discourse in support of a right wing project welded to the interests of corporate and military elites. This theme recalls the 1950s debate about the continuities – or lack of them – between 1950s McCarthyism and the radical and rural (and turn-of-the-century) origins of populist politics. Again, the individual is seen as the front man, but the film itself is, perhaps, cynical rather than liberating in terms of the lack of any sense of media or public challenge to the

Roberts campaign, outside of the incumbent Senator played by Gore
Vidal. The film takes the form of a public-service documentary, albeit one that is more fascinated by than critical of its subject. One
either accepts the notion or not, but it is an emotional 'sell', not
unlike that of the system that the film is criticising. Rather like some
elements of radical media analysis, the film's thesis is inadequately
supported by evidence of a plausible process of politics.

Further contemplation of the American polity from a liberal
stance comes in the studio-made *Bulworth* (1998), Warren Beatty's
fable of a veteran politician's despair with regular politics, and his
subsequent rejuvenation as a man of the people. As often with populist discourse, the notion of 'the people' can have national, nativist
and class connotations, depending on the ideological perspective
adopted. Sixty-year-old Democratic Senator Bulworth is seen as cynical about the rhetoric of electoral process, reflecting Warren Beatty's
own stance on the lack of real political choice in the years since
George McGovern and Robert Kennedy. Out of this despair he decides to speak the brutal truth instead of the usual platitudes; he
tells black Americans, for example, that they have no choice but to
vote for the Democrats. There are echoes of Capra's *Meet John Doe*
(1941) as the Senator decides to end a life made futile by the hypocrisy of the modern electoral process. Liberated from the conventional wisdom of 'getting elected', Bulworth speaks his mind, and is
reborn as a man reflecting the concerns and feelings of the urban
black underclass and its intellectuals. His faith renewed, Bulworth
the holy fool wants to live again, and his campaign revives, only for
him to be assassinated – in accordance with the film's overall assumption that radical change is impossible – by threatened 'special
interests' from the insurance industry. Whether the film is liberating
or merely reinforces a cynicism about the effects of political action
is open to debate. Jesse Jackson felt that it was counterproductive in
suggesting that politics was pointless in such a corrupt system, and
that the only authentic black reaction was 'rage, obscenity and sex'.[19]

Finally, reference can be made to *Wag the Dog* (Barry Levinson,
1997) and Michael Moore's *Canadian Bacon* (1995), both of which
are associated with notions of the effect of the end of the Cold War
on American politics. *Wag the Dog* is a further example of thesis
film-making, where the characters are given little sense of depth or
autonomy, and there is little sense of challenge by media or public to
the campaigns concocted by the White House–Hollywood gurus. The

spin doctors set the media agenda for seventeen days by staging an imaginary foreign war, in order to ensure that the President's dalliance with a 'firefly girl' does not wreck their master's election prospects. The film suggests a hypodermic effect as much as a hegemonic struggle, with the manipulation being shown as total and untraceable. Women immediately break down in tears after hearing the President's war speech, while student basketball players react in kneejerk fashion to news of the mythical hostage. There is much borrowing from real cases (including the hostages crisis of 1980), and to some the satire seemed to be given resonance by the events that followed its release, notably the American cruise missile attacks in the Sudan and Afghanistan in August 1998, and the bombing of Iraq in December of the same year. Both took place against the backdrop of the congressional moves towards impeaching President Clinton. In the film we see the agenda being manipulated without the President – whom we glimpse only once, from behind – being aware. This television-influenced, cartoon-like satire – near to the mocking cynicism that Hart discusses in the media, and arguably a long way from the wit, irony and contemporary 'shock effect' of *Dr Strangelove* (Stanley Kubrick, 1963) – applies even more so to *Canadian Bacon*, a crude satire on a president who attempts to distract attention way from his domestic failures by waging war on Canada.

John Sayles

If it is the commercial potential of independent cinema that has emerged most dramatically since the 1989 Sundance Festival, one film-maker has remained committed to a political notion of cinema throughout this period. John Sayles is straightforwardly one of the baby-boom generation who has maintained a political commitment into middle age. Born in 1950, he began writing novels in the 1970s, and financed his first film from early work as a screenwriter for Roger Corman. *The Return of the Secaucus Seven* (1980) was the first of his eleven films to date as writer-director, a low-budget study of a reunion held by a group from the 1960s college generation. Sayles remembers questioning press reports dismissing the achievements of the 1960s generation and suggesting that many so-called radicals were now in the business of working for Chase Manhattan Bank. He was 'starting to feel the rumblings of that pendulum swing' in the late 1970s, as conservative forces mobilised against elements of the Great Society tradition, and particularly against a beleaguered Democratic presidency and Congress.[20]

Sayles's film work represents better than that of any other filmmaker a form of opposition both to the values of mainstream Hollywood and to dominant thinking about American politics. Whereas mainstream American filmmaking emphasises action and individualism, constant values in Sayles's work in the 1980s and 1990s are notions of community, solidarity and interconnectedness, even in the face of ethnic, racial and class difference, the latter stretching back through the generations. Amid warnings of a decline in various senses of community feeling in America, Sayles has balanced criticism with a degree of social optimism. His most Altman-like study of politics in a city community, *City of Hope* (1991), came out of his personal experiences, but was also a response to Spike Lee's *Do the Right Thing* (1989) – a film he admired – and his desire to depict the police as more complex figures. A mosaic of city life, the film does not avoid political corruption, particularly of the older Irish immigrant power structure, but it is also more hopeful – in comparison, for example, with mainstream Hollywood's *City Hall* (Harold Becker, 1996) – that at least some people will do the right thing. An example of such hope is the idealistic black councilman who learns that his constituency requires strong leadership from him, even at the expense of his own moral doubts. Progress in a divided community – based loosely on Hudson City, New Jersey – is seen as three steps forward, and two back.

Matewan (1987), which re-creates the 1920s industrial conflict of the West Virginia coalfields, stresses solidarity not as left-wing rhetoric – apparent, for all its impressiveness, in the classic independent blacklist-era production *Salt of the Earth* (1954) – but as something constantly in flux, strengthened by a common enemy but weakened by a racial and ethnic difference exploited by employers. The production also represented an implicit comment on Ronald Reagan's own symbolically crucial action in this area when, six months into his presidency, he dealt with the strike of 11,600 members of PATCO, the Air Traffic Controllers' Union, by firing them all.[21] Social progress – not for the last time in Sayles's work – is seen as a slow process, achieved only at great cost to those who went before.

Questions of race recur in Sayles's films, from his low-budget Harlem project *Brother from Another Planet* (1984), via his political epics *Matewan* and, in particular, *City of Hope*, to *Passion Fish*

(1992) and his study of conflicting histories and identities in a Texas small town, *Lone Star* (1996). This last film provides the director's most elaborate dissection of an American community, in this case a Texan border town, but here the writer-director's concern is as much the effect of history and myth on the lives of three interrelated peoples. The gradual decline of the white community, including three generations of sheriffs who figure in the murder mystery, is contrasted with the rising fortunes of those of Hispanic descent, on either side of the border with Mexico, and with a black community attracted by an army base. Appropriately, as far as Texas is concerned, life-chances are shown to be crucially influenced by one's birth either side of 'a line in the sand'. Early on we see parents arguing in a school meeting about the version of history taught in schools, highlighting the practical problems of multiculturalism beyond national rhetoric. Despite demonstrating the weight of history on individuals and communities, Sayles provides his characters with the capacity to defy myth and tradition: the last words spoken are 'Forget the Alamo'.

Sayles has continued to make his own films, financing them by writing screenplays for Hollywood. His last film of the century, *Limbo* (1999), was his most expensive, at $8 million. Again he examines work and society, in this case in an Alaska gearing itself up for the replacement of the fishing industry by a theme park. Sayles has said that he was interested in the idea of failure in a success-oriented culture, and the turn the narrative takes does finally strip the principal characters of the benefits of civilisation, however defined, allowing them to test their real worth in the tradition of American pioneers.

Race, politics and independent voices

Even the success of Eddie Murphy and Whoopi Goldberg in the 1980s could not hide the lack of positive representations of African Americans in American cinema. Yet a key development in the growth of independent cinema from the mid-1980s has been the breakthrough, at least in certain generic forms, of film-making by black Americans. The key influence on this phenomenon has been Spike Lee and his Forty Acres and a Mule production company. Lee's first feature film, *She's Gotta Have It* (1986), was finally completed thanks to an epic fund-raising struggle by the director, a grant from the New York State Council on the Arts, and a deferment of the cost of blowing up the 16 mm negative to 35 mm.[22] Jeff Lipsky of the Samuel Goldwyn Company – which distributed another low-budget film from a new black film-maker, Robert Townsend's *Hollywood Shuffle* (1987) – described *She's Gotta Have It* enthusiastically as a film in which Lee's talent was speaking rather than 'the individual trying to speak for an entire race or for an entire cause'.[23] In the end, Island Pictures signed Lee for a three-picture deal and promoted the film at Cannes, where it appeared alongside other new independents, notably Eugene Corr's *Desert Bloom* (1985), Lizzie Borden's *Working Girls* (1986) and Jim Jarmusch's second feature, *Down by Law* (1986). In fact the film did not 'cross over' substantially to white audiences, but it established Spike Lee as a significant and prolific 'name above the title'.

Spike Lee, Robert Townsend and Julie Dash (with *Daughters of the Dust*, 1991) are all described by Guerrero as 'insurgent' film-makers whose 'guerrilla financing' broke through the 'discrimination that kept African Americans shut out of the movie business'.[24] Townsend's film is particularly related to questions of screen representation, in that it deals with a would-be black actor's struggles in Hollywood to balance his desire for work with his reluctance to add to the stereotypes of pushers, pimps and other city characters seen as saleable to the mainstream white audience.

The late 1980s and the early 1990s saw a wave of films by black film-makers that dealt with the problems of young black men in the inner cities, or with the 'hood'. Most were set in South Central LA, Watts, Brooklyn and Harlem, and most, for all their power and integrity, operated in a narrow area of 'ghetto violence, adventure and pathology'.[25] These films included *New Jack City* (Mario Van Peebles, 1991), *Boyz N' the Hood* (1991), *Straight out of Brooklyn* (Matty Rich, 1991), *Menace II Society* (Allen Hughes/Albert Hughes, 1993), *Juice* (Ernest Dickerson, 1992) and *Just Another Girl on the IRT* (Leslie Harris, 1992). Only the last of these has an African-American woman director, and a focus on female inner-city experiences. These films did reach mainstream multiracial audiences, and they also emphasised an African-American perspective on the notorious and much-debated problems of the inner-city underclass. In John Singleton's *Boyz N' the Hood*, for example, the oppressive and ubiquitous presence of the Los Angeles Police Department (LAPD) is suggested by recurring shots of police patrolmen, searchlights and surveillance helicopters.[26] Without the strong father figure present in

Singleton's film, Massood suggests, escape from the 'Hood' is seen as highly difficult.[27]

The film that shares much with this wave is Spike Lee's *Do the Right Thing* (1989), which was successful at Cannes along with the Palme d'Or-winning *sex, lies and videotape* (Steven Soderbergh). Lee's third feature – made for Columbia Pictures, but with the director maintaining all of his autonomy and independence – came a year after the controversial use of the 'Willie Horton ad' in the successful Republican election campaign, and was prophetic of elements of the Los Angeles 'riots' in 1992. Lee's film provoked a significant debate on relevant social and political issues.[28] Set in Bedford-Stuyvesant in Brooklyn, *Do the Right Thing* portrays a day in the social life of a street community, with the main focus on young blacks, but with key Italian-American and Korean roles. The tensions rise almost imperceptibly during the hot summer day: a black guy objects to an Italian-American Hall of Fame on the wall of the neighbourhood pizza parlour; a white guy driving through overreacts when he is drenched with a fire hydrant by kids; an old man rails against the successful shop opened by Koreans only a year 'off the boat'. The older characters, in particular, are presented with much humanity, but the end of the film brings the political drama, as tension leads to a fight outside 'Sal's Famous Pizzeria', the police arrive and a black man dies at their hands. The crowd self-destructively trash the pizza parlour, and the film ends inconclusively but thoughtfully with the display of two quotations, from Martin Luther King and Malcolm X, on the nature of violence. Lee has remained a prolific director, an activist, and an executive producer of other work by black film-makers; his *Jungle Fever* (1991) was dedicated to Yusef Hawkins, who was shot dead in August 1989 in a racially motivated attack in the predominantly Bensonhurst neighbourhood of Brooklyn. When he needed completion funds for his studio project at Warners, *Malcolm X* (1992), Lee was able to solicit money from a list of African-American artists including Prince, Janet Jackson, Magic Johnson, Oprah Winfrey and Michael Jordan.[29]

Drugs, violence and inner-city racial conflict attracted film-makers and finance in the early 1990s, but it has been harder to tell other stories about African-American life. Charles Burnett has a high reputation in part because of his 1977 film *Killer of Sheep*, but his later films have been few and far between, and have received poor distribution. A producer of his *To Sleep with Anger* (1990) wrote to

black pastors nationwide to try and get support. Burnett wrote and
directed *The Glass Shield* (1995), examining the institutional racism
(and sexism) of the LAPD, as it particularly impinges on an idealistic African-American trainee cop within a white station. Carl
Franklin was more successful in using genre and style – in this case
film noir rather than police-procedural – to comment on a number
of black–white relationships among both criminals and police. His
One False Move (1991) is distinctive not only in its strong sense of
characterisation, but in exploring race and class in deepest rural
Arkansas. Whereas black film can be seen as a notable element of
the success of independent production in the 1990s, the limits of
success, in terms of a more long-term pluralism of images and
representations, are evident. Perhaps *Eve's Bayou* (Kasi Lemmons,
1997) indicates some more hopeful signs. This period study of middle-class black life, produced by Samuel L. Jackson following his
breakthrough with *Pulp Fiction* (1994), was the most successful independent film in America in 1997, and attracted 80 per cent white
audiences.[30]

Outside of avant-garde and experimental film, gay and lesbian
voices were little heard in the 1980s, before the revival in independent
cinema in the early 1990s. *Parting Glances* (Bill Sherwood, 1985) and
Desert Hearts (Donna Deitch, 1986) were exceptions, the later
becoming 'a VCR classic in lesbian living rooms across America',
but creating no immediate trend.[31] AIDS had been first identified in
1981, and over 20,000 Americans had died of the consequences of
the virus before Ronald Reagan made a belated speech on the subject in the mid-1980s. Jerry Falwell, founder of the Moral Majority,
called AIDS 'God's punishment'.[32] The political controversy relating
to several films by gay film-makers provided valuable publicity. A
group of films released in the early 1990s, including *Poison* (Todd
Haynes, 1991), *Swoon* (Tom Kalin, 1991) and *The Living End* (Gregg
Araki, 1992) were seen as part of a 'New Queer Cinema'.[33] Religious Right groups attacked the National Endowment of the Arts
(NEA) grant that Haynes had received to part-fund his $250,000
film, which won the Grand Jury Prize at the Sundance Festival in
January 1991.[34] One strand of Haynes's film – together with the title
– made reference to the AIDS crisis. J. Hoberman of the *Village
Voice* saw *Poison* as 'the toughest, most troubling and least compromised movie on the crisis to date'.[35] As well as creating a niche
market, the debate concerning these films, and their relative com-

mercial success, influenced the mainstream Hollywood agenda, notably with *Philadelphia* (Jonathan Demme, 1993).

Conclusions

The gap between independent and Hollywood film closed in the 1990s, and Manohla Dargis has gone so far as to write about the 'transformation of independent film into a marketing strategy known as "indie film"'.[36] With the development of video and DVD, the profits to be made from 'alternative' entertainment are considerable, while the key independent companies that did so much to market *sex, lies and videotape* (1989), and the other successes from Sundance and elsewhere, are now all owned by major studios. For those film-makers who value their own vision and autonomy, problems of financing and distribution remain significant.

The main successes of independent film in this period were in black film, and in the development of a number of auteurs, from John Sayles to Hal Hartley and Jim Jarmusch. Generally, independent film-makers have examined society in terms of what Shohat and Stam call the 'decentered multiplicity of localised struggles'.[37] Such slices of American life include a Bronx wedding in anthropological detail (Nancy Savoca's *True Love*, 1989), a cautionary Harlem tale (Ernest Dickerson's *Juice*, 1992), the dangers of the drug culture in Portland, Oregon (Gus Van Sant's *Drugstore Cowboy*, 1989), a small-scale vision of racial harmony (*Passion Fish*, 1992), and the culture and African ancestry of the turn-of-the-century Gullah communities (*Daughters of the Dust*, Julie Dash, 1992). The emphasis has been on the small, local truth, as the film-maker sees it, rather than the big stories and ideologies. The story of one working-class man drinking his life away in a Long Island bar, in *Trees Lounge* (written and directed by Steve Buscemi in 1996), is all the more effective for its wit and understatement. Tommy (Buscemi) can joke about his decline. 'I could have been somebody,' he muses, playing Brando, 'instead of an ice cream man, which is what I am, let's face it.'

Some independent film-makers are addressing major political issues. Tim Robbins made *Dead Man Walking* (1995), dealing with the issue of the death penalty, through his own company and a financing deal that preserved his creative autonomy. Other recent films – from Todd Solondz's *Happiness* (1999), to Neil La Bute's rather misanthropic *In the Company of Men* (1997) and Todd

Haynes's unsettling *Safe* (1995) – have looked critically at American middle-class life. Redemptive visions have been rarer, but another film-maker associated with the independent film project, Joel Coen, invests unusual optimism and warmth in his *Fargo* (1996). The film can be seen as providing a communitarian vision, a hopeful model of civic effort and co-operation.[38] Its notion of Minnesota may not be recognised by the locals, but it is a powerful and finally moving vision of 'doing the right thing'. The film highlights the local rather than the global, and humanism – part of that old cinema project back in the days of neorealism – shines through in Frances McDormand's role and performance. William Chaloupka argues that 'the Coens use cinema to provide a glimpse of the daily life generated in a society that takes its civic communitarianism very seriously'. Here, and in John Sayles's evolving work, is a more positive engagement with American civil society, showing practical alternatives to 'bowling alone'.[39]

'I wanna be like you-oo-oo': Disnified politics and identity from *Mermaid* to *Mulan*

Paul Wells

Addressing the potential effects of Disney texts on children, Henry Giroux has persuasively argued that 'the boundaries between entertainment, education and commercialisation collapse through the sheer omnipotence of Disney's reach into diverse spheres of everyday life'.[1] This extraordinary scale of national and global penetration is accompanied by what Elizabeth Bell, Linda Haas and Laura Sells have suggested is 'the "trademark" of Disney innocence that masks the personal, historical and material relationship between Disney film and politics'.[2] This view further suggests that Disney's work is characterised by a highly charged right-wing perspective, resulting in a catalogue of ideological offences including – among the most easily evidenced – sexism, racism, nationalist jingoism and quasi-cultural imperialism. The reactionary nature of Disney's WASP orientations is so obvious, however, that it has become completely naturalised within Disney texts to the point where, contradictorily, it is both self-evident and invisible. It is this contradiction and ambivalence that I wish to address in this chapter, as they operate as the vehicle by which Disney can accommodate 'otherness' in a way that uses the particular language and material conditions of 'animation' to subvert representational differences through a homogeneity of 'style'.

It is important immediately to stress, therefore, that for the remainder of this discussion, I wish to use the term 'Disney' in a more open sense than is readily the case in many analyses. Usually 'Disney' is understood either as '*Walt Disney*', the entrepreneurial animation pioneer – 'the controlling editor',[3] 'the charismatic leader',[4] 'chief designer'[5] and 'the spark plug of production'[6] – or the '*studio*' and its output; or the '*brand*' which is the ideological and commercial imprimatur on a range of cultural artefacts from films to theme parks. I wish to redefine the term 'Disney', however, as a metonym for *an authorially complex, hierarchical industrial process, which organises and executes selective practices within the vocabularies of animated film*. Consequently, this definition seeks to challenge the assumptions of an ideological critique which suggests that 'Disney' offers a coherent position by virtue of any one text being configured within the received framework of its supposedly transparent right-wing orthodoxies. Further, it seeks to interrogate the construction of the assumed 'happiness', within both the text and its reception, which accrues around the Disney cartoons, and which Susan Miller and Greg Rode argue 'is a membrane assuring their coherence as vital organs of cultural continuity'.[7] I wish to argue that there is less ideological coherence in the Disney agenda than is frequently suggested, on the basis that the very process of creating a Disney text militates against such coherence. Thereafter, the homogeneity implied in its reception is similarly questionable. I wish to suggest that any one text evolves its sociopolitical orientation through the assimilation of *cultural resources*[8] within a limited frame of representational appropriation, determined more by the industrialised aesthetic tradition at Disney, and its stylistic inhibitions, than by political sensitivities. 'Technique' subsumes 'Narrative', which, in turn, overwhelms the substantive implications and possibilities of the 'Text' – issues to which I will return throughout my discussion. This is not to suggest, though, that 'cultural resources', however mobilised, are ideologically innocent but, rather, that once subjected to the multiple regulatory codes and artistic conventions expressed by numerous authorial hands within both the animation process itself, and the Disney approach as it has evolved into a 'tradition', the symbolic import of these resources has significantly changed.

Simply, Disney has evolved a production paradigm which, in effect, renders contemporary ideological and political 'specificity' subordinate to the assumptions of Disney's own moral, ethical, cultural, and – most important – *aesthetic* archetypes. The dominant aspects of this paradigm are:

• Encoded caricatural 'norms' signifying simplistic and overdetermined notions of good/evil; serious/funny; effective/ineffective, and so on, which undermine, dilute and resist readings of characters and events at a *significantly specific* politicised and ideological level.

- A mode of 'fairy tale' (which echoes and uses, but does not necessarily draw on a literary fairy-tale tradition) concomitant to the
  principles of 'condensation' in animation,[9] which offers the *maxi-
  mum* degree of suggestion from the *minimum* limits of representational inclusion and selectivity in graphic forms. This also has
  the effect of legitimising non-linear, inconsequential, and often
  undeveloped aspects of narrational and character-driven events to
  operate as substantive models of 'image-based' versatility, but
  without an obligation to representational 'responsibility'.
- The use of songs and choreography, drawn from a utopian musical
  tradition, which in their execution prioritise the use of *spectacle as
  narrative*, and contextualise, filter and/or resist quasi-political
  messages and meanings within the parameters of 'romantic yearning'.

It is the coherence of this creative paradigm, not its 'content', which
on the one hand results in cultural critics like Eleanor Byrne and
Martin McQuillan[10] being able to mount sophisticated, ideologically grounded, deconstructionist readings of Disney texts, while on
the other it encourages the 'mass' audience to persist in its understanding of the 'innocence' of animated spectacle and, more importantly, to note and *only* acknowledge the ritualised components of
the traditionally determined 'cultural resource' now named as
'Disney'. This has major political implications, in the sense that at
one and the same time, Disney may be seen to be endorsing some
of the dominant 'myths' of American political culture – most notably 'populism', with its prevailing tropes of an inclusive political
economy and an intrinsic trust in the political infrastructure – while
it actually *represents* a socially excluding 'reality' where power
resides only with the centrist authoritarianism of an established
conservative elite. Richard Schickel has noted, though, that with
regard to Mickey Mouse during the late 1930s and early 1940s, that
'the political passions occasionally stirred by The Mouse during this
decade indicate the folly of overinterpreting essentially innocent
popular culture material in the light of any ideology – political,
psychological, religious or even literary'.[11] It was largely because
Mickey had been interpreted in such a variety of historically specific
ways in a host of politically diverse nations that his identity lacked
any of the cogency required for a coherent ideologically charged
interpretation that could sustain itself beyond the context within
which it occurred. This is not to deny Mickey, or any other Disney

character or film, political significance or importance, but to suggest that the Disney aesthetic readily challenges any apparently self-evident 'meaning' bestowed upon it by cultural critics. It is also to note that the films thus operate as significantly politicised texts within what may be termed a 'veiled' aesthetic which simultaneously denies this import.

It is clear that the framing of 'Disney' as a seemingly sinister corporate oppressor, constantly celebrating – in Giroux's words – 'deeply anti-democratic social relations',[12] does not, however, seem to tally with the reception of the films. Criticism of the post-1989 Disney *oeuvre* – a period characterised by a deliberate and significant shift in 'authorial' themes and preoccupations from its earlier counterparts – has inevitably been addressed from a leftist perspective, revealing Disney as anything from being a perpetrator of stories in which 'children are taught that cultural differences that do not bear the imprint of white, middle-class ethnicity are deviant, inferior, ignorant, and a threat to overcome',[13] right through to an organisation with an ethos that 'promotes escapism from the indeterminacy of "wild systems" through denial of process and difference'.[14] Clearly, for the cultural critic, it is sometimes difficult to dispute these *interpretations*, but this is ultimately what they are. Martin Barker has sceptically suggested that such work 'is only worth doing if someone, somewhere might be conceived to be in receipt of the thus-discovered plague of reactionary forms', and argues that more work needs to be done on 'why and how people *enjoy* Disney films'.[15] My own work in that very area suggests that audiences recognise and participate in the *difference* afforded by the animated form, and particularise the dominant tendencies of their response, most notably in relation to their emotional reaction to the films.[16] The thought persists that the more interesting issues to explore, therefore, are concerned with why seemingly reactionary, sometimes 'politically incorrect', sometimes culturally inappropriate 'messages' do not become the dominant currency of these films; instead, a kind of quasi-ideological optimism, innocence and security accrue and endure around the texts. Arguably – and, perhaps, crucially – this may be understood as the prevailing effect of a politics of pleasure, where 'emotional' determinacy and agency rather than intellectual or political clarity characterise human ambition and need. This may readily chime, of course, with postmodern notions of the collapse of authoritarian, utilitarian and even democratic discourses within an increasingly de-historicised and sceptical version of sociopolitical understanding in Western cultures. Simplistically, if the 'reactionary' currencies in the Disney texts are obvious, clear and affecting, the Disney audience, however configured, wilfully misreads, ignores or resists such messages. It may also maintain the view that animation is *inevitably* an innocent medium, predominant in children's entertainment, and 'abstract' only in the ways in which, as a medium, it may be differentiated from live action. As Miller and Rode have rightly suggested, though, a culture is composed of *actual* people, who organise and make sense of their experience on their own terms and conditions, using '[R]emembered images' as the 'seeds of cultural formation'.[17] From my own work again, it is seemingly the case that the audience takes with it what may be called a *primary* reading, where it is more important, for example, to endorse the principle of 'freedom' rather than its implications; where it is more satisfying to enjoy the 'playing out' of the protagonists' progress towards fulfilment; and where it is reassuring to believe that notions of 'goodness', 'right', 'truth', and so on, may still exist, *even if* there is a full understanding and tacit acceptance of the potentially illusory or misrepresentative elements of the text. In this, it may be that Disney differs little from the key regimes of American popular cinema from Capra to Spielberg. Any *secondary* reading which interrogates the Disney texts inevitably reads more complexly, and just as inevitably finds these texts open to more critical questions than its conception and execution can support or answer.

Animation is obviously 'artificial'; its characters are 'unreal'; its politics is subordinate to the assumption that the medium, in its conventional forms, promotes 'entertainment' before education, a point often overlooked by critics insisting upon pedagogic intent and affect. Giroux, for example, suggests that Disney is 'profoundly pedagogical in its attempt to produce specific knowledge, values and desires'.[18] It is the notion of 'specificity' that I wish to question here, and not the accusation of educative provocation. The 'primary' reading that I have suggested is the determinate reading in the 'mass audience' is seemingly more 'open'; grounded more in 'emotional' matters; and 'aspirant' rather than contained. Disney, in prioritising 'utopian' *principles* as a narrational and aesthetic norms, distanciates itself from the actual *meanings* implicit in the representational conventions consistently deployed. The *spectacle* of archetypal themes and emotions prevails over a cerebral engagement with *ideas*. It is this which is sometimes frustrating for the animation critic who champions the medium as one of the most subversive repositories for aesthetic and philosophical inquiry, only to have to admit that orthodox animation in the Disney style retains an apolitical veneer, even when it is potentially highly politically charged. Ironically, this legitimises acts of representational subversion *and* reactionary consistency, because the specificity of the technique in making the film still subsumes the process of storytelling. The Western Union, it seems, is still the best place to send messages. Arguably, though, the very 'openness', 'emotionality' and 'aspiration' I have noted that may be drawn from the reception of the Disney text may be viewed as politically liberating. This point is confirmed by different (ironically, almost oppositional) means in Byrne and McQuillan's discussion of *The Little Mermaid* (Ron Clements and John Musker, 1988), where they suggest that '[T]he endless readability of [the] film ... demonstrates the ways in which the Disney text carries within itself a radical ambivalence to the Disney narrative'.[19] In differentiating 'text' and 'narrative' (though only partially exploring its implications), Byrne and McQuillan identify the way in which the Disney 'text' may become overdetermined in its possibilities, while the Disney 'narrative' carries with it a degree of enunciative specificity that appeals to openness, emotional response and aspiration *before* it may be grounded in quasi-political discourses. I wish to argue, then, that the overdetermined nature of the Disney 'text' is the result of the process of animation which accommodates 'authorial' excess even within strict aesthetic regimes; while the Disney 'narrative' is grounded in the particular modes of archetypal and aesthetic expression that speak to the known variables and antitheses of an unreconstructed or – more likely – uncomplex view of right/wrong; good/evil; attractive/ugly; civilised/barbaric, and so on. It is crucial, then, to explore the actual processes that underpin the construction of the Disney animated feature, and I wish to delineate this in some detail to facilitate a discussion of how 'narrative' and 'text' effectively evolve separately.

The animated film, within the quasi-Fordist industrial paradigm created by the Disney organisation, is constructed in stages, often beginning with an initial story idea that is normally drawn from established literary, graphic or historio-mythic sources. This idea is then developed into a scene-by-scene script detailing the key events, context, character exchanges and projected shooting ideas, although in many instances this remains a highly fluid text through the processes of visual and character development. Even these initial stages are informed by collective suggestion and negotiation among the assigned creative teams in order to refine the principal storyline. The pre-production period, thereafter, involves the key personnel – producer, director, designer and art director – defining the proposed 'style' of the film, and determining the nature of the characters, their personalities and design, and possible voice-casting options. At this stage, lead animators are assigned major characters and/or proposed sequences, and are responsible for model sheets of the character showing the dominant physical, gestural and emotive characteristics of the figure. This is a critical stage in the sense that the supervising or lead animation directors and the voice artists, often major Hollywood stars, are the 'actors' who 'work through' the visual personality of the character, as well as its performance elements. In a process where a film is made frame by frame, this 'visual' criterion is crucial, because the emphasis of the narrative and textual events is very much (over)determined by how things might *look* and *move,* rather than by what they may *mean* in themselves or, ultimately, contextually in relation to other characters or events in the film.

This idea may be reinforced by addressing what may be viewed as an untypical example – the influence of British satiric caricaturist Gerald Scarfe on *Hercules* (Ron Clements and John Musker, 1997). His forty inspirational designs, which are all-pervasive in the film, were primarily driven by Scarfe's concerns with anatomy, graphic economy, and the sense of a spontaneous line, before they were seen as representational images which might harbour a range of potentially challenging (political) meanings or connotations. Consequently, the key issue becomes the creative tension which took place between Scarfe's 'brutalist' immediacy in design, and the prevailing imperatives in the Disney personnel to re-create established and traditional visual codings of iconic 'cuteness', and their attempts to ensure a clarity of shape and form in the designs to facilitate ease in the industrial process of *animating*. It is this which becomes the key *ideological* struggle in the film, not the 'political' implications that less specifically emerge out of the final narrative/text. The result in *Hercules* was a compromise which is half-Scarfe, half-Disney, where the 'elegant grotesque' becomes part of the Disney image vocabulary, but carries with it little of Scarfe's anticipated satirical bias. Furthermore – and importantly – nothing in his designs was retained, or found a place in the film, if it could not be made 'simple' enough to facilitate 'complex' choreography in the animation – form necessarily prevailing over content.

While the key personnel in the production process are essentially 'evolving' the film through a number of parallel approaches, storyboard artists begin preparing the key drawings which illustrate the provisionally determined aspects of the script, picturing the stage-by-stage visual narration of the action sequences. These artists effectively construct the initial *mise en scène* of the film and an implicit editorial regime for executing the main events of the story, and must often persuade the director, producer, designer and art director of the appropriateness and effectiveness of the suggested storyboard. These storyboards, if approved, are shot on film to create a provisional 'plot' reel, which may be subject to considerable re-editing, reordering and the addition of material. If work is rejected, then it is literally 'back to the drawing board' for the artists. Once the 'action reel' is approved, individual sequences can be sent to 'layout', where the composition of each shot is provisionally decided, and cinematographic decisions are made, concerning the most effective expression of narrative concepts in purely visual terms. Again, this stress upon 'technique' and the clarity with which the events of the story unfold becomes of greater importance than some of the implications of the design or the proposed plot. The 'clarification' process that both facilitates technique and insists upon ease in understanding 'the story' allows for little nuance or complexity in the semiotic inflections of the visual narrative. 'Cultural resources' become first and foremost the material of technical and story-telling processes, not the material of an ideologically charged, concept-led aesthetic. The multiple 'authors' of the Disney text deploy 'cultural resources' in their own work as part of an ever-evolving conception where the Disney 'style' and its concomitant mode of 'fairy-tale-ing' marshal 'narrative' ideologically through aesthetic decisions, but neglect the ramifications of the 'text'. This is largely the outcome of the 'openness' of the pre-production process, which ultimately creates an openness in the text, which in turn invites layers of interpretation.

The pivotal moment in the pre-production process, sometimes called the 'workbook' phase, is critical here, in the sense that this is when the key personnel decide upon a shot-by-shot breakdown of the film, taking into account all the detail of the *mise en scène* and determining lighting, camera angles and effects – essentially, all visual phenomena which are not 'character' animation. Decisions are also taken about the camera moves for each scene, and the first dialogue recordings are made to establish provisional timings, and begin the process by which all aspects of the soundtrack are delineated. The value and importance of 'sound' and 'voice' in animation cannot be underestimated, and in recent years they have been highly significant in the ideological readings of Disney films. The casting of Whoopi Goldberg, for example, as a villainous hyena in *The Lion King* (Roger Allers and Rob Minhoff, 1994) was read as another element in the 'racist' discourse of the film, where Goldberg's 'blackness' was read into the schemata of the role and function of the character. This kind of interpretation, in some senses, fundamentally ignores the visual text altogether, and merely casts 'the actor' as the condition of reading. This can raise serious issues, but it can be misleading – Phil Harris and Louis Prima, white performers, voice the nominally 'black' troped characters of Baloo the bear and King Louie the ape in *The Jungle Book* (Wolfgang Reitherman, 1967), but how far this informs and extends a 'racist' discourse is certainly open to question. However this is viewed, it is clear that if it is addressed, it becomes part of a 'textual' reading rather than a 'narrative' one, especially as these creative choices are made on aesthetic grounds.[20]

The production initiative takes a long time actually to arrive at the stage of 'text' or 'narrative', but moves forward as a process of accumulative preparation. Lead and supervising animation directors work with animating teams on each scene, using 'model sheets' with key poses for the characters; establishing the nature of the action and movement, and reviewing the dialogue for performance information. Key drawings of a sequence and an exposure sheet showing frame-by-frame information about the proposed animation are prepared, and teams work on before-and-after sequences, overlapping action, and the in-between drawings of the main poses in the action sequences. Rough line drawings are animated and shot for evaluation and correction, and a whole range of decisions may be made in relation to the work before it proceeds to 'final-line' animation, or 'clean-up'. Consistency in the design and detailed execution of a character is fundamental to the continuity of narrative events in the film, and must work well within the designated background context. Numerous checks are made before all work is scanned on to computer for the key personnel to create a composite of all the scenes, modify colour, movement and sound, and so on, and eventually create a text for camera, and the final completion of the film. The inevitable outcome of such a complex 'authorial' process, however hierarchically organised and efficiently executed, is a text which foregrounds its aesthetic and technical achievement, and radically 'simplifies' its ideological project. Perhaps just as inevitably, if this 'simplification' becomes a technical, aesthetic and textual 'tradition', then it begins to constitute a regulated 'site' which presupposes its own orthodoxies as the conditions of its creativity and political position.

Fundamentally, the Disney 'site' may be viewed within the parameters of Richard Dyer's model of utopian entertainment,[21] and may consequently be placed within a context where the *public* and political may be identified with the 'text', while the *personal* and the political may be identified with the 'narrative'. These, of course, sometimes overlap, and allow for the possibility – and, indeed, the inevitability – that ambivalence and contradiction characterise – some might say 'define' – the animated form. The ontological equivalence intrinsic to animated texts compounds this issue, and speaks further to the difficulties of properly assessing political inscription within Disney films – a point to which I will return. Dyer's conceptions of 'energy' (activity as human potential and power); 'abundance' (material well-being for many); 'intensity' (authentic depictions of affective emotion); 'transparency' (clarity of relationships between the protagonists themselves, and in relation to the audience) and 'community' (networks of communication and 'togetherness') in the musical are especially appropriate in helping to unpack these issues further, and may be enabling in determining how the creation of the Disney text, in deploying 'cultural resources' as part of its aesthetic and narrational process, merely uses them as agents of metaphorical allusion to the thematic and personalised aspects of cultural events, rather than the specificity of cultural politics.

Recent Disney animation has seemingly reflected some key social, cultural and national events – *The Little Mermaid* (1989) (the fall of the Berlin Wall and the end of the Cold War); *Beauty and the Beast* (Gary Tousdale and Kirk Wise, 1991) (the opening of EuroDisney); *Aladdin* (Ron Clements and John Musker, 1992) (The Gulf War); *The Lion King* (1994) (the first democratic elections in South Africa); *Pocahontas* (Mike Gabriel and Eric Goldberg, 1995) (Clinton era 'human rights' processes in, for example, Palestine and Ulster); *Toy*

Story (John Lasseter, 1995) (redefining 'frontier' myths in the light of a 'New World Order'); *The Hunchback of Notre Dame* (Gary Tousdale and Kirk Wise, 1996) ('ethnic cleansing' in the Balkan War); *Hercules* (1997) (reasserting American 'heroism' as a Kennedy/Clintonesque mediated phenomenon); and *Mulan* (Barry Cook and Tony Bancroft, 1998) (Disney's corporate expansion into Chinese markets). Each may be viewed as a conscious attempt to enhance the recognition of 'art' in animation by concentrating on the aesthetic complexity of predominantly 'human'-centred stories. Where once Disney uniformly played out dominant human traits through animals, it now plays them out through humans with no readjustment or re-emphasis to take into account the actual complexity of human beings. I wish to argue that this is because of the creative process in animation that I have outlined above, not because Disney is in some way naive about human complexity or the global politics within which it construes its films. Indeed, with full recognition of its position historically, economically and globally, Disney trusts the implicit ambivalence in its mobilisation of cultural resources as the core of its ideological reach and impact.

All these Disney films serve as examples of the ways in which Disney create 'narrative' and 'text' as politicised entities, where 'narrative' and 'text' may be understood entirely separately from each other, interrelatedly or, indeed, oppositionally; but importantly, all embrace Dyer's utopian paradigm as an 'archetypal veil' which overlays deep themes, and disguises the intricacies of political 'metaphor' as they may be (obviously) read through these stories. At one level, these films use their central protagonist (Ariel, Belle, Aladdin, Simba, Pocahontas, Woody, Quasimodo, Hercules and Mulan) *only* as a vehicle to express stasis, frustration, alienation and oppression in the light of a range of oppositional forces mainly concerned with established traditions and seemingly preordained social structures. Each literally 'embodies' social and romantic 'yearning' for change, and is nominally configured as 'good' in their desire to gain what is normally constructed as a self-evident reward for enduring their current predicament or 'lack'. All are thrust into 'public' circumstances which enable them to act upon the cultural and/or environmental infrastructure, and challenge the oppositional forces, which are inevitably configured as 'bad'/'evil', even if they, too, may be subject to more complex readings, or act as part of a higher redemptive scheme for all the characters involved. Ultimately, all succeed in 'revising', 'reconstructing' or 'redetermining' their social circumstances, but crucial to their progress have been the mobilisation and absorption of 'otherness' (both in the characters and, arguably, in the viewing audience) into a consensual drive towards a known resolution akin to Dyer's utopian ideal.

These central figures are the 'energy' of the narrative, galvanising the affective 'action', which is normally a challenge mounted either to maintain or question established power relations and cultural norms. Initially, it is almost always about a longing for something, or the responsibility of *having* to achieve something at the individual level. In achieving 'abundance' – material well-being for many – these protagonists create 'community' as part of their personal need and ambition, accommodating 'otherness' as 'togetherness'. This is where the 'design' orthodoxies in Disney animation become crucial. The anthropomorphisation of animals and objects; the caricatural norms of comic 'cute'; villainous 'angularity' and romantic 'curvaceousness'; and the mood-determining detail of 'real' environments and psychological/emotional contexts, all retain an ontological equivalence within the *materiality* and *flexibility* of the animated text to the point where 'difference' is evaluated only through the terms and conditions of the animated form, *not* at the social level. The central protagonists are the same as the 'others' they align with or oppose. Those who are marked *narrationally* as 'good', 'right', 'true', and so on, and those who may be punished, redeemed or eliminated in the same scheme, become part of a 'melting pot' of accommodation, rather than a 'kaleidoscope' of differentiation.[22] The animated text/form in the Disney style legitimises this process because *its* creative orthodoxies do not change, while social mores do. In consistently promoting the 'magical' properties of animation – essentially its *procedural* and *technological* difference from live action (though some would argue that the impact of animation in live action is once more making this line indistinguishable) – Disney represents what Bryan Appleyard has described as the 'super-normal'; a world which 'doesn't have to be as upsetting as the real one', and works as 'an expression of a pristine moment in a great nation's life when its people really thought they would all live happily ever after'.[23] Even if Disney's imperialist liberalism could be viewed with complete integrity, and the desire to promote the way towards a peaceful, contented, coexistent human existence remained the underpinning motive of its output, it cannot fail to be viewed at best as naive, at

worst as a cynical manipulation of cultural power within the context
of late industrial capitalism. The maintenance of 'magic' is at considerable cost to reality.

The 'design' strategy described above is further reinforced through
the 'transparency' of each individual as a cipher for a dominant trait,
and the ease in identifying the bonding aspects of the relationships
between romantic lovers; hero/heroine and allies; hero/heroine and
villain, and so forth. This model is authenticated by the 'intensity'
– overt depictions of affective emotion – in the songs and chore-
ographic spectacle that underpin the narrative. Disney – to reiterate,
*an authorially complex, hierarchical industrial process, which organ-
ises and executes selective practices within the vocabularies of
animated film* – has, in effect, created a 'fairy-tale' structure of its
own, which it supports through *visual* orthodoxies, also of its own
making, and advances through overdetermined utopian tropes in song
and spectacle. 'Animation' itself is Disney's first defence here, in the
sense that as a 'genre', or 'film form' in its own right, it refuses the
ways of reading available to critics of live-action film. Byrne and
McQuillan are almost surprised, for example, when they describe
Ariel in *The Little Mermaid:* 'She looks up to the camera with doe
eyes and enhanced breasts, which have more to do with animation
than anatomy'.[24] More to the point, this has more to do with the
'received' knowledges of Disney (indeed, classical cartoon) animation,
and its need to create 'industrial' templates of stereotypical femininity by which archetypal veiling and utopian aspiration may take place.
These strategies inevitably promote the primary reading cited above,
and divert audiences from any apparent necessity for secondary reading. It is in secondary reading, of course, that the highly charged
political and ideological minefield resides. Disney's trademark 'innocence', then, is a consequence of a particular manipulation of technology and a specific approach to 'animation'. It remains, therefore,
to explore the *actual* political implications of this are.

In a recent review of *Fantasia 2000* (2000), John Patterson notes
his loathing of Walt Disney's 'saccharine, utopianised Main Street',
and 'his knee-jerk anti-semitism', commenting on '*Song of the South*
... which would probably make a great Ku Klux Klan double bill
with *Birth of a Nation*', and concluding: 'I've stood on Walt Disney's
grave many times. And if the place had been a little emptier I might
have done a few more things on it, too'.[25] This level of vitriol, essentially directed at Walt Disney himself, has emerged largely as a

consequence of the rejection of the Company-approved 'sanitised' biographical material about Disney written by Bob Thomas and Leonard Mosley;[26] the embrace of Marc Eliot's unauthorised and much more damning biography *Walt Disney, Hollywood's Dark Prince*;[27] and the rise of persuasive disconstructive academic criticism, which fully delineates the issues concerning representation in Disney animated films over the last decade or so. Such extratextual material has significantly coloured a negative response to the films themselves in critical quarters, but has done little to impinge upon the positive nature of the mass viewing audience worldwide. This may indicate that the viewing public has little interest in 'authorship' and 'cultural politics', and is opting to engage with and enjoy the 'super-normal' world of the animated form in a *primal* rather than an *interrogative* or *contextual* way. The historical or institutional issues raised by 'Disney' (however, defined, in this instance) have been subsumed into personal rather than cultural metanarratives. Childhood experiences become adult memories, which in turn influence the next generation of childhood experiences, and so on. This continuity is based on an intrinsic trust in Disney's 'form' and the nature of the primary responses outlined above, and not on the repositioning of 'Disney' within the contemporary sociocultural consciousness or political frame. The sense of 'timelessness' in the Disney animated form facilitates the ease with which this attitude to and trust in 'Disney' persist, although it is clear that on closer inspection, all the texts are of their time, and readily reveal their cultural inflections. Even if Muslims object to their portrayal in *Aladdin*, African Americans find deep-rooted racism in *The Lion King*, the French oppose the presence of Disneyland Paris, Christian Fundamentalists rail against Disney's corporate identity, and Virginians successfully resist the imposition of an American History Theme Park, the engagement with and perpetuation of the Disney myth prevails.

Crucially, it may be argued that this has been achieved because Disney was absolutely intrinsic to the emergence and acceptance of an authentic 'popular culture' in the postwar era. The politics of 'past-Art' and its associated pleasures have been so forcefully entwined in the fabric of legitimate sociocultural materiality that they cannot be readily unpicked and recontextualised within an alternative system of appraisal. This may come with time, and may be aided and abetted by the increasing scale of revelation about how the 'magic' is constructed. With each new *The Making of...* documentary, and every associated 'technology' in toys, promotions and spinoffs, comes a gradual erosion of the 'mystification' of creativity. While the 'wow' factor remains, and technological determinacy retains its awe and wonder, the Disney ethic of responsiveness and reassurance stays in place, but once this is merely a known quantity and one shared by other producers and the public alike, a closer address of the 'Disney' teller, and the actual repercussing tale may take place. Disney's aesthetic, and its own metacommentary on art and progress as illustrated in animated film, when immersed in popular and critical acclaim for over forty years, has in effect defined an acceptable, accessible, and – crucially – archetypal 'Art' for mass consumption. This cannot be easily overturned in the necessary attempt to draw key 'producers' into the realms of important critical debates. In many senses, middle-class critical determinism in reconstructing and redefining 'histories' is a comparitively recent phenomenon, and while it is fundamentally necessary in the reclamation of gender, race and class knowledges, it cannot immediately challenge both the *mythic* identity of Disney and the intrinsic *modernity* of the animated form. Disney 'history' is embedded as cultural history, and a key site for a 'populist' value system that seemed to be drawn from self-evident truths, and was rendered *visible* by an 'art form' made out of artisanal imperatives and folk sensibilities. This 'visibility' has been retained, and continues to be embraced, because its 'imagery' has been maintained and reinvested in (American) culture. Its 'meaning' seemingly does not change in the public imagination, while the social and political context within which it finds itself has changed radically.

Again, Giroux has argued that in recent Disney films, 'memory is removed from the historical, social and political context that defines it as a process of cultural production that opens rather than closes down history. It is precisely this pedagogical policing of memory that undercuts its possibility as a form of critical remembrance that positions human agency against the restrictions and boundaries set by the historical past'.[28] This is clearly a valid point, but I would like to argue that while the mass audience may wish to propagate the Disney myth by an identification with its 'visible' ethic, it still lives in a 'real world' that consistently positions and adjusts their perspective on history, culture, and their own memory of it. While it is obvious that the Disney texts may be part of a personal metanarrative that perceives only inclusion, justice and progress, these texts are part of a cultural environment that does not readily evidence these things. In essence, the 'myth' endures above the specificities of representational responsibility because its claims are for a universality of *human* qualities rather than the particular recognition of geopolitical variation. Its 'modernity' merely foregrounds the possible metaphors in which we can address a limited range of psychological and emotional variables rather than those about increasingly important issues concerning personal and cultural identity. It is no surprise, then, that Disney's design strategy is found irredeemably lacking in its cultural sensitivity, since its mythical ethos does not speak to the contemporary ideological discourses in the public domain.

While the audience watching *Aladdin* sees Jafar, cultural critics see Saddam Hussein; while some view *The Lion King*, others see an inept *Hamlet* or, perhaps, a blatant copy of Osamu Tezuka's *Kimba the White Lion* (1965); some, too, may see *Mulan* as a story about a communist girl, loyal to state-soldiery *and* domesticity, while others may determine a discourse on cross-dressing and queer identity; many may see Belle in *Beauty and the Beast* as a victim of oppressive masculinities and a patriarchal culture, while the more perverse ironists may see a girl going out with a buffalo. This cursory – and partially flippant – glance at these texts is included merely to suggest that one unarguable fact to have emerged about Disney texts in the modern era is that they have attracted much more critical attention and have been subject to poststructuralist, postcolonial, (post-) feminist, and postmodern interrogation. This process has insisted that Disney texts *are* political texts, and this revelation alone has provoked the debates outlined in this discussion. It could be argued, however, that subjecting the texts to multiple interpretations that vindicate these critical approaches has merely – perhaps accidentally – reinforced the mythical centre and its ethos, and promoted the reassurance of primary readings. It is much easier, after all, to 'wish upon a star' than to engage with the Clinton-chasing Kenneth Starr, and perhaps the 'Whole New World' offered by Disney in the comfort of cartoon is politically preferable to the one to which it refers.

Part 6

'O! say, does the star-spangled banner yet wave, o'er the land of the free and the home of the brave?' Contemporary conflict and contradiction

Ambiguity and anger: representations of African Americans in contemporary Hollywood film

Mary Ellison

If music of African-American origin is the most original contribution that the United States has made to world culture, not only does film come a close second, but the two have regularly intersected and positively interacted. While black music has been used and appropriated by white, as well as black, directors within the context of film, it has continued to be an identifiably singular voice. It remains the most deeply felt expression of a people who have been enslaved in a nation that purports to be built on the concept of freedom. It signifies the ambiguous nature of being a building block for a new nation, while still being regarded as 'the other'; of co-founding a new American cultural voice, while mostly being thought of as separate and inferior. At the same time, the cinema has screened America's deeply ambivalent feelings towards the people they had once enslaved. In the 1980s and 1990s, there was a proliferation of white Hollywood representations of blackness that either appeased troubled liberal sensibilities or rationalisd racist practice, usually without pressurising the existent power structure for any destabilising level of change. Simultaneously, there was an upsurge in the visibility of proactive black artists in performing as well as film-making roles. Within the framework of both Hollywood and independent enterprises, a counter-hegemonic position has been staked out that redefines the issue of blackness in a white-dominated society and industry.

Film and film music have become the essential cultural spaces where the politics of race and class interact and are reconfigured. Capitalism has come to support subversive elements in black filmic representation and music whenever it seems likely to make more profit than political difference. Music is the heart and soul of

African-American culture, and its pervasive voice sings with ambiguously supportive and oppositional resonances in films which seek to represent aspects of black people's characters or experiences. Call and response, dualism, and masked political subtexts have long signified a realisation that music and film are cultural forms where anger, aspirations and desire could be hidden in plain sight. The centrality of the music is brought into sharpest relief when the lives of real or fictional musicians are explored, but it is often most powerfully evident in recent films tracking the dissonance of black urban youth.

Films directly about music immediately raise the issue of ambiguity over cultural and racial identity. Jazz has long been a many-faceted, sharp as well as muted, voice of black protest against inequality and white discrimination, while also being the most identifiably American music. Many jazz biopics are made by white directors, who compound the ambiguity by using the actual recorded music of great black artists, as well as the interpretative input of the black actors re-creating their lives. Should *Bird* (Clint Eastwood, 1988) be defined as a challenging black movie because of the overpowering impact of Charlie Parker's own genius as a saxophonist, or is it a white conservative cultural product because it was directed by Clint Eastwood? Is it a film that gives the sound and life of Charlie Parker respectful exposure and illumination, or does it merely commodify his genius for commercial gain? It has been suggested that this is, indeed, an ambiguous film since 'Eastwood's work with the soundtrack creates a diametrical split, the figure that moves through the narrative showing little credible connections with the sounds emerging from the alto on the track'.[1] While similar arguments might seem to apply to Bernard Tavernier's *Round Midnight* (1986), it is a very different kind of film, metadiscourse rather than biography being its underlying approach. It is almost a filmic improvisation around the music of Bud Powell, Lester Young and Dexter Gordon, with Gordon himself imbuing the composite lead role with a raw realism, as well impregnating his tenor solos with emotional immediacy. This film about jazz is also an original expression of jazz as an active creative force, and the Herbie Hancock score eloquently voices a great deal of the hopeful joy and angry disillusionment that have rarely been articulated in words. The film won an Oscar for the best score of 1986.

Only one black director has so far placed the career of a modern jazz musician at the centre of a film. It is hardly surprising that this film-maker is Spike Lee. Not only had Lee become the most pre-eminent of young black directors by the time he made this film, but he is also the son of a creative jazz musician who refused to compromise or take session work. When *Mo' Better Blues* was released in 1990, it caused considerable controversy.[2] With a score written by Terrence Blanchard, and most of the trumpet and saxophone solos performed by Blanchard and Branford Marsalis, the music has a lyrical depth and compassion that illustrate precisely what the film's storyline denies – the possibility of reaching great heights as an artist while still leading a full existence as a human being. Indeed, in order to function as a responsible and loving partner and father, Denzel Washington, as Bleek, has brutally to lose his ability to play the trumpet. Yet, it should be recognised that in the character of Shadow, the saxophonist played by Wesley Snipes, Lee creates a dedicated and successful musician who is also a supportive and loving partner to Cinda Williams as Clarke, Bleek's vocally talented ex-lover.

Blues and rhythm and blues have also been the subjects of films attempting to give cinematic recognition to the foundational role they have played in black culture. Some – like Gordon Parks's brilliant but little-seen *Leadbelly* (1976), or Robert Townsend's *The Five Heartbeats* (1991) – failed to get the distribution promised by their studios. Others, such as Mick Jackson's *The Bodyguard* (1992), seem little more than star vehicles for bankable assets like Whitney Houston; while Brian Gibson's *What's Love Got To Do With It* (1993) concentrates on extreme aspects of the private lives of Ike and Tina Turner and, in some odd way, demotes the music. The opposite is true of many of the feature films – like Michael Schultz's *Krush Groove* (1985) – which document the sociopolitical significance of hip hop with real showcasing skills, but are undercut by essentially weak storylines.

The ability of rap to intersect with jazz and blues, and provide soundtracks that seriously enhanced understanding of all the anger and ambiguity within urban black communities, is indelibly evidenced by films from young black directors like John Singleton with *Boyz N' the Hood* (1991), and Albert and Allen Hughes's *Menace II Society* (1993). Neither these, nor Matty Rich's *Straight out of Brooklyn* (1991), Ernest Dickerson's *Juice* (1992), Doug McHenry's *Jason's Lyric* (1994) or Spike Lee's *Clockers* (1995), ever came close to just being gang- and drug-obsessed action films. On the contrary, they represent 'a dynamic site of ideological production'.[3] They all engage

in debates over the relative role of families and the environment in
the choices made by black youth, with hip hop providing an aggressive subtext that empowers audiences either to sublimate their
fantasies of danger or to attempt to work out strategies to diminish
the very real levels of discrimination and deprivation. These are in
the front line of a struggle to overturn the dominant racial discourses
that portrayed black youth as ineluctably criminalised. The high level
of violence is frequently purveyed as a filmic warning against succumbing to nihilism. Most of all, these are films that tussle with the
nature of black male identity and the question of how to move beyond the macho posturing that snakes through hip-hop lyrics, to a
fuller understanding of the dilemmas confronting black masculinity.
Laurence Fishburne's positive advice to his son on the importance of
responsible fatherhood in *Boyz* is underscored by Stanley Clarke's
affirmative music, and ultimately transcends the more commercially
attractive appeal of Ice Cube's despairingly angry persona and lyrics.
This finds echoes in the often transformative affection shown by sons
and brothers in many of the other ghetto action movies, and there
seems to be an underlying awareness that, despite the violent gestur-
ing, 'there is no single issue more crucial to the survival of people of
color in this nation than the daunting challenge of turning young
boys into productive, loving men who accept their responsiblities'.[4]

Ambiguity can be explored as a key to decoding the layered nature
of African-American representation in film during the final two decades of the twentieth century. Its prevalence is apparent in images
created by both black and white film-makers. Some black-directed
and produced films, such as Robert Townsend's *Hollywood Shuffle*
(1987) or Keenan Ivory Wayans's *I'm Gonna Git You Sucka* (1989),
can be read as embittered or straightforwardly comedic parodies of
earlier cinematic straitjackets. Other 'black' comedies – especially
Shawn and Marlon Wayans's *Don't Be a Menace to South Central
While Drinking Your Juice in the Hood* (1995) and Rusty Cundieff's
Fear of a Black Hat (1994) – remodel the 1990s black and white
media images of violent gangsta and rap lifestyle with deconstruc-
tively absurd yet accessible humour.

Perhaps the most obvious ambiguity exists over what constitutes
a 'black film', and it can be argued that the lines between independent or major studio and black or white areas of control have become
blurred. Should, for instance, *Beloved* (1998) be delineated as a black
or white enterprise, when it was written and purchased for produc-

tion by two culturally powerful black women, Toni Morrison and Oprah Winfrey, but directed by white, male Jonathan Demme and produced under the Disney umbrella? It is not irrelevant that its faithfulness to a difficult text gained the approval of the author without succeeding in attracting audience numbers that might have recouped the high levels of financial and emotional commitment invested in the film. As in the book, words and images escape traditional confines, and splay into nightmares that have to be lived through before the pain of guilt and loss can be assuaged. This contrasted fairly dramatically with the relative commercial success of *The Color Purple* in 1985, when Steven Spielberg's much looser interpretation of Alice Walker's novel introduced sentimental elements that elicited a positive audience response. Black critical reactions were ambiguous in that the distortions were deplored, but the exposure to a black writer's reconstruction of Afro-Southern life in the early twentieth century, and to a wealth of strong black women on screen, was more than welcomed.[5] The blues-laden score by Quincy Jones is an unambivalently acclaimed delight. Other white-directed, black-focused historical films are diluted by the casting of a white lead. In some instances, such as Edward Zwick's *Glory* (1989), it is perfectly accurate to depict black soldiers being commanded by a white officer, but in other cases – Spielberg's *Amistad* (1997) in particular – a white character with a high audience recognition factor is overemphasised at the expense of historical truth.

Equally, there is an inherent ambiguity in the situation of those black independent film-makers who have attached their talents to corporate studios, with highly variable consequences for their artistic integrity and their consumer impact. Hollywood corporations have expanded to include multiple smaller enterprises that sometimes foster risk-taking as a way of accessing fresh or diminishing audiences. Indeed, the 1990s have witnessed leading independent film companies being subsumed into powerful conglomerates: in 1993, Disney acquired Miramax for $60 million; while the Turner Broadcasting Corporation purchased New Line Cinema for $600,000 million. Such familiar outlets for black themes and aspiring black directorial talent are being controlled by more condensed corporate authority. Despite official claims to the contrary, autonomy has become a fragile commodity in such circumstances.

This problem is being circumnavigated by black community-based companies such as Master P's No Limits. Master P (Percy Miller)

built a multimillion-dollar base on the recording and marketing of
New Orleans rap before expanding into film. His first movie was –
rather like F. Gary Gray's *Friday* (1995) – a cult classic that relied on
a music-based, ghettocentric style which played with an oppositional
tension between sound and action as well as humour and the serious
choices facing black youth. Unlike *Friday*, Master P's *I'm,'Bout It'*
(1997), appealed almost solely to young black audiences, but still
made a tenfold profit on the small initial investment, with 300,000
video sales. Major distribution companies refused to handle the film
because it was 'too uncompromisingly black', and a leading article
in the black press gave him full support: 'Refusing to allow the film
industry to place limitations on his art, P became the first in a line
of defiant young black entertainment moguls to send their film
projects directly to retail video and music stores.' His next two films,
I Got the Hook Up (1998) and *Foolish* (1999), pulled in a broader
band of ticket purchasers and made profits of between $8 million
and $12 million. *Foolish* also stayed in the national box-office charts
for several weeks. This was still achieved on small budgets, and both
films continued the pattern of being written, directed and produced
by Master P, who also played the lead roles. As the decade closed, his
No Limits Filmworks had *No Tomorrow*, starring himself and Pam
Grier, ready for release. There may well be a case for respecting
Master P's perspective that film-making which reflects black street
life, music and humour, while remaining independent of corporate
control, is essentially counter-hegemonic. Yet there is another layer
of ambiguity in a situation where the power to erode capitalist
manipulation has been acquired only by exploiting the explosive
musical talents and socioeconomic deprivation of frustated New
Orleanian rappers for personal profit. The fact that this profit is
shared by what is effectively a black collective, and is mainly fed
back into black-directed cultural enterprises, may undermine the
prevailing capitalist ethos at the same time as selectively using much
of the standard business infrastructure. Master P was arguably also
masking deconstructive determination with media inflated hype when
No Limits took out a full-page advertisement in *The Source* in July
1999 asking readers to 'SAY NO TO RAP ON RAP VIOLENCE'. It
may be more than coincidental that, in October 1999, Master P was
the only black person listed in *Fortune*'s 40 Richest Under-40 list,
worth apparently $361 million.[6]

Both F. Gary Gray and Master P began by making independent

features that played with the concept of the 'buddy movie', which has long been one of the Hollywood mainstream's most favoured genres. Gray's appealingly offbeat comedy *Friday* is essentially a buddy movie that plays with asking serious questions and is threaded with a musical intertextuality. The film teams Ice Cube with Chris Tucker, and the partnership enables the film 'to resonate with the style of the most extreme elements of black folk culture'.[7] Moreover, the black-directed film that has had the greatest box-office success is undoubtedly a 'buddy movie'. When Sidney Poitier made *Stir Crazy* in 1980, he gave Richard Pryor the freedom to improvise neo-minstrel dialogue with co-star Gene Wilder in a film that was to gross $101,500,000, a sum still unparalleled for a black-directed movie. Poitier had previously starred in dramatic buddy movies with white co-stars. In Stanley Kramer's *The Defiant Ones* (1958), and Norman Jewison's *In the Heat of the Night* (1967), he won the respect and friendship of previously racist and alienated white men. Indeed, his performances in these films was not only allegorical but did actually improve white perceptions of how relationships with black people might progress. Poitier also directed, wrote, produced and starred in series of comedic black buddy movies in the 1970s. It is open to debate whether *Uptown Saturday Night* (1974), *Let's Do It Again* (1975), or *A Piece of the Action* (1977), could be perceived as sharing aspects of W. E. B. DuBois's 'double consciousness' or 'twoness' as fully as *Stir Crazy*.

Stir Crazy itself undoubtedly taps into a black consciousness that slave ancestors were among the first non-native Americans, and this consciousness is almost always offset by an acute awareness of the difficulty of being accepted as fully American. Like DuBois, Poitier seems to be exploring the conviction that the United States might be a country founded on a theoretical ideology of equality, but unequal distribution of wealth, justice and opportunity is the regular experience of the majority of African Americans.[8] The mark of slavery seemed to those experiencing discrimination to have left a disenabling stain that neither abolition nor over a century of civil-rights activism and Black Power movements could remove. During and after slavery, minstrelsy and 'toming' had become complex coping mechanisms whereby identity could be protected by masking and appropriating the very stereotypes that denied black humanity. At the same time, sardonic mockery of supposed superiors and deliberate self-misrepresentation was a specific continuation of African ceremonial ritual. In Hollywood, marginalised black actors came to use their assumed racial inferiority as a performative trope that could subvert hegemonic control from the very margins to which they had been confined. At the same time, the mainstream could be infiltrated with the reappropriated and ambiguous cinematic signifiers. It is crucial that the neo-coon mask employed by Richard Pryor in *Stir Crazy* can be seen as more than just an entertaining disaster-avoidance tool, and is visibly underpinned by his own comedic persona. There are self-referential pointers to the drug-taking, path-breaking stand-up, whose live and recorded routines are revolutionary in their exposure of the intersection of class and racism, who is also responsible for destabilising and reclaiming the 'N' word. Few actors demonstrate more acutely the subversive role of laughter in the arsenal of anti-racism. Pryor's performance in *Stir Crazy* constantly soars into the surreal, and is equally regularly accompanied or pre-empted by the bizarre actions of Gene Wilder. Together they literally and metaphorically make a mockery of the judicial system that has unjustly imprisoned them, bringing to mind the disproportionately high number of young black men in the real America of the 1980s and 1990s who were dubiously incarcerated rather than being productively educated or employed.

It is part of the subtly serious, while comedically outlandish, dualism of this film that race is never an overt issue. The main ally of the creatively aspirational pair (Pryor wants to 'mask' professionally as an actor, and Wilder to write) is a black, gay transvestite (played by George Stanford Brown); they also get vital support in their plan to escape their ludicrous 125-year sentences from other black and American-Indian prisoners. The most feared white mass murderer in the prison is turned around by their unconventional friendship and not only comes to their aid but encodes solidarity for black equality when he sings 'Birmingham Jail' late at night in his cell. The buddy syndrome here is different from many in earlier and later interracial combinations. This centres on a friendship that was unquestionably solid before the action begins, and has an almost symbiotic quality as it continues.

So many other duos – from *The Defiant Ones*, through *48 Hours* (Walter Hill, 1982), to at least the first *Lethal Weapon* (Richard Donner, 1987), as well as *Die Hard with a Vengeance* (John McTiernan, 1995), *New Jack City* (Mario Van Peebles, 1991), and F. Gary Gray's *The Negotiator* (1998) – have to transcend mutual distrust before becoming bonded with their filmic partners. There are, of course, exceptions such as Samuel Jackson's almost symbiotic relationship with John Travolta in Quentin Tarantino's *Pulp Fiction* (1994), where blackness and male bonding epitomise cool, and Jackson philosophises and quotes the Bible as he shoots to kill. In a move that was self-consciously controversial, Tarantino disrupts the easy camaraderie by casting himself as a friend of Jackson's who is married to a black nurse, and feels that this imparts enough blackness to his character to allow him to call a black person a 'nigger'. In reality, this is the one thing that Samuel Jackson found objectionable about the racial interactions in the film.[9] Mario Van Peebles uses an apparently more conventional approach in depicting his two black and white co-stars in *New Jack City* (1991) as initially opposed detective colleagues, but the relationship between Ice-T and Judd Nelson has an unusual degree of equilibrium. This is shaken only by a secondary paternalist-buddy alliance between Ice-T and Chris Rock, as an explosive drug-addicted gang member turned police spy, and is counterbalanced by the unstable and self-destructive buddy connection of the drug-dealing duo, played by Wesley Snipes and Allen Payne.

Buddy movies can be seen as both projecting and defusing some the fears of white America over the consequences of fraternising with black men. This can be true of both white- and black-directed films. The agendas may well be different, but the impact on the audience can often be quite similar, and the influence of black actors on the way their roles are constructed and perceived should not be underestimated. Samuel Jackson as Zeus Carver in *Die Hard with a Vengeance* embodies a physical presence and psychological arrogance that seem threatening until they are rendered harmless by the rapport he develops with Bruce Willis. This becomes possible only once Jackson has challenged Willis about trying to sound black while behaving as overtly racist. Jackson's ability to transcend prejudiced behaviour and attitudes can be seen as a metaphor for communal black forgiveness over centuries of oppression. The illusion is created that black men can now join with white in renegotiating a coherent construction of masculinity.

In Lawrence Kasdan's *Grand Canyon* (1991) an accidental friendship between Danny Glover and Kevin Kline positively transforms and empowers the lives of their initially separate circles of families and friends. Glover again figures in a similar relationship in *Bat 21*

(Peter Markle, 1988). Constantly overseen by helicopters that encode the obscene violence of the Vietnam War, and Danny Glover's filmic determination to use his power as a helicopter pilot to save the life of Gene Hackman's lost intelligence expert, the developing rapport seems under surveillance. The helicopters hover with a more threatening air over the gun and gangsta rap culture that seems the only route to respect for the black youth of Los Angeles, and in so doing they compound the confusion of Glover's troubled nephew. His escape from a future of violence is made possible only because the friendship between Glover and Kline becomes strong enough to draw the two family circles together in a way that enables choice and disempowers discrimination. Similarly, in the *Lethal Weapon* series, Danny Glover is reassuringly unthreatening: he is the solid, dependable family man whereas his white partner, Mel Gibson, is almost psychotic, and relies on him for emotional and physical support. This relationship is given further destabilising ambiguity by the regular homoerotic overtones and the accompanying ambivalent laughter.[10]

Eddie Murphy incorporates a different kind of ambiguity as the almost archetypal 'buddy', whose air of casual ease always retains a dangerous edge. A persistent maverick, he charms his way out of initial rejection into being accepted as wittier, cooler and more capable than his partners in the *48 Hours* or *Beverly Hills Cop* series of movies. Yet to ensure that any sense of real menace is removed, his sexuality is marginalised and his resentment implodes in humour. This is a lesson that has been learnt well by Will Smith and used to finely tuned effect in blockbusters such as Barry Sonnenfeld's *Men in Black* (1997) and *The Wild, Wild West* (1999).

Many 'buddy' movies go further in creating an almost iconic representation of blackness as the site of wisdom. It is Morgan Freeman who is most frequently found personifying sagacity and patience. In *The Shawshank Redemption* (Frank Darabont, 1994) he shares his survival skills with Tim Robbins, enabling him to withstand and then escape from the trauma of prison life, before ultimately sustaining their mutually supportive friendship within the context of freedom. Both David Fincher's *Se7en* (1995) and Gary Fleder's *Kiss the Girls* (1997) project Freeman as a detective possessed of deductive powers, patience and human understanding that can never be matched by that of his partners. Neither Brad Pitt in *Se7en* nor Ashley Judd in *Kiss the Girls* can approach his level of understanding of the complexity and deviance of the human spirit. As William Somerset in *Se7en*, Freeman illuminates the persistently rain-sodden darkness with his meticulously crafted prescience and knowledge, and his slowly increasing determination to remain, to simply be there, as a stubborn obstacle in the path of evil. It is clear that Freeman's blackness is crucial: Richard Dyer points out that, apart from the ambiguous references to *Shaft* (Gordon Parks, 1971) and

> *Lethal Weapon* et al., Somerset also belongs with two other gifted black investigators, Sidney Poitier *In the Heat of the Night* (1967) and Freeman himself in *Kiss the Girls*, films which explicitly pit the education, intelligence and good sense of the black investigator against whites who are both stupid and racist. All this may inadvertently flush out something perhaps inadvertently brushed under the carpet, 'that serial killing is a white thing'.

He is the only one who can fully construe the meaning of the starkly visual, theatrical and literary-rooted evidence that signifies the seven deadly sins. Freeman 'functions as the intellectual and moral voice of the film', yet he sees, like the killer, 'a world drenched in endless wickedness'. He somehow 'remains outside of this, without sin. The film relies, with excellent judgement, on Morgan Freeman to carry off this contradiction: his repose, the expressivity we see in his eyes, the mellow timbre of his voice give Somerset an unforgettable presence.' *Se7en* ends with Freeman's ambivalent statement 'Ernest Hemingway once wrote, "the world is a fine place and worth fighting for." I agree with the second part.' His final decision not to retire to the country but to 'be around', not just to try and save Brad Pitt from perpetual breakdown but to continue to be the erudite, compassionate 'site of wisdom' in a bleak, self-destructive urban wasteland, is a triumph of his basic belief in humanity, despite all the obvious evidence to the contrary.[11] It is a negation of his own cynicism, and an affirmation of the possibility of change and redemption, that moves him to refuse to abandon either his partner or the city he has made it his life's work to comprehend and help.

More unsparingly dark, and specifically anti-hegemonic, is Bill Duke's *Deep Cover* (1992). This forms a logical progression from his début film, *The Killing Floor* (1984), a searching reconstruction of racism, migration and unionism, undercut by a destructive buddy relationship, made when he was at the forefront of an emergent

African-American incursion into mainstream cinema. *Deep Cover* unfolds a disturbingly dysfunctional buddy scenario in which Laurence Fishburne and Jeff Goldblum both become aware of the corruption endemic within American government, and of the degree to which it is dependent on a diplomatically entwined drug cartel. As an undercover police agent forced to trade in the drugs he despises with specific hatred because they were responsible for his father's death, Laurence Fishburne is the heart of a quintessentially ambiguous film. In the closing frames, he challenges the audience to find a way to spend drug profit money that does not compound inequality and criminality: 'The money doesn't know where it came from, but I do. If I keep it, I'm a criminal. If I give it to the government, I'm a fool. If I try and do some good with it, maybe it just makes things worse. Either way I'll probably just wind up getting myself in more trouble. It's an impossible choice, but in a way, we all have to make it. What would you do?' Moments earlier, just before he is killed by Fishburne, Goldblum had hurled a speech of abuse at diplomatically immune drug barons, dismissing their defensiveness as symptomatic of a world which is divided not by ethnicity but by poverty: 'the only important divisions are between rich people and poor people'.[12] The film is a tangential attack on capitalism and the existent power structure and it opens up the question of how to deconstruct a world in which wealth is increasingly polarised. Todd Boyd sees it as parallel-ing the contemporary situation of defiantly posturing young black men who eschew mainstream accommodation but are continually consumed by it. He feels that Fishburne's final question

> is a direct challenge to the producers of black popular culture. It is also a challenge to Black people in America today regarding their general state of cynicism and apathy. With the civil rights movement having resulted in middle class selfishness, accommodation, and isola-tion from the larger community of Black people, and with the at-tempts on the part of the right to reverse the few individual gains made during our time, there are few real choices left.[13]

Fled (1996) could almost have been made as a semi-humorous parody, or even pastiche, of *Deep Cover*. It also stars Laurence Fish-burne as an undercover cop with an initially unwilling white partner in Stephen Baldwin, and was also directed by a young but established black film-maker, Kevin Hooks, who had found a wide audience and critical acclaim with *Passenger 57* (1992). *Fled*, however, is a much lighter affair, with the fast-paced action prefaced by a start reminiscent of *The Defiant Ones* and constant, overt references to similar sequences of events in a series of Hollywood movies. Corruption and treachery, as well as connections with drug barons, are still rife in high places, but this time they are overcome by the mutual trust and integrity of the interracial duo. In *Gang Related* (Jim Kouf, 1997), the bond between two undercover police officers – played by Tupac Shakur and James Belushi – is initially 'closer than family, closer than blood', but it cannot survive the corruption and shedding of blood instigated by the white partner. Here both seem fated to die violent deaths that were set on course by their perpetration of a drive-by murder. The knowledge that this is the last performance by the talented Tupac Shakur before his own fatal drive-by shooting in 1996 gives the film an air of nightmare neorealism. More optimistic resonances of *Deep Cover* were explored by Bill Duke himself when he put Laurence Fishburne at the centre of *Hoodlum* (1997), which again locates him in a drug- and corruption-laden environment. This time, however, he is playing not a detective but a real 1920s gangster, Buppy Johnson, who uses a variety of allies – including numbers queen Cicely Tyson, deliciously evoking all the ambiguity of attempting to be a good person in a bad business – to control crime in 1920s Harlem. Eventually, he finds redemption through his relationship with Vanessa Williams, who enables him to face up to what he has become, and how he can change. While this is an essentially disturbing and violent film, it does – unlike *Deep Cover* – end with the expectation that good intentions can be transformative.

Black women are not absent from the buddy-role syndrome, but just as in movies in general, they have fewer roles and, with the exception of Whoopi Goldberg, a less prominent media profile. Kasi Lemmons, for instance, plays a crucial small role as Jodie Foster's buddy in Jonathan Demme's *Silence of the Lambs* (1991), where she is decisive in enabling her room-mate to find the serial killer. It is also Kasi Lemmons who plays Virginia Masters's buddy and research co-worker in *Candyman* (Bernard Rose, 1992), and she ultimately dies to defer her friend's death at the hands of the legendary black ghost of a man who had been murdered a century earlier because of his love affair with a white woman. In several black-directed films, the concept of buddyism is expanded to four close female friends. F. Gary Gray's *Set It Off* (1996) tracks Jada Pinckett, Queen Latifah, Kimberley Elise and Viveca A. Fox as they spend virtually all their time together, and plan and carry out the kind of robbery more common in male action films. Rather different are Debbie Allen's *Stomping at the Savoy* (1992) and Forest Whitaker's *Waiting to Exhale* (1995), where four women provide a safe base for each other in order to cope with probblems they encounter in every aspect of their lives. In *Savoy*, the power of friendship to destroy, as well as sustain, ends in division and misery as loyalty is driven out by materialistic motivation. In *Waiting*, the four friends all positively empower each other, and the common bond shared by Whitney Houston, Angela Bassett, Lela Rochon and Lorreta Devine transcends the ambiguity and anger that they intermittently feel towards men and life in general.

It is more common, however, to see young black directors using a female buddy duo as background to a central male-dominated storyline. In *Devil in a Blue Dress* (Carl Franklin, 1995), the strong friendship between Jenifer Beals and Lisa Nicole Carson is essential to the complex, cheating-orientated plot that actually revolves around Denzel Washington's politically cynical and embittered detective. *Jason's Lyric* (1994) similarly shows the supportive closeness of Jada Pinckett and Lisa Nicole Carson as being very secondary to the ambiguously demanding love of predatory brotherly bonding. Directed by African-American Doug McHenry, who had previously concentrated on humorous male camaraderie in *House Party 2* (1991), it is full of painful choices and fatal consequences. As in *New Jack City*, there is overt recognition that man is still his brother's keeper in a criminalised environment that has destabilised the tortuously fine balance between self-destruction and salvation.

Salvation and revenge are the rationale for one of the oddest intergender and inter-racial partnerships in *Ghost* (Jerry Zucker, 1990). Here, Whoopi Goldberg becomes the buddy of Patrick Swayze's ghost in order to set his spirit free, save his wife's life, and bring his computer-fraud murderer to justice. The fact that she does this in Oscar-winning, high-comedy, double-consciousness style is a prime example of the fluid structure of the genre. Equally comedic, and only slightly less playful with stereotypical presuppositions, is Cuba Gooding Jr's Oscar-winning performance as Tom Cruise's 'show me the money' football-playing buddy and client in *Jerry Maguire* (Cameron Crowe, 1996). Both performances demonstrate how apparently historically referential, self-deprecating laughter is only masking a gleeful, powerfully self-assertive reclamation of

African-American humour with attitude. Similarly, it is Samuel Jackson in another white-directed film, Renny Harlin's *The Long Kiss Goodnight* (1996), who gives his role as the uncertain buddy of Geena Davis's amnesiac, politically deceived assassin a deeply comedic and deconstructive dimension.

A rather more mythic, heroic buddy role is played by Laurence Fishburne in Andy and Larry Wachowski's *The Matrix* (1999), where he persuades Keanu Reeves to join him in his mission to save humanity from life in a state of virtual reality under the cyborgs that control people's illusions. There may be a degree of compensatory artistic guilt as a motivating factor in the recurring depiction of black men as wise and good saviour figures, instead of the sexually threating, potential rapists of the stereotyped past. In *Terminator 2* (James Cameron, 1991) it is Joe Morton, previously best known as the alien challenging racism in John Sayles's *Brother from Another Planet* (1984), who is cast as the self-sacrificing scientist who chooses to ally himself with Linda Hamilton, and then blow himself up rather than be a crucial tool of mechanical power-brokers. In both films, there is a life-affirming black consciousness that puts the future of humanity well before personal happiness.

More laterally heroic – but no less effective as social commentary, or affective as an empathetic perfomance – is Tupac Shakur's role as Tim Roth's 'buddy' in Vondie Curtis Hall's brilliantly witty and elliptical *Gridlock'd* (1998). Within the broad framework of an anti-establishment buddy movie, this is a sharply focused reminder of decades of black life and cinematic history. Drug addiction and the deaths that track the drug trade are treated with the same mixture of hard-hitting drama, witty irony and absurd playfulness that distinguishes 'gangsta' rap as a genre. The director, Vondie Curtis Hall, had initially impacted on the public as the lone, powerful black presence in the demeaningly black-disregarding *Mississippi Burning* (Alan Parker, 1988), where he was aggressive enough to be many a white man's worst nightmare. Here he casts himself as the worst nightmare of black urban youth – a violent and murderous drug-dealer. Encoded in the frustration of the constant blocks put in the way of withrawal from drugs are the problems that beset Shakur's own mother when she decided that drugs provided only empty and debilitating answers. Even more meaningful is the role of Erica Huggins as co-producer. As a leading member of the Black Panther party in the early 1970s, she had every reason to believe that kicking a drug habit was a denial of white control over black lives. Referencing her belief that the CIA had been instrumental in depoliticising the West Coast black community through drugs, at the same time as the FBI infiltrated and destroyed the Panthers, the film points a fascinating bifocal lens at dehumanising official barriers to positive change.

Reception is one of the vast and multifaceted arenas that impacts on the nature of film, as well as the marketing process. A consequence of corporate involvement is that large-scale test audience responses may lead to demands that a film be altered to remove uncomfortable moments or endings, and effectively appeal to a perceived lower common denominator. It was even suggested to Mario Van Peebles that *Panther* (1995) would improve its audience appeal if it was reformulated to centre on a fictional white hero, possibly casting Tom Cruise as the lead. This would have seemed as counterproductive as it was contraindicated, since both the writer, Melvin Van Peebles, and the director had built their reputations on creating complex black role models in *Sweet Sweetback's Baadasssss Song* (1971) and *New Jack City* (1991) respectively. Similar problems beset Spike Lee's *Malcolm X* (1992) when the studio refused to finance the full cost of the film, and the film had to be slightly shortened, and diminish its revolutionary socialist element, in order to get the approval of both Warner and individual black backers.

Independent films frequently have to contend with business-centred preconceptions about reception, and face difficulties not only in getting produced but also in finding distributors. Charles Burnett's *To Sleep with Anger* (1990), for instance, was never marketed or distributed with any enthusiasm or confidence, despite its provocative evocation of the continuing strength of Southern 'conjure' culture in modern black urban life. Even the presence of Danny Glover as the elementally ambiguous trickster figure did not secure large-scale cinematic exposure, despite critical acclaim. Julie Dash's *Daughters of the Dust* (1992) also received limited screenings because of distributors' ambivalence about the perceived reception of a complex film that very slowly reveals its almost secretively unfolding images of late-nineteenth-century black women's inner and exterior lives in the still-African-dominated Sea Islands.

Despite its layered levels of accessibility, similar nervous uncertainty constrained the marketing of Kasi Lemmons's lyrical and perspicacious *Eve's Bayou* (1997). This subtle exploration of memory, family and gender relationships set in a small all-black Louisiana town was written as well as directed by Kasi Lemmons, and made financially viable by Samuel Jackson's involvement as star, producer and investor. Jackson was attracted not only by his own role as the good looking doctor, but also by the way in which the film implies that guilt and imagination can become the arbiters of memory. At the end, the storyteller draws the conclusion that 'the truth changes color depending on the light and tomorrow can be clearer than yesterday. Memory is a selection of images, some elusive, others printed indelibly on the brain. Each image is like a thread, each thread woven together to make a tapestry and the tapestry is our past.' The story is told and retold by ten-year-old Eve Batiste (Jurnee Smollet), daughter of Louis, Samuel Jackson's philandering doctor, and named after her ancestor African Eve, who was freed from slavery by General Batiste because she saved his life before going on to bear him sixteen children. Set in the 1960s, the film has no white characters and only the evocative classical as well as jazz elements of Terrence Blanchard's eloquent score testify to the town's mixed ancestry. The modern Eve is a prescient child who senses the danger lurking in the way her fourteen-year-old sister's burgeoning sexuality is focused too obsessively on their charming and affectionate father. It is Eve that Sisely goes to after she pushes fantasy into reality and initiates a sexual kiss with her father, only to find that he rejects her with a shocked slap. Her account of what happened amounts to a misremembering, but Eve believes her sister and wishes her father dead. Even though Mozelle (Debi Morgan), her father's sister, tells her: 'You can't kill people with voodoo, that's ridiculous', Eve goes to a voodoo practitioner to seek his death. When he is shot by a jealous husband, Eve blames herself.

The seductive bayou, heavy with Spanish moss and suffused with flickering sunlight, seems to foreground memory, imagination and guilt, but this is just as much a film about gender. It deconstructs the differences between men and women without desexualising either. While black women are celebrated for their joy and capacity for love, so are the men. This is a rare film in that it features black men who combine strength with sensitivity and generosity of spirit. When the film opens, Mozelle is partnered by her warm and loving third husband Harry, played with consummate appeal by Branford Marsalis. After he dies in a car crash, she finds an even more affirming and powerful partner in Julian Grayraven, a generous spirited

part-black, part-Native American artist played with apposite tenderness by Vondie Curtis Hall (who is married to Kasi Lemmons). When
Mozelle initially refuses to marry Julian because she feels that she is
cursed and barren, he responds with the powerful affirmation 'You
are not barren, you are wounded here [touching her heart] and it is
here I will plant my seeds.' Mozelle constantly plays down gender
differences, and argues that she and her brother are 'two of a kind',
'we are the same'. Before he is killed, her brother wrote her a letter
explaining his promiscuity as a need to feel 'heroic'. He understands
that this is an illusion that feeds his ego, and Samuel Jackson himself
has pointed out in an interview:

> he is still someone who loved his wife and children. He was a good
> provider. He cared about his sister and mother. He was very supportive
> of the community. He was always working to give his family a better
> life. I felt it was crucial to depict him as a real man that was missing
> a very important element in his life. He didn't feel like a hero at home.
> And he didn't feel very heroic about himself as a person. See, the
> complexities of an individual are very deep and vast. Your family must
> be part of your foundation. Black men will always possess the need to
> feel heroic … it is almost an ever present obligation. It's very hard not
> to be portrayed as dogs to our children and women.[14]

Films aimed at targeting specifically young black audiences may
find their content and distribution affected by anticipated audience
reception and the perception of theatre owners or management, even
when there is no dependence on large studio production. Hype
Williams, for instance, faced problems as he moved from music
videos into directing *Belly* (1999), a film he intended to contain an
anti-drugs message, only to find his glamorous style created such a
seductive impression that Magic Johnson refused to allow the film to
be screened at his nationwide chain of cinemas located in black areas. Johnson has maintained his refusal to screen *Belly,* but Williams
has acknowledged that his directorial style will in future be affected
by the theatre owner's sense of morality.

A keen awareness of the power of the market and of audience
reception has motivated Spike Lee, the most prolific and influential
black film-maker of the late twentieth century, to diversify into advertising and film product tie-ins to ensure that he can maintain a
high degree of autonomy and control, despite working primarily
within the constraining large-studio system. The necessity for this

became evident once the success of the totally independent, low-budget *She's Gotta Have It* (1986) ensured that Hollywood developed enough interest for Columbia to provide the $6.5 million dollar finance for Lee's next feature, *School Daze,* a bright musical remembrance of the sociopolitical and colour dynamics at Morehouse school. Lee rapidly discovered that there was an artistic price to pay for Hollywood money; cuts in complexity, effects and length were insisted upon by the studio. Despite this, Lee managed to keep in a connection between the deprivation caused by sharecropping in the deep South and apartheid in South Africa, made all the more effective by a verbal confrontation between Samuel Jackson and Laurence Fishburne as representatives of the class divide in black America. Lee simultaneously determined to use the way the existing economic system functioned to establish the financial independence that would ensure artistic expression. As Nelson George has pointed out:

> In the face of modern corporate infotainment monoliths, the most realpolitik counter strategy is to be in business with as many as possible. Diversifying protects you against cooptation by any single corporate entity or industry. With revenue flowing in from commercials, books, music videos, and merchandising, Spike has some major cushion should Hollywood get tired of his methods or his mouth.[15]

It is typical of Lee's richly textured and self-referential style that *Do the Right Thing* (1989) contains a humorous allusion to Nike's Air Jordan trainers – one of the products he has personally advertised on prime-time television. The fact that this politically charged and challenging film should also show the greatest profit – the initial investment of $6.5 million produced $28 million in domestic box-office receipts alone – seemed to indicate a talent for appealing to a broad band of white as well as black audiences. Much of the power of the film lies in the way racial tension is viewed from more than one perspective, and is treated with wit as well as with seriousness and historical immediacy. There is also a warm empathy flowing through the portrayal of the older characters, like Ossie Davis's Da Mayor and Ruby Dee's Mother Sister, which balances the depth given to the wide range of young African Americans, Hispanics and Italians. Humour lightens the portrayal of competing Korean and West Indians, and each group is fired by some kind of anger at racist discrimination, as well as ambiguity about their status in multicultural Brooklyn. One of the most interesting aspects of Spike Lee's work as a film-maker is that although he has black nationalist leanings and has been at the forefront of the New Black Aesthetic, he does not preach in his movies.

The varied layers of images, action, dialogue, sound and music in *Do the Right Thing* offer choices rather than certainty. Samuel Jackson's role as local radio DJ is almost that of an African *griot*. His commentary on events is given historical resonance as he chooses the great blues and soul songs, songs that have encoded every differing response to past discrimination and hope, to float out into the neighbourhood. Even the riot which follows the murder of Radio Raheem by two white policemen seems constrained by uncertainty about violence being the most productive response to violence, despite visual references to the very real Howard Beach murders and the controversial – but now discredited – Tawana Brawley case. Spike Lee's character, Mookie, emodies this ambivalence as he hesitates over hurling the trash can through the pizzeria window. The persistent recurrence of the one photograph that shows Martin Luther King and Malcolm X together suggests options that may involve ideas expounded by both of these essentially radical socialist leaders. The final imprinting on screen of quotations highlighting their conflicting ideas on the role of violence could be regarded as drawing attention to their only substantive ultimate division. The general sense of choice and ambiguity is underscored by most of the saxophone solos in the film. While the overall score, composed by Bill Lee and expertly produced by Delfeayo Marsalis, tends to reinforce the action, the solos by Branford Marsalis add an oppositional tension and lyrical intensity to the mood of most of the significant scenes. The power and variety of the music, which embraces styles from the punching message of Public Enemy's 'Fight the Power' through to drifting, ethereal solo sax, clearly added to the market appeal of this film, which actually managed to create a perceptible shift in white attitudinal responses to black people. Its anti-hegemonic stance was clearly 'masked', or blended sufficiently subtly into its fabric, for it to create a positive impression: audience surveys indicate that white racism was diminished by the film in that the majority of non-black viewers evinced greater understanding of the black urban situation after seeing it.[16]

Lee's determination to engage the audience as active participants in the cinematic experience is rarely more evident than in *Jungle Fever* (1991), where he opens up an array of questions about interracial sex, mixed-race offspring and perceptions of racial difference (with a significant subtext about dysfunctional families and drug abuse). The discussion is not just focused on the central relationship between Wesley Snipes and Anabella Sciorra, but includes in the debate a wide range of opinions. It evokes echoes of the earliest screened interracial relationships between Dorothy Dandridge and Michael Rennie and Harry Belafonte in *Island in the Sun* (Robert Rosen, 1956), but is far more honest in its assessment of the issue. It cannot fairly be compared with far more straightforward recent films about succesful black and white connections. Films such as *Mr and Mrs Loving* (Dick Friedenberg, 1996), with its legally ground-breaking marriage between Lela Rochon and Timothy Bottoms, and its alternately edgy and romantic score by Branford Marsalis, or Jesse Nelson's fraught but committed romance between Whoopi Goldberg and Ray Liotta in *Corrina, Corrina* (1994), are very different, since they centre firmly on two specific individuals. Others, such as Alison Swan's *Mixing Nia* (1998), show the kind of journey that is necessary to resolve a confusion about racial identity if you were born to a black and a white parent, and have relationships with black and white men. These are films with resolutions; *Jungle Fever* is not, and had no intention of providing answers, but it does raise almost all the relevant questions.

Many – if not all – of Spike Lee's films reflect aspects of his own life, as well as his attitudes and interests. In *Jungle Fever*, some comments may reflect his own reaction to his father's second marriage to a white woman. *Crooklyn* (1994) was co-written with two of his siblings, and undoubtedly recorded some of their responses to their mother's premature death while they were still young children forced to come to terms with tragic loss and unaccustomed responsibility. Most of his films are actually set in Brooklyn, where he himself grew up, and when he moves outside his home territory, it is because the topic makes this imperative. *Get On The Bus* (1998) is a story about finding identity and a sense of community on a journey from Los Angeles to the Million Man March in Washington. What is even more constant than the setting is the power and ambiguity of the music. Lee's films have exceptional density of sound and aural significance, because the basic score is given constant dialectical tension by a resonant use of individual songs and arresting singers. The songs for *Jungle Fever* were provided by Stevie Wonder, and while his genius for distilling the essence of commodified urban greed is as apparent in his voice as in the lyrics for 'Living for the City', it is startling and confusing to hear the young Marc Dorsey almost replicating his sound on 'People Make the World Go Round' in *Crooklyn*. Dorsey went on to compound the double impact of his loaded nuances in *Clockers* and *Get On the Bus*. But the most telling musical ambiguities are juxtaposed in *He Got Game* (1998). Here the conflicting emotions of a father and son bound together, yet separated, by a sense of guilt about their roles in the accidental death of Martha/Lonette McKee, Denzel Washington's wife and Ray Allen's mother, are eloquently underscored by the quintessentially American concertos of Aaron Copland. Copland himself felt that the only way to make his compositions uniquely American was to incorporate jazz and blues, because they were the most original of all New World sounds. Contradicting the harmonious flow of the Copland score are the angry, deconstructive rap songs fired out by Public Enemy. Lyrics such as 'But damn the game, if it don't mean nothing. What is Game? Who got Game?' or 'Fuck the game, if it ain't saying nothing … Folks don't even own themselves, paying mental rent to corporate presidents,' express outrage at the corruption and racism that corrode black youth through sport as much as through the unjust judicial system. This intelligent film is deeply ambiguous, and it is the music that creates the most effective dialogue between the opposed positions.

As the twenty-first century begins, racism is still rampant, and poverty is still a condition that affects a disproportionately high number of African Americans. The genuine affection with which Will Smith is regarded by the American public is marked by a sense of relief that racism can so easily be denied if it means identifying with such a likeable, funny and warm family man. His role as heroic saviour of an alien-threatened earth in *Independence Day* (Roland Emmerich, 1996) is the core of the highest-grossing film with a black lead. It took $305,400,800 in US box-office sales, and his buddy movie, *Men in Black* (Barry Sonnenfeld, 1997), earned the second-largest income for a domestic theatrical release with a black star. He has won a reputation as a serious actor in complex roles with *Six Degrees of Separation* (Fred Schepisi, 1993) and the politically paranoid *Enemy of the State* (Tony Scott, 1998). His buddy movies have built on his acceptability in *The Fresh Prince of Bel Air*, and reduced fear of association with at least one black person, without perceptibly diminishing levels of discrimination and deprivation for black people in general. His style and mannerisms have been appropriated by the acquisitive white gaze, but he remains grounded in his career as a musician, and has continued to make award-winning rap records that are as unthreatening as they are marketable.

Other black actors have also established their identities as attractive or compelling, but the success of men such as Samuel Jackson, Denzel Washington, Morgan Freeman, Wesley Snipes, Danny Glover, James Earl Jones, Cuba Gooding Jr, Omar Epps, Taye Diggs or Eddie Murphy has never been matched by any parallel group of black women. Despite the beauty and talent of Halle Berry, Angela Bassett, Nia Long, Jada Pinckett, Lynn Whitfield, Alfre Woodard or Vanessa Williams, the only women who have acquired any degree of instant recognition or universal acclaim have been the comedic Whoopi Goldberg and the nostalgia-rooted Pam Grier in Tarantino's *Jackie Brown* (1998). It would seem that sexism still has as much bearing on film as either class or race. It may, indeed, be the intersection of all three that has constrained the progression of black women either on or behind the screen. Less attention has been paid to Whoopi Goldberg when she has played a political activist in films like *The Long Walk Home* (Richard Pearce, 1990) or *Ghosts of Mississippi* (Rob Reiner, 1996) than in her humorous roles. The blurring of at least some of the identifiable delineations between the work of white and black directors seems a more frequent occurrence as the new century begins. There seemed, for instance, to be a less than marginal difference in the way in which the *Sister Act* (1992) and *Sister Act 2* (1993) were used by white Emile Ardolino or black Bill Duke to allow Whoopi Goldberg to formulate a new take on an old minstrel act. The fact that in both films she could play a singing whore and nun meant that male fantasies could be combined into one feisty, self-mocking parody that audiences are able to perceive as walking a fine line between deconstructing and reinforcing the double-consciousness-driven stereotypes.

In a not wholly dissimilar way, Pam Grier's dignity and authority in *Jackie Brown* are largely dependent on playing with her blax-ploitation image as a sexually aggressive, vengeance-seeking warrior in *Foxy Brown* (Jack Hill, 1974), with the eras evocatively linked by the assertive 1970s soul songs that reinforce her determination to control the pattern of her own future. To some she has become a feminist icon; to others she remains an erotic male fantasy. She has a higher recognition factor than Teresa Randle, who starred in Spike

Lee's *Girl 6* (1996), which did make an adventurous attempt to map out the spaces where a woman could seek to establish the extent of her sexual desires and the boundaries of her needs. Accompanied by the hungrily sensual music of Prince, the film continues the search for female identity haltingly begun in *She's Gotta Have It* (1986), but delves more deeply into the cinematic iconography of black women by reconfiguring Randle as Dorothy Dandridge and Pam Grier in moments of yearningly imagined daydreams.

Among black women directors, Leslie Harris won accolades for *Just Another Girl on the IRT* (1993), in which she put a teenage black girl's responses to an unwanted pregnancy vividly on the screen, but she did not make a star out of Ariyan Johnson. This is just as true of Alison Swan's *Mixing Nia,* which features Karyn Parsons, already known to many viewers as one of Will Smith's 'family' in *The Fresh Prince of Bel Air*, but it had too little theatre distribution to re-create her image as a black woman seeking her own voice within the framework of the cinema, as well as that of her life in the film itself. Despite major studio backing, Darnell Martin's *I Like It Like That* (1994), received almost as little exposure as the other films written and directed by black women. It is a searching look at the shifting Hispanic as well as black cultural space occupied by Lauren Velez, and the ambiguity of her search for identity and survival. Every shift in mood or cultural alliance was accompanied by music that said more than any words or actions. It seemed appropriate that Velez's greatest triumph as a record producer's assistant was to have two Hispanic brothers record Otis Redding's powerfully dualistic 'Try a Little Tenderness', especially since her transvestite brother had pleaded for understanding from his rejecting mother while Otis sang his achingly yearning original version in the background. Similar containment and tensions seem to have constrained the ability of most of the other female-authored or -focused movies over the last two decades of the twentieth century. It is anomalous that during the years when black women increased their visibility in public life, they became proportionately less visible on the once silver screen. The situation seems unchanged. While Oprah Winfrey fended off more or less all intrusions into her primacy on the small screen, the cinema remains a male-dominated arena. Halle Berry produced and starred in the critically acclaimed *Introducing Dorothy Dandridge* (1999), but had to rely on funding from cable television's Home Box Office.

The need for greater scope for expressing a wider range of black experiences in a cinematic context was recognised by Todd Boyd, the black academic who co-authored *The Wood* (1999) with director Rick Famuyiwa. While the film is centred on the ambiguities within the relationships of three young, middle-class black men, the feelings of women are paid serious attention. It is set in Inglewood, the home of the feared 'Bloods' gang; life on the street is not ignored, but it is deliberately played down in an intended move away from the violence of 'hood' films. Boyd believes that such films played a valuable role in drawing attention to the deprivation and injustice that engendered extreme anger: 'the problem was not the content of the films. The problem was that they were the only films that were being made.'[17] The number 1 film in the US box-office in the last week of October 1999 was Malcolm D. (cousin of Spike) Lee's richly textured and politically complex *The Best Man*. The critical question is whether the reception of any one genre is seen in some kind of balanced relationship to the real lives of black people. Film cannot purport to be realistic; even a documentary is only a partial, selected record of chosen events, and black film-makers and actors can only represent their own individual perspectives. But some films have links to existing reality that are close enough to touch chords of perceived experience, and raise significant questions. It is evident that many of these are reactive responses to dominant white depictions of black people, and others are primarily shaped by commercial strategies, but all are part of composing a new and complex imagery of blackness on the screen that is spearheaded by proactive film-makers attempting to give voice in both film and film music to the ambiguity that informs most black responses to life in America. Randall Kenan reinforces the idea that being a black American, on or off the screen, is a paradox that has yet to find full expression: 'the culture of being black … remains fascinating and elusive, multi-faceted and ever-changing, problematic and profound. Despite its Old World origins, black American culture, the language, the art, the music, the customs, ad nauseum, is a New World creation, as varied as the geography of the Americas, and belonging to all. It is a part of America.'[18]

The adversarial imagination

Phil Melling

War created the United States, argues Michael Sherry, and since the late 1930s the country has lived under its 'shadow'. War in general, and the Cold War in particular, 'defined much of the American imagination'. It was 'the blank screen on which unrelated concerns were often projected' and 'the paradigm in which Americans defined themselves, pursued change, or resisted it'. If 'the fear of war' 'penetrated' the American sense of self, then 'the achievements of war' 'anchored it', forcing the nation to 'routinely' declare war 'on all sorts of things' that did 'not involve physical combat at all'. The demands of national security created a 'compelling urgency'. This, and the need for 'action' against real or imagined enemies remains the imperative that continues to excite the popular imagination in the current age.[1]

For Harold Pinter, militarism in the United States has generated profound emotional dependencies:

> The U.S. was really turned on by the idea of Soviet aggression. It justified everything. It was there with the cornflakes every morning. It was part of the American way of life. You had an enemy and you loved him. You had a knife at his belly but you hugged him to you because he was your lover in death. You needed him.[2]

After 1989, the sense of frustration at the loss of a lover was palpable, agrees Ronald Steel. In the United States, 'the Cold War was not supposed to end at all', and when it did, it was a major disappointment. The demise of the Soviet empire in Europe happened too quickly, and left a residual frustration in the mind of an opponent who was used to equating 'the dissolution of the Soviet State'

with 'a catastrophic defeat in war'.[3] When Pinter asked the United
States in 1990 what it was 'going to do' now that it 'no longer' had
'a good fat enemy' to spend 'billions of dollars on', the White House
provided – it seemed – an immediate answer.[4] Saddam Hussein's
invasion of Kuwait, says Bruce Cummings, 'touched off an astonish-
ingly rapid intervention, as if the force had been pre-placed at the
ready'.[5]

   War with Saddam, nevertheless, was no substitute for a replay of
the Cold War, and the search for an errand behind which the nation
could unite remained a terminally elusive quest in the next decade.
In a society where the machinery of war had created vast, un-
expended energies, the desire for confrontation and climax proved
relentless. Hollywood, in particular, devoted itself to meeting the
challenge of the demon lover by exploring the need for military vigilance as well as providing a forum for its critique. It lamented the
loss of a Cold War culture while contextualising the Cold War theatre as a pathological site, one which attracted the manic energies of
those who searched for cathartic action in border operations.

   Hollywood managed to look both ways during the 1990s: it was
critical of yet complicitous with those who saw the Cold War conflict
as the *raison d'être* of a militarised state. It exposed the dependencies of those who found it difficult to free themselves of the ideological constraints of recent history. On other occasions, it appeared
to be the victim of constraint itself, and struggled to lift the veil of
'historical interpretation' which for over fifty years had 'imprisoned
the imagination and intelligence of the country'.[6] Ron Howard's
Apollo 13 (1995) is a nostalgic film which reacquaints its audience
with the sexual energy of the Cold War and the political willingness
to dramatise the conflict through phallic technologies and an iconography of penetrative tools. *Apollo 13* is also a reminder of the
value of accepting Cold War risk and the benefits that accrue from
competing with the Soviets on technological projects that are funded
on an epic scale. The race to the moon was not only a ritualised
affair, it was also, says Henry W. Cooper, a 'clear and direct military
contest'. NASA found its organisational model and inspiration for
the space race in the Manhattan Project of World War II, when
Roosevelt promoted aircraft production and authorised the building
of atomic bombs. NASA, adds Cooper, recruited scientists and engi-
neers 'as if it were building an army for war', and selected its astro-
nauts from the military.[7] It also drew heavily on the armed forces

work in rocketry and space technology, and expanded an aerospace industry that was essential to the armed forces in Vietnam.

Apollo 13 is a valedictory and a lament for a Cold War culture in which the United States was prepared to fund a $20 billion programme in order to win the hearts and minds of a global public. The Apollo programme is dramatised as visual theatre, unlike the secretive and sacrificial experiments conducted by the Soviet Union on its human and animal cargos. In its race to the moon, the United States balances the interests of lunar imperialism with a Marine-style ethic which protects elite US citizens from the ravages of nature. 'I'm not going to be responsible for leaving an American in space,' says the controller, who brings his astronauts back to earth unharmed, after their spacecraft malfunctions and the crew are faced with delinquent Communist children who populate the films and fiction of the 1990s. In Wolfgang Peterson's *Air Force One* (1997), the ultra-radicals of Kazakhstan crave the return of the Soviet empire as a global power. Unfortunately, they respect only the values of gangsters, a moral failing which shows up when they kidnap the President and his family on their return from a Summit meeting in Moscow. In Piers Paul Read's novel *A Patriot in Berlin*, set in the aftermath of the failed 1991 coup against Gorbachev, peace remains a chimera, and Eastern European freedoms are tenuous. Russia is a despotic power, and the maverick nationalists of Chechnya share the same derangement that we find in Stuart Baird's film *Executive Decision* (1996). Here, David Suchet becomes involved with Chechen terrorists who seek vengeance on America for its war on Islam.

Other film-makers who came in from the cold via Chechnya include Tony Scott with *Crimson Tide* (1995), a remake of Tom Clancy's novel *The Hunt for Red October*. *Crimson Tide* features a Chechen freedom fighter (with a resemblance to the ultra-nationalist Vladimir Zhironovsky) who takes control of a Russian submarine which is intercepted by the USS *Alabama*. In anticipation of his own pre-emptive strike, the US commander (Gene Hackman) tells his crew that 'the peace' is over, and that the United States is 'back in business', thereby signalling to them his moral right to remain distrustful of ex-Communists. When the nationalist leader threatens nuclear war, the commander is prepared to accommodate him. The gung-ho style conflicts with that of his second-in-command (Denzel Washington), who refuses to carry out his orders, thereby saving the world from mutually assured destruction. The film is reluctant to apportion blame and, despite a smug pro-American message, remains ambiguous on the question of whether Hackman has behaved irresponsibly, suggesting America's right to launch a nuclear attack in circumstances which safeguard the country's national security interests. Scott's message to his audience, says Mark Lawson, seems to be that nuclear films make more plausible viewing when those who control Soviet technologies are 'insecure'. The 'doomsday' narrative becomes more 'plausible' in a world where small nations are seeking to construct or acquire the bomb 'than was the case during the Cold War when checks and balances were in place'.[8]

Fear of the Soviet nuclear fleet and the continuing threat of nuclear emission began with the explosion at Chernobyl on 26 April 1986. Chernobyl seemed to demonstrate that Communism was not only in the process of self-destruction, but posed a threat that was also indiscriminate and just as likely to contaminate Western countries – land, livestock and water supplies – as those in the East. The inability to control the nuclear process within the damaged reactor unit at Chernobyl led to a widespread anxiety that other sources of combustible energy would soon be released, the impact of which would be felt beyond the borders of Belarus and the Ukraine. In 1995, the United Nations Secretary-General revealed that the humanitarian problems sparked by Chernobyl were still growing, and that the healthcare system could not cope – in 1990 80 per cent of rural hospitals and polyclinics still had no hot water. The report also indicated that no systematic monitoring had occurred of the army of Soviet 'liquidators' – almost 200,000 strong – each of whom suffered ninety seconds of intense radiation inside the hulk of the Chernobyl Number 4 reactor as they attempted to shut it down. The 'liquidators' had dispersed; many were untraceable, leaving behind a dramatic source of anecdotal evidence and high levels of morbidity, leukaemia and thyroid cancer.[9]

In a world that had lost its Cold War borders, the memory of the 'liquidators' entered the post-Cold War imagination of the West. It was as if Chernobyl had created a lost generation of Soviet citizens, an army of refugees who were wandering the planet and carrying within them an incurable sickness. They bring to mind the paintings of Cornelia Hesse-Honnegar and the mutant insects of Chernobyl that metamorphose and roam the earth with the original spores of the reactor unit inside their body. The wandering of plant 'liquidators' whose illnesses could not be monitored gave rise to other fears:

the toxic menace posed by rogue or degenerate populations when the borders that contain them are breached and badly neglected. The demolition of the Berlin Wall and the removal of East–West border controls only heightened the fear among America's right-wing communities that the nation was at risk from migrant hordes desperate to travel from the Third World to the First. The disasters at Chernobyl and Bhopal and the Exxon oil spill, coupled with an increase in viral epidemic and cross-border infection, gave the age a 'deeper' and 'darker' meaning, says Marina Benjamin.[10]

John McTiernan's *Die Hard with a Vengeance* (1995) confronts the problem of what to do with the shattered political energies that Communism left behind, and the deranged idealism of the newly liberated who find themselves without a job. A central scene shows insect-like, gas-masked bank robbers marching through the underground rubble of America's National Reserve, coolly stealing the country's wealth while its heroes, Bruce Willis and Samuel Jackson, career around pointlessly up above. The aliens burrowing into America's heart are disillusioned ex-soldiers from East Germany, made jobless by the Cold War's end, who have come to America in search of easy pickings.

In *Die Hard with a Vengeance*, the infiltration of America by Eastern Europeans is less specific than it generally is in orthodox Cold War films. In John Milius's *Red Dawn* (1984), for example, the Soviet force that invades America poses a coherent threat to American national security interests. Here, 'the mood of encirclement' and the 'anxieties about US weakness', says Stephen Prince, are largely ideological.[11] In Joseph Zito's *Invasion USA* (1985), however, a subtle change has begun to take place, and we sense the arrival of a new phenomenon: the ideological giving way to the multicultural, and the political threat beginning to merge with the racially plural. In *Invasion USA*, an army of thugs led by a renegade Soviet officer spread terror throughout the USA until they are successfully dispatched by military units who work alongside a solitary cowboy (Chuck Norris) with backwoods manners. Cold War invasion anticipates Third World invasion. Rostov, the leader of the force, is Russian, but his gang is an anonymous collective consisting of black, Oriental and Latino gangsters. Their motive is random violence – they blow up churches, shopping malls, families at home, and unleash anarchy in the hope that the rule of law will collapse and the government will fall into enemy hands. Made at a time when boatloads of Cuban and Haitian refugees were fleeing to the United States, *Invasion USA* played upon feelings of anxiety among indigenous communities, and affirmed the need for political vigilance on America's southern borders. What makes it a 1980s film, however – and an endorsement of Reagan's presidency – is that it 'works to certify the validity of the security apparatus: police, army, FBI, CIA, those groups which work together to stop Rostov and which form the infrastructure of a militarized Cold War state'.[12]

The idea that American borders can be policed by the institutions of local and national security, and that politicians with no experience of military life can properly conduct security operations, is not something one readily associates with popular culture of the 1990s. In the later period, which sees less overt and specific impact from military leaders, struggles for power often provoke multicultural conflict and the need to address a variety of sensitivities, which in turn necessitates far more covert strategies of interference and control.

In *Executive Decision* (1996), the threat of invasion is indiscriminate and largely unflattering to political elites in Washington. At the heart of the film lies the problem of racial degeneracy and the discontent which accompanies the arrival in America of those groups whose spiritual and ethnic traditions lie outside the West. In *Executive Decision*, Islamic radicals want to repeat the success of 1993, when they attacked the World Trade Centre in New York with a car bomb. To accomplish this task they form a suicide pact in order to deliver 'the true vengeance of Islam into the belly of the infidel'. They hijack a passenger-carrying 747, fill it with enough explosive to wipe out the Eastern seaboard, then prime it to detonate on arrival in Washington. Special forces units are sent to intercept and enter the plane in mid-flight. The hijackers are assassinated, the rescue mission is accomplished, and the bomb is defused with a display of technical bravura of which even the scientists working on Apollo 13 would have been proud. On the surface, the executive branch of government remains in control of the rescue operation. Underneath, the politicians are little more than bystanders. Their strategy of wait-and-see is unimaginative, and calculated on the basis of public approval ratings. Their static trade-offs contrast vividly with the maverick energies of a freelance engineer and a secret-service para-military unit whose self-reliance and inventiveness save the plane and the nation from devastation. The film suggests that the nation's gratitude can be claimed less easily by those who pull the political strings

– the fatuous worthies who claim the credit for rescue missions – than those who work behind the scenes and live on the margins of political tolerance in military environments. In the light of the events of September 11 the film has taken on new relevance. The profound effects of a real attack have rendered the outcomes of the film super-ficial at best, but nevertheless such a story does draw attention to the very real and palpable difficulties of maintaining a clear 'political' agenda in the face of events and issues which resist this clarity. *Executive Decision* exposes political insecurity and hypocrisy, and sug-gests that heroic endeavour can thwart 'the other' and its implied ideological unacceptability. Real life has suggested that this may not be possible, and that heroic endeavour may only be visible and know-able in those who try to recover an already irredeemable situation. The easy solutions offered by Hollywood only reveal further the fundamental lack of understanding in addressing such issues, and the deep-rooted fears that are seemingly appeased by simple adven-ture narratives, but horribly exposed by irresolvable real world events.

If *Executive Decision* is cynical of those who aspire to high office – the murdered presidential candidate, Senator Mavros, is the victim of his own conceit – Roland Emmerich's *Independence Day* (1996) is a savage parody of those who hold it. In *Independence Day*, the President (Bill Pullman) is a Gulf War veteran and a family man who leads from the front. As a fighter pilot, he is capable of taking de-cisive action, yet he is willing to share the limelight with farm boys and Vietnam veterans and, when the safety of the world is at risk, to give a redneck from the sticks (Randy Quaid) the chance to act as saviour of the planet. The buffoonery of the film is unapologetic, and in a way its runaway success reveals a genuine sadness in the country. Behind the failure of political will in military theatres like Bosnia and Rwanda – and perhaps because of it – lies a desperate need for a heroic presidential style: a Chief Executive who is not bedevilled by right-wing attacks on his moral authority, fitness for office or political impotence in moments of crisis. The President in *Independence Day* leads his nation in combat against the alien in-vaders of outer space. His is a Shakespearian gesture, an attempt to re-masculinise the American male by investing the presidency with the charisma and persona of Henry V. Unlike Bill Clinton, the Presi-dent is a war veteran 'with balls' behind whom the nation can rally. He gives the orders and fights the enemy with any means at his disposal (a clear reversal of what politicians did to the military in

Vietnam), but only because he has worked in the military. His unilateralism in launching an attack is also important, since it dispenses with the need for UN mandates and Security Council resolutions.

In the 1990s, Hollywood performed a search-and-rescue mission on the presidency, but only in ways that could be justified militarily. Jonathan Freedland may be correct in arguing that *Independence Day* and *Air Force One* can be read as 'a coded cry of panic'[13] over the illegal migrants heading for America's southern border, but only because the executive in Washington appears oblivious to the threat of trespass. These films are a wake-up call to politicians. They show us the disparity between what an invented president can do (in defence of the nation) and what a real president, like Bill Clinton, is prepared to do in order to retain political power. Where Clinton is accused of a failure of political will in war zones like Somalia, or the US–Mexican border, in action movies like *Air Force One*, he is a Vietnam veteran who launches his own paramilitary crusade against Communist subversives and terrorist attackers.

In *Air Force One*, heroic leadership skills are integral to the presidency, and territorial sovereignties are defended single-handed. In Costa Gavras's *Betrayed* (1988), however, the legacy of Vietnam has a much more complex effect on the veteran, transforming him into a psychopathic killer who fights to defend the agrarian heartland against foreign invasion. *Betrayed* strips away the pretence of a wish-fulfilment presidency in order to expose the pathological addictions of those who defend America's borders. As a political thriller, *Betrayed* focuses on the rise of agrarian resistance movements in the United States and, in particular, the emergence of the Posse Comitatus, a radically decentralised vigilante movement dedicated to protecting the interests of farmers threatened with foreclosure. In *Betrayed*, America's family farms are in crisis and, on the eve of the New World Order, the government appears to have lost interest in their survival. The frustration felt by farmers when their self-sufficiency is undermined and their farm income drops below subsistence level places an intolerable strain on a community which, for generations, has equated hard work with stability. Deprived of self-respect and legitimate economic aspiration, the farmer turns to a politics of vendetta replete with all the racist contradictions of small-town America. In the farmers' support for the Posse Comitatus, the film provides a cogent explanation as to why the banks are foreclosing on farms. Jews incapable of farming, it is argued, have managed to control the world's monetary system in order to control the global food supply.

Betrayed, however, is more than a populist expression of anti-Semitism. From the outset, the film presents us with a group of likeable Illinois farmers who have fallen on hard times, and are forced to create a self-help militia in an attempt to identify the reason for economic decline. The local militia operates as an individual cell in a larger, underground network. In order to preserve its anonymity, this resistance network meets once a year at a summer camp. Here it professes a racist creed, practises military drill, trades weapons, and promotes ideas on revolution and violence.

This quasi-fascist philosophy is seemingly confirmed at the outset when Sam Kraus, a Jewish talk-show host in Chicago, is gunned down and murdered for attacking a right-wing fundamentalist on a phone-in. Other executions follow, such as that of a black youth who is kidnapped in Chicago and taken to the country, where he is set loose and then hunted with dogs. The need for vigilantism is underwritten by an Old Testament God whose word is interpreted by a righteous ministry in the cornbelt. In his sermons, the Reverend Russell Johnson tells his congregation that they are descended from the Lost Tribes of Israel, and must protect themselves from the 'mud people': the immigrants and Jews, who are descended from Cain. Pulpit paranoia is superficially popular, especially with men like Shorty who, through no fault of his own, lost a farm to the bank and a son to Vietnam. Underneath the racist rhetoric, however, the real enemy of the farmer is not Vietnam. It is a government which has been corrupted by overseas influence, and is unresponsive to the needs of an agrarian hinterland. The xenophobia of the community is inconsistent, and its racist persona is full of discrepancies. The legacy of Vietnam is also a contradiction. The militia leader, Gary Simmons, had a distinguished career in Vietnam, but has returned home sympathetic to many of the strategies employed by rural guerrilla movements. As a Christian patriot, Simmons vilifies Communists and Jews but, as a point man in the war, has considerable respect for the military discipline and moral character of the Vietnamese. At camp, Simmons finds the neo-Nazi paramilitaries in their fascist uniforms little better than make-up artists, and despises their posturing and childish theatricality. Like the Vietnamese, Simmons is fighting to defend his land against the forces of corporate capitalism. As a patriot, he is determined to preserve the jobs, the products, the industries and the living standards of the American working man, many of which are being swallowed up, as he puts it, by Arab tycoons with easy money from places like 'Abu Dhabi'. As a result, Simmons carries with him a considerable empathy for the NVA grunts and Vietcong guerrillas, and he resists any attempt by adolescent fascists to hijack the disciplines and military proficiencies that are earned in battle.

In *Betrayed*, patriotic fantasies combine with fears of sociocultural and economic trespass in a community that feels alienated by a government that is unduly sympathetic to the claims of immigrants, the aspirations of foreigners, and multicultural agendas. *Betrayed*, says Andrew Sullivan, shows how, since the late 1980s, a vocabulary of violence and 'incendiary' talk has been directed at the complacency of the federal government and its inability to stop illegal immigration by Asians, Africans and Central Americans.[14] Right-wing nationalists have loaded their speeches with 'fighting words', says Sullivan, arguing the need to bear arms against trespassers. The fiction that the United States is 'an occupied country', adds Christopher Hitchens, has been based on a spurious and dangerous claim which justifies the need for witch-hunts against foreigners.[15]

Behind the fear of foreigners lies a wider fear of mass conspiracy, one articulated by Linda Thompson, lawyer and right-wing chair of the American Justice Federation in Indianapolis. Thompson believes that Americans are 'under siege' from their own government; as proof of this she distributes a video to warn her members that the government is actively plotting to strip the people of their freedom, perhaps even to kill some of its own citizens. To achieve this, she claims, the government is colluding with the United Nations to establish the 'one-world' New World Order. Thompson argues that the Clinton administration [planned] to import 100,000 Russian and Chinese troops, under United Nations control, to disarm ordinary American citizens, and that the Crips and Bloods, the Los Angeles-based Hispanic and black street gangs, are currently being recruited and trained for the same purpose. In the order to implement this strategy, black helicopters scan the country as part of a vanguard of military units, while underground prisons have been built and highway signs have special 'troop transport' markings in secret code.[16]

In the front-line communities of the United States – especially those on the US–Mexican border – rural communities see themselves as being in a 'war zone', with little in the way of self-protection.[17]

'That border between the US and Mexico is like a war. Remember, remember that,' Don Ramón, the voice of experience in Gregory Nava's film *El Norte* (1983), tells the protagonist Enrique. The border is patrolled by officials, many of whom have experience of war zones like Vietnam. For Joseph Wambaugh, the border patrol agents see themselves as soldiers and the immigrants as 'armies'.[18] Border patrol agents are difficult to control, says William Langewiesche, and are the most 'unsupervised and undisciplined law-enforcement agency in the country. They think they are above the law,' he continues. 'They think they can get away with anything.' Their tactics of search and destroy are more suitable to 'combat' zones, and fabricate a narrative that re-mythologises a Cold War psychosis. Vietnam prevails as a metaphor in the narration of the border. According to Wambaugh, Chicano activists from San Diego call the border 'the Vietnam of the Southwest'. The border patrol use infrared scopes; the agents drive Broncos. An immigration official, who calls his work a civilian version of Vietnam, complains to Langewiesche that this makes it the second losing war he has fought.

For America's right-wing conservatives in the 1990s, vigilante and military strategies were the methods required to prevent the infiltration of indigenous communities by plague-ridden migrants. For Pat Buchanan and Pat Robertson, the border is a site of degeneracy, and without its closure the country risks being tainted by what Martin Wollacott refers to as the new combinations of 'intimacy' that occur when 'societies' are 'penetrated by each other'.[19] In *The Turning Tide* (1993), the evangelical fundamentalist Pat Robertson prophesies that plague and virus will soon enter the United States as a result of the movement of human and animal populations in border states like New Mexico. The virus-carrying rodents that cross the Mexican border, he argues, remind us of the black rats that travelled from Asia into Europe during the fourteenth century and carried infected fleas as a result of poverty, overcrowding and poor sanitation.

On the Mexican border, the accompanying movement of Latino populations from regions affected by atmospheric warming, widespread pollution, environmental destruction, war, AIDS and famine has created the fear of a refugee crisis and a swirling broth of cross-border infections. In the 1996 presidential election Pat Buchanan, the Republican winner of the New Hampshire Primary, advocated a five-year moratorium on legal immigration and the construction of a security fence along a stretch of the US–Mexican border to halt the transmission of viruses.

In 'hot' zones like the border,[20] mainstream politicians have been much slower to realise the dangers posed by infectious diseases and pathogens. Peter Hutchings describes how, in March 1998, representatives of several United States federal agencies met to discuss an imaginary scenario involving the release of deadly virus along the Mexican border. At the same time, says Hutchings, President Clinton was waking up to the menace of biological warfare after reading Richard Preston's *The Cobra Event* (1998). The government's relatively late discovery of the political implications of cross-border movement and the spread of infectious disease only served to fuel the paranoia of right-wing extremists.

For those who are committed to defending American borders, like Colonel McClintock in Wolfgang Petersen's film *Outbreak* (1995), the violation of bodily sites is beyond the control of political elites in the nation's capital. McClintock (Donald Sutherland) has spent too long in the military, and believes that the public is in need of the moral and physical discipline which only military regimes can impose on lax societies. The arrival in the USA of a monkey infected with the Motabo virus in Zaïre (another war zone) provides him with an opportunity to quarantine the local population when it escapes into the woods outside San Francisco. McClintock uses a quasi-containment strategy to control and traumatise the civilian population. Reluctant to abandon the psychosis of the Cold War years, he becomes obsessed with the 'casualties of war', the public who are victims of Third World infection, together with a belief that the military are 'the immune system of the body politic', and have the ability to control the crisis.[21]

McClintock's militarised policies of enclosure and incarceration are partly explained by what happened on the west coast of the United States as a result of the bombing of Pearl Harbor on 7 December 1941. The subsequent decision to round up over 100,000 Japanese Americans (two-thirds of them American-born citizens) was taken on the basis that they were enemies of the state, despite overwhelming evidence to the contrary. Alan Parker's film *Come See the Paradise* (1990) shows how the creation of internment camps dislocated the Japanese-American community socially and psychologically. In David Guterson's *Snow Falling on Cedars* (1994), political retaliation is governed by economic concerns – fears of capital accumulation and financial independence by the Japanese community in the Pacific Northwest – and a populist paranoia that views Third World societies as a threat to public health.

McClintock's real problem is that, like so many veterans of the Vietnam and Gulf wars, he is living in an age where the opportunities for direct action are fast receding, and the military disciplines of Cold War theatres have little immediate relevance to civilian life. In Quentin Tarantino's *Pulp Fiction* (1994) the veteran's status in American life is defined by the work of crime syndicates, and the difficulty of living in cities that are being invaded by gangs and migrants from Third World communities.

In *Pulp Fiction*, America's Third World border shifts to the urban hinterland of Los Angeles, a place where traditional gangster enclaves are just as vulnerable to alien attack as the frontier communities of the old Southwest. No one in the city is exempt from the effects of migration. Even criminal enclaves are obliged to protect themselves, says Claire Sterling, from unauthorised and indiscriminate entry by the 'brash' and 'greedy'[22] – especially in California, where the ethnic groups have moved in, 'spreading fear'. They bring with them a memory which ranges from ethnic cleansing to military dictatorship, from revolution to civil strife. According to James Willwerth:

> In the bizarre and bloody world of Southern California gang life, armed and alienated children are guerilla warriors. Cambodian gangs battling Hispanic gangs is but the newest infection. I. R. A. Reiner, district attorney for Los Angeles County (pop. 8,776,000), estimates that 130,000 gang members operate in his jurisdiction alone. They range from subteen 'peewees' to as many as 13,000 hard-core killers. Last year in the county (1990) the gangs accounted for 18,059 violent felonies and 690 deaths.

In Los Angeles, Willwerth continues, Cambodian and Hispanic gangs are among the most assertive in defending and extending their territory: 'Many Cambodian gang members became hardened to violence during their escape from the killing fields of Southeast Asia. Many families literally walked out of Cambodia knowing, even as children, that if they didn't keep up with the adults, they'd be lost forever.'[23]

In *Pulp Fiction*, the threat from an internal and external Third World turns out to be real when a pair of 'hillbilly psychopaths', Zed and Maynard, succeed in penetrating the defences of Marsellus Wallace, a gang leader who momentarily wanders off base. Reno Smith's fears of bodily weakening and contamination as a result of trespass, in John Sturges' *Bad Day at Black Rock* (1955), are now realised. Cultural dispersal gives way to sexual trespass and the threat of virus. Forgetting to protect his back, Marsellus chases a gang member who has double-crossed him. Although 'hot on his ass', Marsellus falls victim to rectal entry and is sodomised in a pawn-shop. In a random and indiscriminate attack on his sexuality, Marsellus finds himself mounted in the 'dungeon' of a 'Mason–Dixon' store.[24]

In *Pulp Fiction* the threat to the community from aliens with fetishes and sodomites who wander ever more widely is explicit. Marsellus is taken below the belt and below the border. The external world in the 1990s is a threat to everyone's security, both personal and public. As Marita Sturken argues: 'The rigid bodily boundaries of the immune system … are directly related [to our] depiction of the external world as inherently hostile.' In the social life of *Pulp Fiction* 'there is no room for … transgression' and 'foreignness is portrayed as threatening to the viability and wholeness of the body'.[25]

Marsellus does everything in his power to minimise the risk of attack. In his raw bid for power, he understands the role of strong leadership. A theatrically compelling – almost priestly – individual, he redeems the cult of the strong man at a time of weak leadership in the United States. He is the man of action the country yearns for in an era when presidential politics has conspicuously failed to pro-vide effective direction in overseas theatres. He also shows that cor-porate strategies among black entrepreneurs are alive and well on the nation's streets, and that power is translated most effectively through military initiatives. As a black godfather, Marsellus has an intuitive knowledge of the importance of war iconography in the establish-ment of crime syndicates. He protects his market share with a mili-tary style that relies heavily on the use of dress codes – the business suit as military uniform – search-and-destroy missions, synchronised killing, 'mopping up' operations in troublesome environments, and a war rhetoric which emphasises the importance of errand and the need to subjugate the other with biblical Scripture. (The text memo-rised from Ezekiel 25: 17 is an example of how Marsellus applies a righteous errand to a criminal task.) Where the Roman warrior Marcellus checked the progress of Hannibal in the Second Punic

War, Marsellus Wallace conducts his operations in the field with
military precision and without bureaucratic interference from corrupt law-enforcement agencies. At a time when – as Jonathan
Freedland puts it – 'men feel embattled'[26] in the United States,
Marsellus Wallace is 'everybody's boss', an urban warlord whose
name 'sounds between a gangster and a king'.[27]

Where modern society is – as Norman Mailer tells us in *The
Naked and the Dead* – 'largely a continuation of the army by other
means',[28] gangsters must demonstrate their suitability as theorists
and tacticians of violence. They must also distinguish themselves
from a mainstream political leadership whose response to military
problems in the post-Cold War era has been variously criticised as
fumbling and ineffectual. (Such was the nation's despair over the
quality of leadership, especially during the first Clinton administration, that it even contemplated the prospect of electing Colin
Powell to the presidency.) In Los Angeles, Marsellus Wallace must
communicate his understanding of war and, at the same time, demonstrate what it takes to be a war leader who can cope with the
battle-hardened style and reputation for violence that Asian and
Hispanic gangs have acquired. Clarity of purpose is essential; so too
is the ability to speak in a language ordinary people can understand
– a language not of prevarication (the charge frequently lodged
against President Clinton during the Bosnian crisis) but of populist
decisiveness.

Pulp Fiction is a Cold War story of the world as a dangerous
place. It is also an AIDS story. Los Angeles is a life-threatening
environment where vulnerable communities rely heavily on a powerful system of defence. Immune systems are established like military
organisations, since bodies and territories are under constant siege
from voracious adversaries. Besieged by an army of potential enemies,
Marsellus operates his own system of protection to mimic that of the
human body, and 'enlists a remarkably complex corps of internal
bodyguards to battle the invaders'. His wish is that they 'cleanse' his
organisation 'of foreign particles', rid it of 'infectious micro-
organisms', and 'weed tissue of renegade cancer cells'.[29] In order to
accomplish this, Marsellus offers opportunities for terminal action
to the families of veterans such as Butch Coolidge and soldiers of
fortune like Jules Winnfield (who may well be a Vietnam veteran).
The offer is accepted at a time when the nation's veterans are struggling to improve their self-esteem economically, and facing com-

petition in crime syndicates from Third World immigrants. Through-out *Pulp Fiction,* Jules behaves like a soldier on active duty, as if he is on patrol or walking point for his commander, Marsellus Wallace. Jules is a cleansing agent, ridding the body of its social impurities. Where Vincent Vega, his associate, mumbles and shuffles and has sloppy manners, Jules is clean, athletic and outspoken. He has an erect gait, and executes his missions with impeccable precision. He insists that his watch is synchronised before an attack, and that an action is commenced exactly 'on time'. When The Wolf gives 'orders', Jules obeys and goes to work on 'brain detail'.[30] Vincent, who is careless and a drug addict, cannot accept the imposed discipline and answers back, delaying the mission.

One of Jules's main targets is a group of college kids who have developed bad habits and bad manners, including a 'preppy-looking type', a black youth and a 'surfer with a "flock of seagulls haircut"'. Each of the 'seagulls', bar one, is killed. Marvin, who is black, survives (although he dies accidentally in a later scene). His survival is important. He must carry the memory of the scene with him, and narrate to his brothers the style in which the killing has occurred.[31] What Marvin witnesses is a hit man who is able to blow his oppo-nents away with casual ferocity, as well as a storyteller who handles the event with controlled power and traumatises his opponents into silence.

The fusion of avenging angel and aficionado of popular culture invokes a tradition of gallows humour. Jules Winnfield manipulates this discourse for reasons that are not self-serving and wilfully deter-mined, but in order to demonstrate authority and claims to power. Jules involves us in a charade. He pretends to distract us from the errand Marsellus has assigned to him by discussing the merits of the Big Kahnua Burger that Brett, his victim, is eating for breakfast. The breakfast is the food of a condemned man, and the boy's last supper. The distraction is a ploy. The travel trivia we are given on French and American popular culture give way to a Scripture lesson and a read-ing from Ezekiel. In a country where Marsellus is 'king', Jules becomes the state prosecutor who hides his true identity behind the fake bonhomie of the gourmet gangster. That identity is revealed the moment Vincent Vega, Jules's partner, opens a briefcase containing the stolen goods Marsellus is after. Jules switches his attention from food to politics. At that moment he adopts the persona of grand inquisitor or, more specifically, security agent, 'interrogator' and border policeman. He asks Brett: 'What country you from!', and Brett is described as 'petrified' and confused. Jules then asks him: '"What" ain't no country I know! Do they speak English in "What"?'[32] These are the questions one might normally ask an illegal immigrant, not, one suspects, a white college boy. The questions are for public consumption, and meant to be repeated elsewhere (by Marvin) to those – less literate members of society – who are not present at the meeting, but are likely to hear about it.

Jules does two things here. First, he targets the gangland criminal as an illegal immigrant. He signifies his interest not merely in the problem of immigration but in the covert practices of non-English-speaking immigrants, the boat people who, as Asians and Hispanics, are the principal rivals of Marsellus Wallace. Jules, in other words, conveys his hostility to immigrant America through a coded piece of populist paranoia, and exploits the middle-class fear of illegal immigration in order to give the impression that he, too, is troubled by it. Secondly, Jules signifies his disdain for those who lack his status in society and his command of English. A guardian of the nation's borders, Jules wishes to show us that he has a duty of care to protect America from the very foreigners of whom America's conservatives are fearful in the New World Order. Narrative authority is important. Before Jules shoots, he tells a story, illustrating that he is a scholar of sorts who knows the Bible and understands the narrative purpose of the canon. There is something of the saviour as sociopath here, the murderous poseur as border policeman. Jules assembles his victims like a black Winthrop. Before he sends them forth to meet their Maker, he explains the mistakes that have caused their undoing. His speech inverts Winthrop's sermon on board the *Arbella*. The boys are told they have not fulfilled their compelling commission from God, and have succumbed, instead, to the sloth and indolence of an urban wilderness.

Jules Winnfield shares the same misgivings as the conservative Right in his assault on America's youth and his biblical complaint about its lack of discipline, moral character and speech patterns. In the same year as *Pulp Fiction* appeared, another assault was launched on the moral laxness of Clinton's America and the soft-centred liberalism which the Clinton administration appeared to uphold. Robert Zemeckis's *Forrest Gump* was the biggest cinema hit of 1994, and struck the nerve of right-wing conservatism dead on. As a homage to patriotism, capitalism and the family, it stressed the extent to which Americans were prepared to entrust moral authority not to a politician but to a Vietnam veteran, one who opposed drugs, invested wisely, took regular exercise and wore his country's uniform with pride.

Behind the success of *Forrest Gump* lay the fear of promiscuity and the spread of AIDS – the scourge of Forrest Gump's sweetheart, who is punished for taking drugs and hanging out with anti-Vietnam types. Her death in the film marks the symbolic end of the counter-culture movement of the 1960s – a period of perceived waywardness, profligacy and laxness – and the triumph of moral conservatism. The message mirrors the work of Christian fundamentalists who, throughout the 1990s, sought to retrieve the nation from the slough of moral despond into which the Clinton presidency had fallen, and the financial scandals and sexual peccadilloes that dogged the White House. For the New Right, the Clinton administration was a repository for what Newt Gingrich has called 'the nihilistic hedonism of the counter culture'.[33] For Gingrich, its trademarks were secrecy and promiscuity, and the kind of treachery which the Right associates with the AIDS virus. Those who knowingly carry HIV and infect their partners are no different from the alien menace in Roger Donaldson's *Species* (1995), a film in which a human hybrid gives in to her genetically programmed instincts to maim and kill her lovers.

In Pat Robertson's *The Turning Tide*, there are fifteen indexed references to homosexuality, each of which refers to its degrading and debilitating influence, from the politicised world of radical multi-culturalism to the cloistered corridors of the US navy, where homosexual, radical elements are trying to gain public recognition for covert activities. In the right-wing imagination, HIV 'hides in order to survive', and so do homosexuals. They, like the viruses they carry, are regarded by Jesse Helms and Pat Robertson as 'strategic and cunning' and 'envious', their body a post-ideological site where the new Cold War is acted out. In the adversarial world of the HIV virus, 'the immune system' is 'a nation under siege, and HIV … a Cold War spy, terrorist, or guerilla fighter', who is striving to over-run the nation's borders. HIV becomes fascinating, says Marita Sturken, because it is 'invisible to the naked eye', and the desire to visualise the virus is powerful. 'Metaphors of sight permeate descriptions of the immune system' – which must recognise intruders – in order to understand them – but 'popular accounts describe HIV as hiding in cells, concealing itself from sight and disguising itself to avoid detection'. HIV is menacing 'primarily because of its ability to hide from view', to become inextricably part of the personality of the victim, who may not even know he is infected, or may go under-cover to avoid detection.[34] The AIDS virus 'is so adept', agrees Paula Treichler, that 'we might even acknowledge our own historical mo-ment more specifically' by giving it 'a postmodern identity: a terror-ist's terrorist, an Abu Nidal of viruses'.

The religious Right had a profound effect in shaping the Ameri-can political and cultural landscape when the fear of AIDS was at its greatest in the early 1990s. During that period, Hollywood was un-willing to remove the threat of AIDS as a terrorist or Cold War virus. On the contrary, AIDS appears to have been read by Holly-wood as an illness which targets those who allow their bodies to be violated by alien presences, and knowingly expose themselves through dangerous or 'perverse lifestyles'. Before *Philadelphia* (1993), Hollywood found it difficult to make the case for AIDS by its si-lence, and allowed the illness to be seen as a metaphor of social breakdown. AIDS had 'the potential to kill America'. As the initia-tor of breakdown in American life, it had the capacity to destroy an individual, as well as 'the health care structure, the family, the con-tinuity of generations' – a frequent complaint of Pat Robertson and Jesse Helms.[35]

The first mainstream Hollywood film to deal with the subject of AIDS – and one of the few to feature gay characters in a serious dramatic context – was Jonathan Demme's *Philadelphia*, which came out in 1993. *Longtime Companion* (1990) was produced for television when no studio would touch it; Bill Sherwood's *Parting Glances* (1986) and Greg Arakis's *The Living End* (1992) were made inde-pendently. Before 1990, Hollywood reduced homosexuals to cliché, and consistently refused to educate an audience whose thinking about AIDS and gay life had been shaped by notions of perversion and Divine retribution. The industry's refusal to acknowledge its own decimation – many of its actors, writers, publicists and studio execu-tives had been mown down by AIDS – seemed like a kind of denial, a deliberate attempt to marginalise its own. As Marita Sturken says: 'Hollywood's inability to address AIDS as a primary issue in the 1980s and 1990s powerfully demonstrates the homophobia that ex-ists in an industry in which, as Rock Hudson's life bears witness, celebrities cannot come out of the closet without tarnishing their image.'[36] Even *Philadelphia* was tentative in its treatment of gay life, and featured only one brief kiss between Tom Hanks and his lover (Antonio Banderas). The audience learned little of the nature of the homosexual community, and instead witnessed a courtroom drama and a story about homophobia.

Hollywood has been less willing to extend the same consideration to the victims of HIV as it has to those contaminated by extra-terrestrial viruses. Alien abduction narratives largely externalise the threat to human societies. They combine sexual and body trespass with metaphors of illegal migration, and take the Cold War invasion narrative to a sci-fi dénouement in blood fetishism and genetic hybridity. Tales of abduction and bodily takeover – James Cameron's *Aliens* (1986) or David Fincher's *Alien³* (1992), for example – loop back to Hollywood's fear of the multicultural, and, at a time of Third World migration, can best be understood – as Annalee Newitz has argued – as 'cautionary racial fables'.[37] In *Men in Black* (1997), the link between aliens and non-citizens has an ethnic configuration when a Mexican who is caught sneaking into the USA in a truck is really an alien from outer space. In David Twohy's *The Arrival* (1996), the association between aliens and Latino immigrants is developed less satirically. The aliens disguised as Mexicans who are employed in American research corporations also work in a plant south of the border that is committed to destroying the environment by making the planet hotter. The idea that the United States is the twin victim of ultraviolet rays from the sun and a secret force of Latino invaders refers us back to earlier fears of degradation and the migrant threat to the American heartland in post-Cold War conspiracy narratives. *The Arrival*, says Jodi Dean, 'channels anxieties around security, otherness, and immigration into a story of extraterrestrial invasion. The audience can express its squeamishness about aliens without experiencing guilt over racism or political incorrectness.'[38]

Whichever way we read them, alien invasion narratives are largely hysterical devices which clearly speak to our needs and fears in the early twenty-first century. In a still-insecure world, malign plots and conspiracies externalise our fear of invasion and are couched in militarist terms which terminate in scenes of Cold War contagion. Films which target aliens and cover-up tend to foment, says Elaine Showalter, 'an atmosphere of conspiracy and suspicion and prevent us from claiming our full humanity as free and responsible beings'. They distract us 'from the real problems and crises of modern society', and undermine a respect for evidence and truth.[39]

Notes

Introduction

1 Susan Mackey-Kallis, *Oliver Stone's America* (Boulder, CO and Oxford: Westview Press, 1996), p. 2.
2 Stephen Powers, David Rothman and Stanley Rothman, *Hollywood's America: Social and Political Themes in Motion Pictures* (Boulder, CO and Oxford: Westview Press, 1996).
3 Martin Barker, *From Antz to Titanic: Reinventing Film Analysis* (London and Sterling: Pluto Press, 2000), pp. 177–8.
4 Interview with the author, June 1988.
5 John Patterson, 'Bruckheimer Goes to War', *Guardian Review* (27 October 2000), pp. 2–4.
6 Powers, Rothman and Rothman *Hollywood's America*, p. 246.
7 Michael Medved, *Hollywood vs America: Popular Culture and the War on Traditional Values* (New York: HarperCollins, 1992).

American cinema, political criticism and pragmatism

1 Amy Taubin, 'So Good it Hurts', *Sight and Sound*, vol. 9, issue 11 (November 1999), p. 18.
2 Susan Jeffords, 'Can Masculinity be Terminated?', in Steven Cohen and Ina Rae Hark (eds), *Screening the Male* (London: Routledge, 1993), p. 25.
3 Ina Rae Hark, 'Animals or Romans', in *ibid.*, p. 153.
4 Jeffords, 'Can Masculinity be Terminated?', p. 245. For an account of the ways in which concepts of power and violence are equated with or articulated through images of nationhood and masculinity in American cinema, especially in the figure of the (national) hero, see Richard Slotkin, *Regeneration through Violence* (Middletown, CT: Weslyan University Press, 1973); Susan Jeffords, *The Remasculinization of America* (Bloomington: Indiana University Press, 1989); and Robert

Burgoyne, 'National Identity, Gender Identity, and the "Rescue Fantasy" in *Born on the Fourth of July*', *Screen*, vol. 35, no. 3 (Autumn, 1994), pp. 34–48.

5 Amy Taubin notes in relation to *Fight Club* that the film's transgressive possibilities radiate from the fact that it puts 'a brain on the screen as an exhibit – especially when the exhibit is connected to the loss of self, in particular the loss of the masculine self'. It seems to me that it is not the loss of masculinity *per se* that is of political interest, but the particular version(s) of masculinity which is being negotiated. See Taubin, 'So Good it Hurts', p. 18.

6 Jude Davis, 'Gender, Ethnicity and Cultural Crisis in *Falling Down* and *Groundhog Day*', *Screen*, vol. 36, no. 3 (Autumn 1995), p. 214.

7 Jeffords, *The Remasculinization of America*.

8 Susan Jeffords, 'The Big Switch: Hollywood Masculinity in the Nineties', in, Jim Collins, Hilary Radner and Ava Preacher Collins (eds), *Film Theory Goes to the Movies* (London: Routledge, 1993), p. 197.

9 *Ibid*. I am sensitive to and largely sympathetic towards Jeffords' own qualification of this reading put forward later in the same article, as well as to the one articulated by Donna Haraway, who argues that 'the image of the sensitive man calls up, for me, the male person who, while enjoying the position of unbelievable privilege, also has the privilege of gentleness'. Quoted in Jeffords, 'The Big Switch', pp. 206–7.

10 Carol Clover, 'White Noise', *Sight and Sound*, vol. 3, issue 5 (May 1993), p. 9.

11 Richard Dyer, 'White', *Screen*, vol. 29, no. 4 (Winter 1988). Interestingly, Dyer also includes a similar disclaimer to his work, pointing out that he is at pains to avoid the double-sprung trap of 'guilt and me too-ism' (p. 45).

12 Clover, 'White Noise', p. 9.

13 Robert Hughes, *Culture of Complaint* (New York: Oxford University Press, 1993), p. 17.

14 Respectively, the quotations are from: David Denby, *The New Yorker*; Gregory Weinkauf, *New Times L.A*; Kenneth Turan, *L.A. Times*; and Robert Ebert, *Chicago Sun Times*.

15 Alexander Walker, *Evening Standard*, quoted in 'How to Start a Fight', *Fight Club* DVD sleeve notes (Twentieth Century Fox Home Entertainment, 2000).

16 A comparable – if not as hyberbolic – critical reaction can be traced in relation to *Magnolia*. Where *Fight Club*'s pathos was explained away by reference to juvenilistic, anti-Semitic and fascistic adjectives, *Magnolia* was commonly described as a film *about* patriarchy. While to some extent I would go along with this, simply wheeling out such a loaded term masks more than it reveals. For it fails to tackle a host of other terms, such as humiliation, cruelty, kindness, hope, despair,

joy, sadness, happiness, misery, loneliness, and so forth, which lie just
below the frozen surface of 'patriarchy'.

17 Michael Lerner, 'The Crisis of Values in America: Its Manipulation by
    the Right and its Invisibility to the Left', in David Batstone and
    Eduardo Mendieta (eds), *The Good Citizen* (London: Routledge, 1999),
    p. 65.
18 *Ibid.*, p. 66.
19 *Ibid.*, p. 72.
20 *Ibid.*, p. 72.
21 *Ibid.*, p. 66.
22 Taubin, 'So Good it Hurts', p. 18.
23 *Ibid.*
24 Lerner, 'The Crisis of Values in America', p. 74.
25 Richard Rorty, 'The End of Leninism, Havel and Social Hope', in *Truth
    and Progress: Philosophical Papers Volume 3* (Cambridge: Cambridge
    University Press, 1998), p. 230.
26 *Ibid.*, p. 232.
27 Paul Willemen, 'An Avant-Garde for the 90s', in *Looks and Frictions*
    (London: BFI, 1994), p. 152.
28 *Ibid.*, p. 152.
29 Alan Ryan, 'Socialism for the Nineties', *Dissent* 37 (Fall 1990), p. 442.
30 Andrew Feenberg, *Questioning Technology* (London: Routledge, 1999),
    p. 104.
31 Although it is formulated in a slightly different context, I think Feen-
    berg's call to develop our critical accounts 'with a view to constructive
    change rather than romantic retreat' captures the reformist impulses
    and pragmatic stance I am trying to communicate here (*Questioning
    Technology*, p. 179).
32 Jürgen Habermas, *Die nachholende Revolution* (Frankfurt: Suhrkamp,
    1990), p. 203.
33 Hughes, *Culture of Complaint*, p. 73.
34 Douglas Kellner, 'Film, Politics and Ideology: Toward a Multiperspec-
    tival Film Theory', in James Combs (ed.), *Movies and Politics: The
    Dynamic Relationship* (London: Garland, 1993), p. 73.
35 Hughes, *Culture and Complaint*, p. 75
36 *Ibid.*, p. 73
37 Rorty, 'The End of Leninism, Havel and Social Hope', p. 238.
38 A lot of what follows plays out Rorty's call to separate out public from
    private vocabularies when we talk about political matters in the con-
    text of film theory: 'The vocabulary of self-creation is necessarily pri-
    vate, unshared, unsuited to argument. The vocabulary of justice is
    necessarily public and shared, a medium for argumentative exchange
    ... But there is no way to bring self-creation together with justice at
    the level of theory' (*Contingency, Irony and Solidarity* (Cambridge:

Cambridge University Press, 1989), p. xiv). See also Richard Rorty, *Objectivity, Relativism and Truth* (Cambridge: Cambridge University Press, 1991), especially Part III; *Essays on Heidegger and* Others (Cambridge: Cambridge University Press, 1991); and *Truth and Progress*, especially Part III.

39 Rorty, 'The End of Leninism, Havel and Social Hope', pp. 231–2.
40 Richard Rorty, 'Derrida and the Philosophical Tradition', in, *Truth and Progress*, p. 330.
41 Nicholas Garnham, *Capitalism and Communication: Global Culture and the Economics of Information* (London: Sage, 1990), p. 15.
42 This tendency towards scepticism and despair arises, I think, out of a too-literal interpretation of a brand of postmodern philosophy of which Baudrillard is perhaps the highest priest.
43 Timothy Corrigan, *A Cinema Without Walls: Movies and Culture After Vietnam* (London: Routledge, 1991), p. 197.
44 *Ibid.*, pp. 197–8.
45 Terry Eagleton, *Ideology: An Introduction* (London: Verso, 1991), p. 30.
46 Roger Silverstone, *Why Study the Media?* (London: Sage, 1999), p. 143
47 Noel Carroll, *A Philosophy of Mass Art* (Oxford: Oxford University Press, 1998), p. 361. I also agree with Carroll when he says that non-pejorative conceptions of ideology – such broad brush definitions which simply equate ideology with symbolic activity, make it co-extensive with culture, or refer to it a 'a system of beliefs' – are of little heuristic or political use to the cultural critic just in so far as there is no tool available from which one can disintricate the ideological from the non-ideological. And if 'everything' is ideology, then why bother? I think that Carroll is right when he points out that the *only* definition of ideology with any critical mileage must be a pejorative one – that is, one which in some way propagates a 'false view' of the world in favour of some practice of social domination. However, I disagree with Carroll's claim that ideology still has a useful role to play in social criticism. It seems to me that while it was once useful, the word 'ideology' has simply become too fuzzy and too equivocal to be profitable and, moreover, that all the useful functions that are performed by Carroll's redefinition of the term might be achieved equally well, and far more directly, by being content to ask questions such as 'to what extent is this cultural artefact useful to a liberal description of the world?'
48 For writers like Eagleton, it is not possible take out a 'third-party' Marxist or a 'comprehensive' ideological critical policy without being underwritten by metaphysical insurance precisely to the extent that they require a fixed point, an unswerving pivot which distinguishes objective political beliefs from distorted or ideological ones. The only

criteria for untangling facts of the matter from social constructs are provided by metaphysical concepts such as 'truth' and 'reality'. Better, I think, to abandon metaphysics once and for all, accept that everything is a social construct, agree with Wilfred Sellars's claim that 'all awareness in a linguistic affair' (Eagleton, *Ideology*), and concentrate our efforts on which social constructs are useful to social democracies, which impede freedom and cause pain, and which new constructs might help us to improve our lot and that of our community.

49 The 'correct' forensic skills of the film critic are more or less those of deconstruction.

50 This description of the ambiguous complexity of ideological readings and the difficulty for film critics is taken from Jacinda Read's account of the way *The Accused* and *Thelma and Louise* construct a 'popular feminism'. I certainly do not wish to imply that Read's work is characteristic of the sort of ideological critique which I am suggesting we drop. On the contrary, it is an excellent example of the more provisional, localised and modest political analysis I advocate below. See Jacinda Read, 'Popular Film/Popular Feminism: The Critical Reception of the Rape-Revenge Film', *Scope:ONlineFilmJournal*,http://www. nottingham. ac. uk/film/journal/articles/popular_feminism. htm (14 February 2000).

51 Slavoj Žižek, *The Sublime Object of Ideology* (London: Verso, 1989), p. 49.

52 Jude Davies and Carol R. Smith, *Gender, Ethnicity and Sexuality in Contemporary American Film* (Edinburgh: Keele University Press, 1997), p. 7.

53 Douglas Kellner and Michael Ryan, *Camera Politica: The Politics and Ideology of Contemporary Hollywood Film* (Bloomington: Indiana University Press, 1990)

54 *Ibid.*, p. 16.

55 *Ibid.*, p. 1.

56 *Ibid.*

57 Paul Wells usefully describes this apparent discrepancy between what the audience sees and what the trained eye of the critic sees in relation to the putative dubious ideology of Disney in terms of the cultural critic's preoccupation with the materiality of the text set against the primacy of narrative for the audience. See his chapter in this volume.

58 Of course, this narrative of sociopolitical progress is judged by our own lights – but they are the only ones available for us to describe our own history. Given this, one can argue with Rorty that what we need is not a social transfiguration – a new communal *foci imaginarius* – but more, and wider, distribution of the things we have already: freedom, wealth, tolerance, and so on. This means accepting the idea – which sends a Marxist's stomach into convulsions – that 'the rich

democracies of the present day already contain the sorts of institutions necessary for their own reform', and that

> communication among the citizens of those democracies is not 'distorted' by anything more esoteric than greed, fear, ignorance and resentment. This amounts to saying that that the instruments of perfectibility are already, in the rich North Atlantic constitutional democracies, in place – that the principal institutions of contemporary democratic societies do not need 'unmasking', but rather strenuous utilization, supplemented by luck. (Rorty, *Truth and Progress*, p. 326)

59 These four quotations are from (in the order they appear): Kellner and Ryan, *Camera Politica*, p. 266; Robyn Weigman, 'Race, Ethnicity and Film, in John Hill and Pamela Church Gibson (eds), *The Oxford Guide to Film Studies* (Oxford: Oxford University Press, 1998), p. 158; Robin Wood, *Hollywood from Vietnam to Reagan* (New York: Columbia University Press, 1986), p. 50; and, Douglas Kellner, 'Film, Politics and Ideology', in James Combs (ed.), *Movies and Politics: The Dynamic Relationship* (New York: Garland, 1993), p. 73.

60 Paul Willeman, 'Notes on Subjectivity', in *Looks and Frictions* (London: BFI, 1994), p. 70.

61 Nick Couldry, *Inside Culture* (London: Sage, 2000), p. 116.

62 Elspeth Probyn, *Sexing the Self* (London: Routledge, 1993), p. 3.

63 Anna Yeatman, 'Justice and the Sovereign Self', in M. Wilson and A. Yeatman (eds), *Justice and Identity: Antipodean Practices* (New South Wales: Allen and Unwin, 1995), p. 207.

64 Judith Butler, *Gender Trouble: Feminism and the Subversion of Identity* (London: Routledge, 1994).

65 Couldry, *Inside Culture*, p. 116.

66 Davis and Smith, *Gender, Ethnicity and Sexuality in Contemporary American Film*, p. 5.

67 Anna Yeatman, *Postmodern Revisions of the Political* (London: Routledge, 1994), p. 48.

68 John Rawls, 'Justice as Fairness: Political not Metaphysical', *Philosophy and Public Affairs*, no. 14 (1985), p. 230.

69 *Ibid.*, pp. 225–6.

70 Robyn Weigman, 'Black Bodies/American Commodities: Gender, Race and the Bourgeois Ideal in Contemporary Film', in Lester D. Friedman (ed.), *Unspeakable Images: Ethnicity and the American Cinema* (Chicage: University of Illinois Press, 1991), p. 309; and Rorty, *Truth and Progress*, p. 11.

71 Richard Rorty, *Contingency, Irony and Solidarity* (Cambridge: Cambridge University Press, 1989), p. 85.

72 Again, Amy Taubin is the only critic I am aware of who has picked up

on this crucial distinction between public and private selves when she argues: 'Since Tyler's bombs are as reliable as Jack is as a narrator, this is what you might call, if you think about it carefully, an open ending.' I think Taubin is absolutely right to call into question the veracity of the explosive visual ending precisely to the extent that Tyler is running the show. For if Tyler is *only* a quasi-self, then he cannot actually be holding Jack hostage. This is another example of critics being too quick to read the politics of a film off a particular character – in this case a character who doesn't even exist ('So Good it Hurts', p. 17).

73 Richard Rorty, *Truth and Progress*, p. 19.

74 Rorty was actually reworking a phrase by Lorenz Krüger when he argues that philosophy might be seen as 'the professionalised conscience or consciousness of the world in which democracy has become a possibility.' See, 'The contingency of philosophical problems: Michael Ayers on Locke', in *Truth and Progress*.

75 George Berkeley, quoted in Richard Rorty, *Truth and Progress*, p. 78.

76 John Rawls, quoted in Richard Rorty, The priority of democracy to philosophy', in *Objectivity, Relativity and Truth: Philosophical Papers Volume 1* (Cambridge: Cambridge University Press, 1991).

Hollywood in elections and elections in Hollywood

1 Senator Joe Lieberman, speech to Democratic National Convention, 16 August 2000.

2 Robert Reich, 'How Bouncing Bush Has Cornered Gore', *Observer* (15 August 2000), p. 25.

3 Quoted in Danielle Decker Jones and Chris Cillizza, 'Talking Heads', *National Journal* (5 August 2000), p. 2561.

4 Jonathan Freedland, 'Trying to Fill Bill's Shoes', *Guardian* (16 August 2000), p. 19.

5 Quoted in Jones and Cillizza, 'Talking Heads'.

6 Reich, 'How Bouncing Bush Has Cornered Gore'.

7 Quoted in Ed Vulliamy, 'The Hollywood Hitman', *Observer* (20 August 2000), Review section, pp. 1–2.

8 Freedland, 'Trying to Fill Bill's Shoes'.

9 Burt Solomon, 'They Spoke, We're Late', *National Journal* (19 August 2000), p. 2675; Tom Brokaw quoted in James A. Barnes, 'As NBC Fidgeted, Senators Droned On and On', *National Journal* (19 August 2000), p. 2675.

10 Martin Kettle, 'Presidents in Thrall to the Silver Screen', *Guardian* (19 July 2000), p. 3.

11 Damian Whitworth, 'Kennedys Back Gore's New Frontier', *The Times* (17 August 2000), p. 18.

12 Ben Macintyre, 'JFK's Daughter Revives Memory', *The Times* (16

August 2000), p. 15.

13 Duncan Campbell, 'Kennedys Deliver Family Values', *Guardian* (17 August 2000), p. 14.

14 Ed Vulliamy, 'Gore gives America a Stark Choice', *Observer* (20 August 2000), p. 23.

15 Vulliamy, 'Gore Gives America a Stark Choice', p. 23.

16 Andrew Sullivan, 'Clinton Steals the Show and Leaves Party in Identity Crisis', *Sunday Times* (20 August 2000), p. 24.

17 Peter Preston, 'A Wimp Acts Superman', *Observer* (20 August 2000), p. 22.

18 John Patterson, 'Democrats and Dream Demons', *Guardian* (25 August 2000), G2, p. 23.

19 Quoted in Grace Bradberry, 'Lieberman Challenged Over Film Censorship', *The Times* (29 August 2000), p. 11.

20 'Dole for President' leaflet distributed in 1996 Iowa caucus campaign, from author's archive of election materials.

21 Mark Morris, 'Guns and Posses', *Observer* (2 April 2000), Screen section, p. 7.

22 Martin Kettle, 'Gore Goes Back to Basics', *Guardian* (17 August 2000), p. 2.

23 Andrew Sullivan, 'Jewish Gamble May Cost Votes', *Sunday Times* (13 August 2000), p. 25.

24 Ruth Marcus, 'Partied Out, but Happy', *Washington Post National Weekly Edition* (28 August 2000), p. 13; Amy Wallace and Josh Meyer, 'Let the Parties Begin – and Bring a Checkbook', *Los Angeles Times* (13 August 2000), website, http://www. latimes. com/news/politics/elect2000/demconven/lat_mor.

25 Ben Macintyre, 'Clinton's Stars Steal Limelight from Gore', *The Times* (11 August 2000), p. 18.

26 Ben Macintyre, 'Clinton, Doing it His Way to the Last Note', *The Times* (12 August 2000), p. 18.

27 Martin Walker, *Clinton: The President They Deserve* (London: Vintage, 1997), pp. 5, 8, 111.

28 Speech, *Hansard*, 11 November 1947, col. 206.

29 Ben Fenton. 'Critical Gore is Now a Fan of Hollywood', *Daily Telegraph* (21 September 2000), p. 21.

Oliver Stone's presidential films

1 Tom Wicker, 'Does "JFK" Conspire Against Reason?', *New York Times* (15 December 1991), section 2, pp. 1, 18.

2 James Petras, 'The Discrediting of the Fifth Estate: The Press Attacks on *JFK*', *Cineaste*, vol. xix, no. 1 (1992), p. 15.

3 Bernard Weintraub, 'Nixon Family Assails Stone Film as Distortion',

New York Times (19 December 1995), p. C18.
4 Garry Wills, 'Dostoyevsky Behind a Camera: Oliver Stone is Making Great American Novels on Film', *Atlantic Monthly,* July, 1997, pp. 96–101.
5 William Grimes, 'What Debt Does Hollywood Owe to Truth?', *New York Times* (5 March 1992), pp. C15–22.
6 Norman Mailer, 'Footfalls in the Crypt', *Vanity Fair* (February 1992), pp. 124–9, 171.
7 Lance Morrow and Martha Smilgis, 'Plunging into the Labyrinth', *Time* (23 December 1991), pp. 74–6.
8 Eric Hamburg (ed.), *Nixon: An Oliver Stone Film* (New York: Hyperion, 1995).
9 Bernard Weintraub, 'Professor Stone Resumes His Presidential Research', *New York Times* (17 December 1995), section 2, pp. 11, 26.
10 David Denby, 'Movies: Thrill of Fear', *New York Magazine* (6 January 1992), pp. 50–1.
11 Janet Maslin, 'Film Review: Stone's Embrace of a Despised Nixon', *New York Times* (20 December 1995), pp. C11, 20.
12 Anthony Summers, *Conspiracy* (New York: Paragon House, 1989), p. 11. This book has been reissued with the new title, *Not in Your Lifetime: The Definitive Book on the JFK Assassination* (New York: McGraw-Hill, 1998).
13 *Ibid.*
14 Richard Reeve, *President Kennedy: Profile of Power* (New York: Touchstone, 1994), p. 514.
15 *Ibid.*, p. 620.
16 *Ibid.*, p. 662.
17 Frank E. Beaver, '"Citizen Nixon" – Oliver Stone's Wellesian View of a Failed Public Figure', in Don Kunz (ed.), *The Films of Oliver Stone* (Lanham, MD: The Scarecrow Press, 1997), pp. 275–84.
18 Fawn M. Brodie, *Richard Nixon: The Shaping of His Character* (Cambridge, MA: Harvard University Press, 1983), p. 76.
19 Jack Mathews, 'Anatomy of a Tragic Man, In "Nixon" America's Most Enigmatic leader', *Newsday* (20 December 1995), pp. B3, 9.

Gender and family values in the Clinton presidency

1 Betty G. Farrell, *Family: The Making of an Idea, an Institution, and a Controversy in American Culture* (Boulder, CO: Westview Press, 1999), p. 15. For other notable and politically divergent views of the family see John R. Gillis, *A World of Their Own Making: Myth, Ritual, and the Quest for Family Values* (Cambridge, MA: HarperCollins, 1996); and Betty Friedan (ed. Brigid O'Farrell), *Beyond Gender: The New Politics of Work and Family* (Baltimore, MD: The Woodrow Wilson

Center Press/Johns Hopkins University Press, 1997).

2 Hillary Rodham Clinton, Commencement speech, Wellesley College (29 May 1992), quoted in Norman King, *The Woman in the White House* (New York: Birch Lane Press, 1996), p. 6.

3 Susan Faludi, *Backlash: The Undeclared War against Women* (London: Chatto & Windus, 1992).

4 Hilary Radner, 'Pretty is as Pretty Does: Free Enterprise and the Marriage Plot', in Jim Collins, Hillary Radner and Ava Preacher Collins (eds), *Film Theory Goes to the Movies* (London: Routledge, 1993), pp. 56–76.

5 Jude Davies and Carol R. Smith, *Gender, Ethnicity and Sexuality in Contemporary American Film* (Edinburgh: Keele University Press, 1997), p. 10.

6 Sharon Willis, 'Hardware and Hardbodies, What do Women Want? A Reading of *Thelma and Louise*', in Collins *et al.*, *Film Theory Goes to the Movies*; Yvonne Takser, *Working Girls: Gender and Sexuality in Popular Cinema* (London: Routledge, 1998); Philip Green, *Cracks in the Pedestal: Ideology and Gender in Hollywood* (Amherst, MA: University of Massachusetts Press, 1998).

7 Susan Jeffords, *The Remasculinization of America: Gender and the Vietnam War* (Bloomington: Indiana University Press, 1989), p. xi; see also Elizabeth G. Traube *Dreaming Identities: Class, Gender and Generation in 1980s Hollywood Movies* (Boulder, CO: Westview Press, 1992).

8 Frank Krutnik, 'The Faint Aroma of Performing Seals: The "Nervous" Romance and the Comedy of the Sexes', *Velvet Light Trap* 26 (1990), pp. 57–72.

9 See Jude Davies and Carol R. Smith, 'Race, Gender, and the American Mother: Political Speech and the Maternity Episodes of *I Love Lucy* and *Murphy Brown*', *American Studies*, vol.39, no. 2 (1998), pp. 33–63.

10 Dan Quayle, 8 September 1994, quoted in Judith Stacey, *In the Name of the Family: Rethinking Family Values in the Post Modern Age* (Boston, MA: Beacon Press, 1996), p. 83.

11 Bill Clinton, 9 September 1994, quoted in Stacey, *In the Name of the Family*, p. 84.

12 See especially Robert E. Denton Jr and Rachel L. Holloway (eds), *The Clinton Presidency Images, Issues, and Communication Strategies* (Westport, CT: Praeger, 1996).

13 Stacey, *In the Name of the Family*, p. 102. See also Barbara J. Risman, *Gender Vertigo: American Families in Transition* (New Haven, CT: Yale University Press, 1998).

14 Faludi, *Backlash*.

15 Virginia Wright Wexman, *Creating the Couple: Love, Marriage and*

Hollywood Performance (Princeton, NJ: Princeton University Press, 1993), p. 43.

16 Chrys Ingrahams, *White Weddings: Romancing Heterosexuality in Popular Culture* (London: Routledge, 1999), p. 139.

17 For a paradigm of how non-white ethnicity is represented negatively in the service of the preservation of white feminity within the marriage narrative see D. Soyini Madison, '*Pretty Woman* through the Triple Lens of Black Feminist Spectatorship', in Elizabeth Bell, Lynda Haas and Laura Sells (eds), *From Mouse to Mermaid: The Politics of Film, Gender and Culture* (Bloomington: Indiana University Press, 1995), pp. 224–36.

18 See Denise M. Bostdorff, 'Clinton's Characteristic Issue Management Style: Caution, Conciliation, and Conflict Avoidance in the Case of Gays in the Military', in Denton and Holloway, *The Clinton Presidency*, pp. 189–223; David A. J. Richards, *Identity and the Case For Gay Rights: Race,Gender, and Religion as Analogies* (Chicago: University of Chicago Press, 1999).

19 Quoted in Ingraham, *White Weddings*, p. 160.

New York City in American film

Portions of this essay appeared in a different form in Leonard Quart, 'Spike Lee's *Clockers*:: A Lament for the Urban Ghetto', *Cineaste*, vol. 22, no. 1, pp. 9–11; and Leonard Quart and William Kornblum, 'Film and the Inner City', *Dissent* (Spring 2000), pp. 97–104.

1 Leonard Quart and Albert Auster, 'A Novelist and Screenwriter Eyeballs the Inner City: An Interview with Richard Price', *Cineaste*, vol. 22, no. 1, p. 16.

2 'City's Jobless Rate is Lowest Since '88', *New York Times* (19 May 2000), p. B7.

3 Dennis Hevesi, 'Average Cost of Apartments Hits $700,000', *New York Times* (19 May 2000), pp. B1 and 7.4); Mia L. Mask, 'Buppy Love in an Urban World', *Cineaste*, vol. 25, no. 2, pp. 41–4.

Dixie's land: cinema of the American South

1 P. Gerster, 'Stereotypes', in C. R. Wilson and W. Ferris (eds), *Encyclopedia of Southern Culture*, vol. 3 (New York: Anchor Books, 1991), p. 494.

2 D. Webster, *Looka Yonder: The Imaginary America of Populist Culture* (London and New York; Routledge, 1988), p. 73.

3 J. G. Cawelti, 'That's What I Like about the South: Changing Images of the South in the 1970s', in Elsebeth Hurup (ed.), *The Lost Decade:*

America in the Seventies (Aarhus: Aarhus University Press, 1996), pp. 12–13.

4 Editorial, *Cineaste*, vol. 17, no. 4 (1989), p. 2.
5 E. Guerrero, 'The Slavery Motif in Recent Popular Cinema', *Jump Cut* 33 (1988), pp. 55, 56.
6 M. L. Mask, 'Eve's Bayou: Too Good to be a "Black" Film?', *Cineaste*, vol. 23, no. 4 (1998), p. 27.
7 G. Brown, 'Fried Green Tomatoes at the Whistle Stop Cafe', *Sight and Sound*, vol. 1, no. 11 (1992), p. 46.
8 G. Essler, *The United States of Anger* (London and New York; Routledge, 1997), p. 320.

Independent cinema and modern Hollywood

1 Emanuel Levy, *Cinema of Outsiders: The Rise of American Independent Film* (New York: New York University Press, 1999), pp. 39–40.
2 Geoff Gilmore, Sundance programmer, interviewed in *Sight and Sound*, vol. 5, no. 5 (May 1995), pp. 22–3.
3 Levy, *Cinema of Outsiders*, p. 3.
4 Douglas Kellner, 'Film, Politics and Ideology', in James Combs (ed.), *Movies and Politics, The Dynamic Relationship* (New York: Garland Publishing, 1993), p. 71.
5 Michael Ryan and Douglas Kellner, *Camera Politica: The Politics and Ideology of Hollywood Film* (Bloomington: Indiana University Press, 1988), p. 282.
6 Arthur Schlesinger, Jr, *The Disuniting of America: Reflections on a Multicultural Society* (New York: W. W. Norton, 1992).
7 Roderick P. Hart, *Seducing America: How Television Charms the Modern Voter* (Thousand Oaks, CA: Sage, 1999), pp. 57–8.
8 See Levy, *Cinema of Outsiders*, Appendix 2, pp. 527–37.
9 Justin Wyatt, 'The Formation of the "Major Independent", Miramax, New Line and the New Hollywood', in Steve Neale and Murray Smith (eds), *Contemporary Hollywood Cinema* (London: Routledge, 1998), p. 74; John Pierson, *Spike, Mike, Slackers and Dykes: A Guided Tour across a Decade of Independent American Cinema* (London: Faber & Faber, 1996).
10 Thomas Schatz, 'The New Hollywood', in Jim Collins, Hilary Radner and Ava Preacher Collins (eds), *Film Theory Goes to the Movies* (New York: Routledge, 1993), p. 10.
11 Schatz, 'The New Hollywood', p. 23; Thomas Schatz, 'Show Me the Money: In Search of Hits, The Industry May Go Broke', *The Nation* (5–12 April 1999), pp. 26–8.
12 Wyatt, 'The Formation of the "Major Independent"', p. 84.
13 M. Poster, ed., *Jean Baudrillard: Selected Writings* (Cambridge: Polity

Press, 1988).

14 Gabriel A. Almond and Sidney Verba, *The Civic Culture, Political Attitudes and Democracy in Five Nations* (Princeton, NJ: Princeton University Press, 1963), p. 440; Joseph S. Nye, Jr *et al.*, *Why People Don't Trust Government* (Cambridge, MA: Harvard University Press, 1997), p. 1; E. J. Dionne, *Why Americans Hate Politics* (New York: Simon & Schuster, 1991).

15 Jeffrey C. Goldfarb, *The Cynical Society: The Culture of Politics and the Politics of Culture in American Life* (Chicago: University of Chicago Press, 1991), p. 28.

16 Hart, *Seducing America*, p. 70.

17 *Ibid.*, p. 26.

18 *Manufacturing Consent: Noam Chomsky and the Media* (1992) was directed by Peter Wintonik and Mark Achbar.

19 Jesse Jackson, in Gary Wills, 'Bulworth', *New York Review of Books* (16 July 1998), pp. 24–5.

20 Gavin Smith, *Sayles on Sayles* (London: Faber & Faber, 1998), p. 58.

21 Haynes Johnson, *Sleepwalking through History: America in the Reagan Years* (New York: Doubleday, 1992), pp. 153, 163–5; Smith, *Sayles on Sayles*, p. 123.

22 Pierson, *Spike, Mike, Slackers and Dykes*, pp. 46–50.

23 *Ibid.*, p. 60.

24 Ed Guerrero, 'A Circus of Dreams and Lies: The Black Film Wave at Middle Age', in Jon Lewis (ed.), *The New American Cinema* (Durham, NC: Duke University Press, 1998), p. 328.

25 *Ibid.*, p. 337.

26 Paula J. Massood, 'Mapping the Hood: The Genealogy of City Space in *Boyz N' the Hood* and *Menace II Society*', *Cinema Journal*, vol. 35, no. 2 (Winter 1996), p. 90.

27 *Ibid.*, p. 91.

28 See 'Critical Symposium on *Do the Right Thing*', *Cineaste*, vol. 27, no. 4 (1990), pp. 32–9.

29 Spike Lee, speaking in the video production, 'The Edge of Hollywood', *American Cinema*, vol. 5, The New York Center for Visual History, 1995.

30 *Sunday Telegraph* (22 February 1998), p. 11.

31 Sarah Schulman, *My American History: Lesbian and Gay Life During the Reagan/Bush Years* (New York: Routledge, 1994), p. 155.

32 Kenneth MacKinnon, *The Politics of Representation: Reagan, Thatcher, AIDS, and the Movies* (London: Associated University Presses, 1992), pp. 158, 165.

33 Schulman, *My American History*, p. 254.

34 *Variety* (15 April 1991).

35 J. Hoberman, *Village Voice* (9 April 1991).

36 Manohla Dargis, 'Unpleasantville, 1998's Hot Indies Turn Hollywood Upside Down', *The Nation* (5–12 April 1999), p. 44.
37 Ella Shohat and Robert Stam, *Unthinking Eurocentrism: Multiculturalism and the Media* (London: Routledge, 1994), p. 328.
38 William Chaloupka, *Everybody Knows: Cynicism in America* (Minneapolis, University of Minnesota Press, 1999), p. 168.
39 Robert D. Putnam, 'Bowling Alone: America's Declining Social Capital', *Journal of Democracy*, vol. 6, no. 1 (1995), pp. 65–78.

'I wanna be like you-oo-oo'

1 Henry Giroux, 'Are Disney Movies Good for Your Kids?', from Shirley Steinberg and Joe Kincheloe (eds), *Kinderculture: The Corporate Construction of Childhood* (Boulder, CO and Oxford: Westview Press, 1997), p. 55.
2 Elizabeth Bell, Linda Haas and Laura Sells (eds), *From Mouse to Mermaid: The Politics of Film, Gender and Culture* (Bloomington and Indianapolis: Indiana University Press, 1995), p. 5.
3 Robin Allan, *Walt Disney and Europe* (London: John Libbey, 1999), p. 1.
4 Alan Bryman, *Disney and His Worlds* (London and New York: Routledge, 1995:, pp. 14–15.
5 Jack Zipes, 'Breaking the Disney Spell', in Bell, Haas and Sells (eds) *From Mouse to Mermaid*, p. 29.
6 Paul Hollister, 'Genius at Work: Walt Disney', in E. Smoodin (ed), *Disney Discourse* (London and New York: Routledge, 1994), p. 38.
7 Susan Miller and Greg Rode, 'The Movie You See, The Movie You Don't See', in Bell, Haas and Sells (eds), *From Mouse to Mermaid*, p. 86.
8 I am grateful to Martin Barker for introducing me to this concept.
9 This concept is more fully explored in Paul Wells, *Understanding Animation* (London and New York: Routledge, 1998), pp. 76–80.
10 See Eleanor Byrne and Martin McQuillan, *Deconstructing Disney* (London and Sterling: Pluto Press, 1999).
11 Richard Schickel, *The Disney Version* (London: Pavilion, 1986), p. 186.
12 Giroux, 'Are Disney Movies Good for Your Kids?', p. 62.
13 *Ibid.*
14 Patrick D. Murphy, 'The Whole Wide World was Scrubbed Clean: The Androcentric Animation of Denatured Disney', from Bell, Haas and Sells (eds), *From Mouse to Mermaid*, p. 126.
15 Martin Barker, *From Antz to Titanic: Reinventing Film Analysis* (London and Sterling: Pluto Press, 2000), p. 189.
16 See Wells, *Understanding Animation*, pp. 222–42.
17 Miller and Rode, 'The Movie You See…", in Bell, Haas and Sells (eds),

From Mouse to Mermaid, p. 87.

18 Henry Giroux, 'Memory and Pedagogy in the "Wonderful World of Disney"', in Bell, Haas and Sells (eds), *From Mouse to Mermaid*, p. 48.

19 Byrne and McQuillan, *Deconstructing Disney*, p. 35.

20 I have written more emphatically elsewhere that I do not believe that the personae of Tom Hanks and Tim Allen impact significantly upon Woody and Buzz, the characters they voice in the *Toy Story* movies, in relation to their status as animated characters and ultimately as 'stars' in their own right. As Brad Bird – director of many *Simpsons* episodes and the full-length feature, *The Iron Giant* (1999) – notes, 'What is typically lost in discussions about animation is the fact that when you watch an animated film, the performance you are seeing is the one that the animator is giving you' (Ed Hooks, *Acting For Animators* (Portsmouth: Heinemann, 2000), p. vi).

21 Richard Dyer, 'Entertainment and Utopia', in *Only Entertainment* (London and New York: Routledge, 1992), pp. 17–35.

22 For a useful explanation of these metaphoric positions see Jason Macdonald, 'Conceptual Metaphors for American Ethnic Formations', in Philip John Davies (ed), *Representing and Imagining America* (Keele: Keele University Press, 1996), pp. 84–92.

23 Brian Appleyard, 'Disney Family Values: The Triumph of Niceness', *Sunday Times* 'How Disney Makes Magic' Supplement, Week One: Creating Character, 1998, p. 8.

24 Byrne and McQuillan 1999, *Deconstructing Disney*, p. 24.

25 John Patterson, 'Sport, Cash, Mice and Uncle Walt', *The Guardian* (7 January 2000), Review section, p. 19.

26 See Leonard Mosley, *The Real Walt Disney* (London: Grafton Books, 1985); Bob Thomas, *Walt Disney* (London: W. H. Allen, 1976).

27 Marc Eliot, *Walt Disney, Hollywood's Dark Prince* (London: André Deutsch, 1993).

28 Giroux, 'Memory and Pedagogy in the "Wonderful World of Disney"', p. 47.

Ambiguity and anger: representations of African Americans

1 Frederick Garber, 'Fabulating Jazz', in Krin Gabbard (ed), *Representing Jazz* (Durham, NC and London: Duke University Press, 1995), p. 90.

2 Kalamu Ya Salaam, 'If Only Mo Betta was Better', *Wavelength* (September 1990), pp. 9–11; Amiri Baraka, 'Spike Lee at the Movies', in Manthia Diawara (ed), *Black American Cinema* (New York and London: Routledge, 1993), pp. 151–2.

3 S. Craig Watkins, *Representing: Hip Hop Culture and the Production of Black Cinema* (Chicago, University of Chicago Press, 1998), p. 197; see also Mark A. Reid, *Redfining Black Film* (Berkeley: University of California Press, 1993), pp. 133–4.

4 Edmund Lewis, 'Listen Up, Brothers', *Louisiana Weekly* (13–19 September 1999), p. 4.

5 Michele Wallace, *Invisibility Blues: From Pop to Theory* (London: Verso, 1990), p. 245.

6 'There Are No Limits', *Louisiana Weekly* (11–17 July 1999), pp. 1–6; No Limits advertisement, *The Source*, no. 118 (July 1999), p. 120; Edward Helmore, 'No Limits for Master P', *Observer* (17 October 1999), Business section, p. 7.

7 Todd Boyd, *Am I Black Enough For You? Popular Culture from the Hood and Beyond* (Bloomington, Indiana University Press, 1997), p. 139.

8 W. E. B. DuBois, *The Souls of Black Folk* (London: Bantam, 1989), pp. 154–79.

9 Quentin Tarantino, *Pulp Fiction* (London: Faber & Faber, 1994), pp. 146–8; Andrew Anthony, 'You Can Call him "Nigga", Just Don't Call Him "Nigger"', *Observer* (8 March 1998), Review section, p. 6.

10 Sharon Willis, *High Contrast: Race and Gender in Contemporary Hollywood Film* (Durham, NC and London: Duke University Press, 1997), pp. 31–56; Hazel Carby, *Race Men* (Cambridge, MA and London: Harvard University Press, 1998), pp. 169–78.

11 *Se7en* (New Line, 1995); Richard Dyer, *Seven* (London: British Film Institute, 1999), p. 77.

12 *Deep Cover* (First Independent, New Line Cinema, 1992).

13 Boyd, *Black*, p. 129.

14 Misty Brown, 'Bayou Spellbounds Jackson', *Louisiana Weekly* (10–16 November 1997), p. 11; *Eve's Bayou* (Jackson/Lemmons Production, 1997).

15 Watkins, *Representing*, pp. 92–111.

16 Richard Merelman, *Representing Black Culture,* (London: Routledge, 1995), p. 123.

17 Lee Hubbard, 'It's All Good...', *Louisiana Weekly* (19–25 July 1999), p. 10.

18 Randall Kenan, *Walking On Water: Black American Lives at the Turn of the Twenty-First Century* (London: Little, Brown & Co., 1999), p. 638.

The adversarial imagination

1 Michael S. Sherry, *In The Shadow of War: The United States Since the 1930s* (New Haven, CT: Yale University Press, 1995), pp. ix–x.

2 Harold Pinter, 'Yanquis Go Home!', *Independent on Sunday* (8 May 1995), p. 11.
3 Ronald Steel, 'The End and the Beginning', in Michael J. Hogan (ed.), *The End of the Cold War: Its Meaning and Implications* (New York: Cambridge University Press, 1992), p. 104.
4 Pinter, 'Yanquis Go Home!', p. 11.
5 Bruce Cummings, 'The Wicked Witch of the West is Dead. Long Live the Wicked Witch of the East', in Hogan (ed.), *The End of the Cold War*, p. 90.
6 Malcolm Bradbury, 'Frontiers of Imagination', *The Guardian* (15 February 1990), p. 21.
7 Henry W. Cooper, 'Annals of Space', *New Yorker* (2 September 1991), p. 63.
8 Mark Lawson, 'Cold Warriors Never Die', *Guardian* (10 November 1995), G2, p. 2.
9 David Holloway, 'The Politics of Catastrophe', *New York Review* (10 June 1993), p. 37. See also Julia Voznesenkaya, *The Star Chernobyl* (London: Quartet, 1987).
10 Marina Benjamin, *Living at the End of the World* (London: Picador, 1998), p. 44.
11 Stephen Prince, *Visions of Empire: Political Imagery in Contemporary American Film* (New York: Praeger, 1992), p. 57.
12 *Ibid.*, p. 62.
13 Jonathan Freedland, 'Aliens Are Coming Home', *Guardian* (11 July 1996), G2, p. 7.
14 Andrew Sullivan, 'Loud and Angry', *Sunday Times* (30 April 1995), Section 3, p. 7.
15 Christopher Hitchens, 'Look Over Your Shoulder', *London Review of Books* (25 May 1995), p. 12.
16 Sharon Churcher, 'USA Confidential', *Penthouse* (November 1995), pp. 56–74. See also Jim Smolowe, 'Enemies of the State', *Time* (8 May 1995), pp. 58–68.
17 William Langewiesche, 'The Border', *Atlantic* (May 1992), p. 74.
18 Joseph Wambaugh, *Lines and Shadows* (New York: Bantam, 1984), p. 14.
19 Martin Wollacott, 'Living in the Age of Terror', *Guardian* (22 April 1995), p. 22.
20 Richard Preston, *The Hot Zone* (London: Corgi, 1995), pp. 373–4.
21 Peter Hutchings, 'Satan Bugs in the Hot Zone: Microbial Pathogens as Alien Invaders', in Deborah Cartmell, I. Q. Hunter, Heidi Kaye and Imelda Whelehan (eds), *Alien: Exploring Differences in Film and Fiction* (London: Pluto, 1999), p. 20.
22 Claire Sterling, *Crime Without Frontiers* (London: Little, Brown, 1994) p. 123.

23 James Willwerth, 'From Killing Fields to Mean Streets', *Time* (18 November 1991), p. 103.

24 Quentin Tarantino, *Pulp Fiction: Three Stories About One Story* (London: Faber & Faber, 1994), pp. 121, 124.

25 Marita Sturken, *Tangled Memories: The Vietnam War, the AIDS Epidemic, and the Politics of Remembering* (Berkeley: UCLA Press, 1997), p. 224.

26 Jonathan Freedland, 'Divided Nation Leaves Leaders With Problem', *Guardian* (26 November 1994), p. 14.

27 Tarantino, *Pulp Fiction*, p. 159.

28 Norman Mailer, *The Naked and the Dead* (New York: Penguin Books, 1948), p. 324.

29 Peter Jaret, 'Our Immune System: The Wars Within', *National Geographic* (June 1986), p. 702.

30 Tarantino, *Pulp Fiction*, p. 159.

31 *Ibid.*, p. 24.

32 Martin Walker, 'America's Reverse Gear Revolution', *Guardian* (26 November 1994), p. 14

33 Sturken, *Tangled Memories*, pp. 225, 228, 231, 244.

34 Paula Treichler, 'AIDS, Homophobia, and Biomedical Discourse: An Epidemic of Signification', in Douglas Crimp (ed), *AIDS: Cultural Analysis/Cultural Activism* (Cambridge, MA: MIT Press, 1988), p. 60

35 Sturken, *Tangled Memories*, pp. 247–8.

36 *Ibid.*, p. 177.

37 Annalee Newitz, 'Alien Abductions and the End of White People', *Bad Subjects Site*, issue no. 5 (May 1993), p. 6.

38 Jodi Dean, *Aliens in America: Conspiracy Cultures from Outerspace to Cyberspace* (New York: Cornell University Press, 1998), p. 155.

39 Elaine Showalter, *Hystories: Hysterical Epidemics and Modern Culture* (London: Picador, 1997), p. 206.

Filmography

Absolute Power (Clint Eastwood, 1997)
Air Force One (Wolfgang Petersen, 1997)
Aladdin (Ron Clements and John Musker, 1992)
Alien³ (David Fincher, 1992)
Aliens (James Cameron, 1986)
American Beauty (Sam Mendes, 1999)
Amistad (Steven Spielberg, 1997)
Angi Vera (Pal Gabor, 1978)
Apollo 13 (Ron Howard, 1995)
Armageddon (Michael Bay, 1998)
Arrival, The (David Twohy, 1996)
Bad Boys (Michael Bay, 1995)
Bad Day at Black Rock (John Sturges, 1955)
Band Wagon, The (Vincente Minnelli, 1953)
Basic Instinct (Paul Verhoeven, 1991)
Bat 21 (Peter Markle, 1988)
Batman Returns (Tim Burton, 1992)
Beauty and the Beast (Gary Tousdale and Kirk Wise, 1991)
Being John Malkovich (Spike Jonze, 1999)
Belly (Hype Williams, 1999)
Beloved (Jonathan Demme, 1998)
Best Man, The (Malcolm D Lee, 1999)
Betrayed (Costa Gavras, 1988)
Bird (Clint Eastwood, 1988)
Birdcage, The (Mike Nichols, 1996)
Bob Roberts (Tim Robbins, 1992)
Bodyguard, The (Mick Jackson, 1992)
Boyz N' the Hood (John Singleton, 1991)
Bringing Out the Dead (Martin Scorsese, 1999)
Brother from Another Planet, The (John Sayles, 1984)

Bulworth (Warren Beatty, 1998)
Cage aux Folles, La (Édouard Molinaro, France, 1979)
Canadian Bacon (Michael Moore, 1995)
Candyman (Bernard Rose, 1992)
Cape Fear (J. Lee Thompson, 1961)
Cape Fear (Martin Scorsese, 1991)
Carolina Skeletons (James Erman, 1991)
Citizen Kane (Orson Welles, 1941)
City Hall (Harold Becker, 1996)
City of Hope (John Sayles, 1991)
Civil Action, A (Steven Zaillian, 1998)
Clock, The (Vincente Minnelli, 1953)
Clockers (Spike Lee, 1995)
Close Encounters of the Third Kind (Steven Spielberg, 1977)
Coal Miner's Daughter (Michael Apted, 1980)
Coalmining Women (Elizabeth Barrett, 1982)
Color Purple, The (Steven Spielberg, 1985)
Come See the Paradise (Alan Parker, 1990)
Cookie's Fortune (Robert Altman, 1999)
Corrina, Corrina (Jessie Nelson, 1994)
Country (Richard Pearce, 1984)
Crimson Tide (Tony Scott, 1995)
Crooklyn (Spike Lee, 1994)
Daughters of the Dust (Julie Dash, 1991)
Dave (Ivan Reitman, 1993)
Days of Thunder (Tony Scott, 1990)
Dead Man (Jim Jarmusch, 1995)
Dead Man Walking (Tim Robbins, 1995)
Deep Cover (Bill Duke, 1992)
Deerhunter, The (Michael Cimino, 1978)
Defiant Ones, The (Stanley Kramer, 1958)
Deliverance (John Boorman, 1972)
Desert Bloom (Eugene Corr, 1985)
Desert Hearts (Donna Deitch, 1986)
Devil in a Blue Dress (Carl Franklin, 1995)
Die Hard with a Vengeance (John McTiernan, 1995)
Disclosure (Adrian Lyne, 1994)
Distinguished Gentleman, The (Jonathan Lynn, 1992)
Do the Right Thing (Spike Lee, 1989)
Dr Strangelove (Stanley Kubrick, 1963)
Don't Be a Menace to South Central While Drinking Your Juice in the Hood
    (Shawn and Marlon Wayans, 1995)
Down by Law (Jim Jarmusch, 1986)
Driving Miss Daisy (Bruce Beresford, 1989)

Drugstore Cowboy (Gus Van Sant, 1989)
Dumb and Dumber (Farrelly Brothers, 1994)
El Norte (Gregory Nava, 1983)
Enemy of the State (Tony Scott, 1998)
Erin Brockovich (Steven Soderbergh,2000)
Eve's Bayou (Kasi Lemmons, 1997)
Executive Decision (Stuart Baird, 1996)
Falling Down (Joel Schumacher, 1992)
Fantasia 2000 (Various, 2000)
Fargo (Joel Coen, 1996)
Father of the Bride (Vincente Minnelli, 1950)
Fear of a Black Hat (Rusty Cundrieff, 1994)
Fight Club (David Fincher, 1998)
Five Heartbeats, The (Robert Townsend, 1991)
Flashdance (Adrian Lyne, 1983)
Fled (Kevin Hooks, 1996)
Foolish (Master P (Percy Miller), 1999)
Forrest Gump (Robert Zemeckis, 1995)
48 Hours (Walter Hill, 1982)
Foxy Brown (Jack Hill, 1974)
Friday (F. Gary Gray, 1995)
Fried Green Tomatoes at the Whistle Stop Cafe (Jon Avnet, 1991)
From Here to Eternity (Fred Zinnemann, 1953)
Fugitive, The (Andrew Davis, 1993)
Game, The (David Fincher, 1997)
Gang Related (Jim Kouf, 1997)
Get On The Bus (Spike Lee, 1998)
Ghost (Jerry Zucker, 1990)
Ghosts of Mississippi (Rob Reiner, 1996)
Gingerbread Man, The (Robert Altman, 1998)
Girl 6 (Spike Lee, 1996)
Gladiator (Ridley Scott, 2000)
Glass Shield, The (Charles Burnett, 1995)
Glory (Edward Zwick, 1989)
Grand Canyon (Lawrence Kasdan, 1991)
Gridlock'd (Vondie Curtis Hall, 1998)
Happiness (Todd Solondz, 1998)
He Got Game (Spike Lee, 1998)
Hercules (Ron Clements and John Musker, 1997)
Hoffa (Danny De Vito, 1992)
Hollywood Shuffle (Robert Townsend, 1987)
Hoodlum (Bill Duke, 1997)
House Party 2 (Doug McHenry, 1991)
Hunchback of Notre Dame, The (Gary Tousdale and Kirk Wise, 1996)

I Got the Hook Up (Master P (Percy Miller), 1998)
I Like It Like That (Darnell Martin, 1994)
I'm,'Bout It' (Master P (Percy Miller), 1997)
I'm Gonna Git You Sucka (Keenan Ivory Wayans, 1989)
In and Out (Frank Oz, 1997)
In the Company of Men (Neil La Bute, 1997)
In the Heat of the Night (Norman Jewison, 1967)
In the Line of Fire (Wolfgang Petersen, 1993)
Independence Day (Roland Emmerich, 1996)
Insider, The (Michael Mann, 1999)
Introducing Dorothy Dandridge (Halle Berry, 1999)
Invasion USA (Joseph Zito, 1985)
Island in the Sun (Robert Rossen, 1956)
It's A Wonderful Life (Frank Capra, 1946)
Jackie Brown (Quentin Tarantino, 1998)
Jagged Edge (Richard Marquand, 1985)
Jason's Lyric (Doug McHenry, 1994)
Jaws (Steven Spielberg, 1975)
Jerry Maguire (Cameron Crowe, 1996)
Jezebel (William Wyler, 1938)
JFK (Oliver Stone, 1991)
Juice (Ernest Dickerson, 1992)
Jungle Book, The (Wolfgang Reitherman, 1967)
Jungle Fever (Spike Lee, 1991)
Jurassic Park (Steven Spielberg, 1993)
Just Another Girl on the IRT (Leslie Harris, 1992)
Just Cause (Arne Glimcher, 1995)
Kids (Larry Clark, 1995)
Killer of Sheep (Charles Burnett, 1977)
Killing Floor, The (Bill Duke, 1984)
Kimba the White Lion (Osamu Tezuka, 1965)
Kiss the Girls (Gary Fleder, 1997)
Krush Groove (Michael Schulz, 1985)
Last Action Hero (John McTiernan, 1993)
Last Temptation of Christ, The (Martin Scorsese, 1988)
Laws of Gravity (Nick Gomez, 1992)
Leadbelly (Gordon Parks, 1976)
Leaving Las Vegas (Mike Figgis, 1995)
Lethal Weapon (Richard Donner, 1987)
Let's Do It Again (Sidney Poitier, 1975)
Limbo (John Sayles, 1999)
Lion King, The (Roger Allers and Rob Minhoff, 1994)
Little Mermaid, The (Ron Clements and John Musker, 1988)
Living End, The (Gregg Araki, 1992)

Lone Star (John Sayles, 1996)
Long Kiss Goodnight, The (Renny Harlin, 1996)
Long Walk Home, The (Richard Pearce, 1990)
Magnolia (Paul Thomas Anderson, 1999)
Malcolm X (Spike Lee, 1992)
Manhattan (Woody Allen, 1979)
Matewan (John Sayles, 1987)
Matrix, The (Andy and Larry Wachowski, 1999)
Mean Streets (Martin Scorsese, 1973)
Meet John Doe (Frank Capra, 1941)
Men in Black (Barry Sonnenfield, 1997)
Menace II Society (Allen Hughes/Albert Hughes, 1993)
Miss Firecracker (Thomas Schlamme, 1989)
Missing (Costa Gavras, 1981)
Mississippi Burning (Alan Parker, 1988)
Mississippi Masala (Mira Nair, 1992)
Mr and Mrs Loving (Dick Friedenberg, 1996)
Mixing Nia (Alison Swan, 1998)
Mo' Better Blues (Spike Lee, 1990)
Mulan (Barry Cook and Tony Bancroft, 1998)
Murder at 1600 (Dwight Little, 1997)
My Best Friend's Wedding (P. J. Hogan, 1997)
My Cousin Vinnie (Jonathan Lynn, 1992)
Nashville (Robert Altman, 1975)
Natural Born Killers (Oliver Stone, 1994)
Negotiator, The (F. Gary Gray, 1998)
New Jack City (Mario Van Peebles, 1991)
Nil By Mouth (Gary Oldman, 1998)
Nixon (Oliver Stone, 1995)
No Tomorrow (Master P (Percy Miller), 2000)
Officer and a Gentleman, An (Taylor Hackford, 1982)
On the Town (Stanley Donen and Gene Kelly, 1949)
One False Move (Carl Franklin, 1991)
Outbreak (Wolfgang Petersen, 1995)
Panther (Mario Van Peebles, 1995)
Parting Glances (Bill Sherwood, 1985)
Passenger 57 (Kevin Hooks, 1992)
Passion Fish (John Sayles, 1992)
Patriot, The (Roland Emmerich, 2000)
Pearl Harbor (Michael Bay 2001)
Philadelphia (Jonathan Demme, 1993).
Piece of the Action, A (Sidney Poitier, 1977)
Places in the Heart (Robert Benton, 1984)
Platoon (Oliver Stone, 1986)

Pleasantville (Gary Ross, 1998)
Pocahontas (Mike Gabriel and Eric Goldberg, 1995)
Poison (Todd Haynes, 1991)
Pretty Woman (Garry Marshall, 1990)
Primary Colors (Mike Nichols, 1998)
Public Housing (Frederick Wiseman, 1997)
Pulp Fiction (Quentin Tarantino, 1994)
Raiders of the Lost Ark (Steven Spielberg, 1981)
Rambo (George Pan Cosmatos, 1985)
Red Dawn (John Milius, 1984)
Reservoir Dogs (Quentin Tarantino, 1992)
Return of the Secaucus Seven, The (John Sayles, 1980)
River, The (Mark Rydell, 1984)
Rock, The (Michael Bay, 1996)
Roger and Me (Michael Moore, 1989)
Round Midnight (Bertrand Tavernier, 1986)
Safe (Todd Haynes, 1995)
Saving Private Ryan (Steven Spielberg, 1998)
Schindler's List (Steven Spielberg, 1993)
School Daze (Spike Lee, 1987)
Set It Off (F. Gary Gray, 1996)
Se7en (David Fincher, 1995)
sex, lies and videotape (Steven Soderbergh, 1989)
Shaft (Gordon Parks, 1971)
Shawshank Redemption, The (Frank Darabont, 1994)
She's Gotta Have It (Spike Lee, 1986)
Silence of the Lambs (Jonathan Demme, 1991)
Sister Act (Emile Ardolino, 1992)
Sister Act 2 (Bill Duke, 1993)
Six Degrees of Separation (Fred Schepisi, 1993)
Sliver (Phillip Noyce, 1993)
Smokey and the Bandit (Hal Needham, 1977)
Snow Falling on Cedars (Scott Hicks, 1994)
Speechless (Ron Underwood, 1994)
Species (Roger Donaldson, 1995)
Steel Magnolias (Herbert Ross, 1989)
Stir Crazy (Sidney Poitier, 1980)
Stomping at the Savoy (Debbie Allen, 1992)
Storyville (Mark Frost, 1992)
Straight out of Brooklyn (Matty Rich, 1991)
Straight Story, The (David Lynch, 1999)
Strange Days (Kathryn Bigelow, 1995)
Striptease (Andrew Bergman, 1996)
Summer of Sam (Spike Lee, 1999)

Sweet Dreams (Karel Reisz, 1985)
Sweet Sweetback's Baadasssss Song (Melvin Van Peebles, 1971)
Swoon (Tom Kalin, 1991)
Terminator 2 (James Cameron, 1991)
Thelma and Louise (Ridley Scott, 1991)
30 Seconds Over Tokyo (Mervyn Le Roy, 1944)
Titanic (James Cameron, 1997)
To Sleep with Anger (Charles Burnett, 1990)
Top Gun (Tony Scott, 1986),
Tora! Tora! Tora! (Richard Fleischer, 1970)
Toy Story (John Lasseter, 1995)
Trees Lounge (Steve Buscemi, 1996)
True Love (Nancy Savoca, 1989)
U Turn (Oliver Stone, 1998)
U571 (Jonathan Mostow, 2000)
Under Fire (Roger Spottiswoode, 1983)
Uptown Saturday Night (Sidney Poitier, 1974)
Wag the Dog (Barry Levinson, 1997)
What's Love Got To Do With It (Brian Gibson, 1993)
Waiting to Exhale (Forest Whitaker, 1995)
Wonder Boys (Curtis Hanson, 2000)
Wood, The (Rick Famuyiwa, 1999)
Working Girls (Lizzie Borden, 1986)
WW and the Dixie Dance Kings (John G. Avildsen, 1975)
You've Got Mail (Nora Ephron, 1998)

Index